S0-ABM-718

Life before Death

and Other Sermons at Harvard

1998-1999

Peter J. Gomes

Plummer Professor of Christian Morals and
Pusey Minister in The Memorial Church

THE MEMORIAL CHURCH
HARVARD UNIVERSITY

Printed for the University
Cambridge, Massachusetts

Volume V

Photograph by William Tobey

President Bok escorts Professor Gomes to his induction as Minister in The Memorial Church, Harvard University Sunday, November 10, 1974

Dedication

Derek Curtis Bok

J.D. '54, A.B. '71 (hon.), LL.D. '92 (hon.)

Twenty-fifth President of Harvard University
1971-1991

For twenty years the First Citizen of our Republic of Letters,
he taught by precept and example the virtuous life

TABLE OF CONTENTS

Introduction

This is the fifth volume in the series that consists of my sermons preached in The Memorial Church on the Sundays of the academic year.

When in September 1994 we issued the first volume, we did so with a sense of risk and adventure. The sermon, as so much other considered speech, had long ceased to be a form of popular discourse, and collections of sermons preached in one place by one person were to be found only in theological libraries and clerical yard sales. For many years previously we had as a matter of routine printed the sermons on a weekly basis and, like all preachers, I was flattered when the occasional request was made for a copy. No one had ever asked for a whole year's worth of my preaching. Nevertheless, I offered the first volume both 'for the record,' as it were, thinking that it might be of interest to someone to see what was said about the Christian faith in a secular university toward the close of the twentieth century, and as a contribution to the preaching literature of our time. In retrospect I admit as well to the preacherly ambition of overcoming the essentially ephemeral nature of the preaching occasion by preserving it in print.

We were sufficiently encouraged by the response to that first volume that we have continued the series in four successive volumes. In my teaching and lecturing on the subject of preaching it has proven useful to be able to submit not only my theories and ideas about preaching, but the record of my own work, to the examination of a critical and curious public. I should hasten to add that although these sermons have been preached in an academic setting, and follow the contours of the academic year, they are not intended to be heard or read as either academic or model sermons. They were preached to real and living congregations, in a particular time and place, about real and living faith and its encounters with the real world. They are not systematic in the sense of the development of a general theological or creedal position, but are meant to apply the principles of the Christian faith and the witness of the Bible to the lives and concerns of a university congregation, which itself cannot be assumed to conform to any one theological, liturgical, or biblical tradition. Such an enterprise is bound to be episodic and repetitious, and it is fair to say that certain large themes and endeavors are addressed year after year and give shape to this work.

Of these themes and endeavors I will speak to but two. First, the longer I preach the more I am convinced of the profound inconsistency between the assumptions of the Christian faith and the assumptions of modern life. To hear the gospel for the first time is to hear something out of sync with the basic assumptions of the times in which we live. The gospel says "Do not be anxious," and most people are defined by their anxieties. The gospel says that we should anticipate the future with joy and patience, and most people are joylessly impatient and terrified of the future. The gospel invites us to embrace change, and most people resist change with all of their might. The gospel invites us to a wide imagination both for ourselves and for God, yet most people embrace the parochial experience of their own experience as the only reality worth taking seriously. In the cultural slang of our time this differnce between what people believe that they are expected to believe, and what they really do believe, is called a 'disconnect,' an ugly but clear concept. Preaching is meant to confront that 'disconnect,' and to help us to move beyond it.

The second theme to which I find myself returning over and over again concerns not so much the authority of the Bible but the experience of the Bible. Much theological blood has been spilt and continues to be spilt on notions of the 'authority' of scripture, a concept which, if not carefully parsed, leads almost inexorably to a bibliolatry, an idolization of text and precedent that denies the power of the spirit in the text and gives it to those whose current interpretation prevails. This is a particularly lethal temptation among Protestants, who want to take the Bible seriously and crave the appeal of its authority. The biblical experience, however, is something else. The utility of the Bible is that within the experiences it records we find the anticipation of much of our own life. We take the Bible seriously, therefore, because it takes the divine encounter with the human dilemma seriously. The Bible's authority is not derived from its textual perfection, but rather from the validity of the experiences that it records and the light that those experiences cast upon our own. The task, therefore, in preaching from the Bible these days, is to steer a course between Bible worship and biblical ignorance, and to do so with reverence, integrity, and imagination. This task I have embraced as my own; and although I may not always succeed, to fail in this enterprise is better than to succeed in some others.

The title of one of my sermons, *Foolish Wisdom for Timid People*, perhaps best summarizes my preaching ambition. It is the title of a sermon preached this spring, which was itself a fluke in the preaching schedule, that took as its text I Corinthians 1:27; "...but God chose what is foolish in the world to shame the wise, God chose what is weak in the world to shame the strong..." For more than a year Dr. Billy Graham had been scheduled to preach in The Memorial Church on February 7, 1999, the first Sunday of the Spring Term, which would have been his third visit to Harvard and the first in which he was to preach at a morning service. We had all been looking forward to the occasion, an enormous congregation had been anticipated, and our disappointment can only be imagined when on Friday morning Dr. Graham was forced to postpone his visit due to ill health. It fell then to me to preach to a congregation expecting to hear one of the greatest preachers of our century, an experience made especially humbling when I chanced to overhear one visitor ask another at the close of the service, "Who was that person who substituted for Billy Graham?"

Preaching is the world's foolish wisdom, but it is meant to give courage to the weak whom the world in its own wisdom is content to ignore. Such foolish wisdom is no less needed within the precincts of Harvard Yard and 02138, by people in this most opinionated zip code in the world, than by those who first heard the apostle Paul, or who hear him still in the small and suffering places.

The title of this volume, *Life before Death*, is taken from one of my sermons in the Easter season when, as indeed on every Sunday, I try to communicate to the faithful and the curious the good news that Jesus calls us to a religion of life and not of death. Without making an idolatry of this present life, I am persuaded that people should hear of a faith that is relevant for them not yesterday nor tomorrow, but today. Living life well before death may just be the greatest challenge of our time.

Three of my predecessors in the Plummer Professorship submitted their sermons to public scutiny in the form of published collections. The most prolific was Francis Greenwood Peabody (1886-1913), whose volumes *Mornings in the College Chapel* and *Sundays in the College Chapel* reached thousands, and were classics of their kind in the last quarter of the nineteenth century. Dean Willard Learoyd Sperry (1929-1953), produced two collections of sermons preached at Harvard in the 1940s and 1950s; and Dr. George Arthur Buttrick (1954-1960), upon his retirement from Harvard, published *Sermons Preached in a University Church*. These volumes of mine I hope will take their place in that succession.

The dedication of this book will strike many, including the dedicatee, as unusual if not eccentric. Derek Bok would not care to be defined as 'churchy,' and during his presidency he most certainly was not, but he did three things for which I wish to pay him the tribute of this dedication. First, in 1974 he appointed me the first Minister in The Memorial Church and the ninth Plummer Professor of Christian Morals, and I shall always be grateful for that vote of confidence. Second, by his judicious reorganization of the University's religious life, of which my appointment was a part, he preserved The Memorial Church for a future of vigorous utility, and I can only hope that he takes some satisfaction in the ministry that he enabled. Third, in difficult and demanding times he always set before the University a high example of public service and rectitude wherein values, reason, and civility helped to shape those wise restraints that kept us free. He fostered an institutional environment and culture within which it was possible for this Church to do its work, and for that all of us who value both Harvard and its Church owe him a debt of thanks.

Peter J. Gomes

The Lodge
Plymouth, Massachusetts
July 1, 1999

Acknowledgements

A sermon requires a congregation, and a preacher a listening and a thoughtful one. With such attentive colleagues I have been blessed in The Memorial Church, and for them I am very grateful.

I acknowledge with great appreciation the continuing editorial services of Cynthia Wight Rossano, who has brought yet another of my books into print.

PJG

PART ONE

Sermons for the Fall Term

YOU CAN IF YOU WANT TO

The Fourteenth Sunday after Pentecost
Freshman Sunday

The Lesson

Ecclesiasticus 6:32-37 (REB)

If it is your wish, my son, you will be instructed; if you give your mind to it, you will become clever. If you are content to listen, you will learn; if you are attentive, you will grow wise. When you stand among the assembled elders, see who is wise and stick close by him. Listen gladly to every godly conversation; let no wise maxim escape you. If you discover anyone who is wise, rise early to visit him; let your feet wear out his doorstep. Ponder the decrees of the Lord and study his commandments at all times. He will instruct your mind, and your desire for wisdom shall be met.

Do no evil, and no evil will befall you; keep clear of wrong, and it will avoid you. Do not sow in the furrows of injustice, for fear of reaping a sevenfold crop.

YOU CAN IF YOU WANT TO

Text: If you are willing, my child, you can be disciplined; and if you apply yourself, you will become clever.

Ecclesiasticus 6:32 (The Apocrypha)

My text is the thirty-second verse of the sixth chapter of the book of Ecclesiasticus, that venerable book of the Apocrypha; and you will find in your bulletins this morning a card with verses thirty-two through thirty-seven written out for you to take home. We hope that you will find a place for it on refrigerator doors in homes and offices, and that all of you freshmen will find a prominent spot for it amongst the clutter in your new rooms. It is wisdom that is useful to all ages, wisdom that is worth referring to again and again.

If you are willing, my child, you can be disciplined,
And if you apply yourself you will become clever.
If you love to listen you will gain knowledge,
And if you pay attention you will become wise.
Stand in the company of the elders:
Who is wise? Attach yourself to such a one.
Be ready to listen to every godly discourse,
And let no wise proverb escape you.
If you see an intelligent person, rise early to visit him;
Let your foot wear out his doorstep.
Reflect on the statutes of the Lord,
And meditate at all times on his commandments:
It is he who will give insight to your mind,
And your desire for wisdom will be granted.
Do no evil, and evil will never overtake you;
Stay away from wrong, and it will turn away from you.
Do not sow in the furrows of injustice,
And you will not reap a sevenfold crop.

Now to you freshmen, members of the Class of 2002: all of your hard work and a little of your conniving have brought you here this morning. We sense your pleasure, we sense your relief, and we sense also something of your apprehension, for if you are like most newcomers to an ancient and venerable place such as this one, you will have by now some small hints of intimidation, some sense of queasiness. Not all of you have it, of course, for there are those among you who regard yourselves as doing us a great favor for coming here in the first place — you actually believe what your mothers say about you, and what your letters of reference have to say about you, and for you there is little that we can do. All of these emotions, mixed and mingled as they are, are right and proper. This is the season of great expectations: you have a right to expect much of Harvard, for after all you are paying a lot and you should expect a lot, and we expect a lot of you. Last June we turned out another class of tired old seniors, and from you we expect renewal. Harvard is like Count Dracula: we here thrive on new blood, namely, on yours!

For the great generality of you just about now, however, I suspect that there is that suspicious hint, that feeling you get when the roller-coaster has climbed its long slow ascent up to top of the highest and first terrifying loopety-loop and pauses there for a second, and you think that perhaps this wasn't the best of all possible ideas after all, or the best of all possible places in which to try out the best of all possible ideas. What about that friendly little co-ed college in the midwest or in Maine or in Ohio, you think, that begged you, even paid you, to come? What about them? What about State U., with its promise of fun and learning at half the price? Harvard, after all, has been known to ruin almost as many people as it may have helped, and at the very least, Harvard can ruin your reputation back home.

Consider the following letter from one of your predecessors, addressed to that great philosopher of our time, Miss Manners, which appeared in her column in *The Boston Globe* of October 3, 1985, just a few weeks after Freshman Sunday. I clipped it because of its eternal usefulness, and this is how it read:

> *Dear Miss Manners:*
> *I am afflicted with a peculiar social stigma, due to attending a well-respected university.*
> *I may as well confess that the university is Harvard...*
> *When my Harvard affiliation is revealed, I have several*

times received one of three reactions:
"You must be rich."
"You must be a brain."
"Wow! Should I get on my knees and worship you?"

The letter concludes with this plaintive observation:

> *This problem has never been mentioned in any of Harvard's brochures or catalogues. What is the proper way to respond?* (*The Boston Globe*; October 3, 1985; P. 68)

The substance of Miss Manner's reply is beside the point, with the exception of her view that the administration supplies no help in this matter because most Harvard students soon learn how to answer evasively. "Where do you go to school?" "Back east." "Where, back east?" "Have you ever heard of Boston?" "Yes." "Well, it's near to Boston." "Oh, you go to MIT." "No, it's nearer to Leslie College..." Eventually the truth will out and you will be required to reveal that you come here. Undergraduates are always worried about mentioning Harvard; graduates, of course, never stop mentioning Harvard. The real problem, however, is not the place, problematic as that might be, but what you bring to the place: you bring too high an expectation of Harvard, and too low an expectation of yourself.

Having thought about it over the years, I believe that my colleagues and I do you no good and actually do you some real harm by telling you how bright and clever you are. We will spend all of this week massaging your egos and flattering you further into the belief that you are the best thing for Harvard since sliced bread, when what we ought to be telling you is that you bring to us great but unrealized potential, that you have much to learn and we have much to teach, and that we haven't much time and so we should get on with it immediately. We should massage not your egos, which are plenty large enough already, but we should massage your ambitions, your aspirations, and affirm what I know is your basic and fundamental desire to learn to live and to learn well. Every one of you at this point enters upon this moment in your life with high hopes, high aspirations, and high expectations; and rightly you should.

What, then, is the purpose of Harvard College? Its purpose is as President Eliot said it was nearly a century ago, "To cultivate within each of you young men and women the durable values and satisfactions of life;" and I emphasize that and ask that you remember it. The task before us consists not in what you can do for Harvard or even in what Harvard can do for you, but rather in what you can do for yourself with a little help from God and your friends. You can do it if you want to.

If you will look with me at today's lesson, the one on the card that we had printed up for you, you will find among the many bits of advice three points worth remembering. The first is that if you listen you will learn something: "If you love to listen you will gain knowledge, and if you pay attention you will become wise."

That may seem a very simple thing, the sort of thing you might say in grammar school, maybe even in high school, but not at Harvard College. Listening is very hard to do at Harvard: some of you are having a hard time doing it right now. Here people are judged, at least superficially, by the quantity of their words, and you may have already found that to be true among your roommates. The idea is that the more you talk, and the louder and faster, the smarter you will be thought to be. That is why so many of you, even at this stage of your young careers, want to go on to law school where you are paid by the word. The lesson, however, says that you ought to cultivate the art of listening because you just might learn something from somebody else. What is the old saying, a cliché worth remembering around here? "It is better to be thought a fool by keeping silent than to remove all possible doubt by speaking."

When you keep your mouth shut and your ears, your mind, and your heart open, you have a chance of actually learning something, experiencing something, contemplating something, and then of saying something perhaps worth hearing when finally you do speak. Shooting from the lip around here is a dangerous and pernicious disease. The book of Ecclesiasticus tells us that it is first and foremost wise to listen, from which one learns, after which one might dare to speak.

Some of you know the story of the little boy who never said a word until he was three years old, no gurgles, no comments, no conversation at all. His poor parents thought there was something wrong with him. Then, one Sunday at dinner, to the consternation of everybody at the table, the child said, "There are lumps in the mashed potatoes." "My God!" said his father: "You can speak! Why haven't you spoken before?" "Because," replied the boy, "up to now everything has been fine."

You do not have to wait for something to go terribly wrong, you do not have to be silent here at Harvard, but in this talkers' paradise that is Cambridge the text gives some very useful advice:

"Be ready to listen to every godly discourse, and let no wise proverb escape you."

Be alert to what you can learn by listening.

The second thing the lesson invites you to do, in a very subtle way, is to go to class. It doesn't say so in so many words, and of course at Harvard there is no mandatory attendance requirement in lectures and classes as there was in high school, but if you want to be wise and become clever, the text tells you:

"If you see an intelligent person, rise early to visit him; let your foot wear out his doorstep."

That's a subtle way of saying that you might attend these classes for which your parents are paying so much money — even if they're in the morning! Not all wisdom here is confined to what occurs in the classroom, however, and wise people are to be found in the oddest places — the laboratory, the library, the lecture hall, the section room, and even in the dining hall — and these are the places in which you should be willing to spend a great deal of your time. Do not, my dear young friends, chain yourselves to that little blinking screen on your desk. Do not think that the only reality there is is the one to which you can connect with a little mouse, to join in the strange and bizarre invisible universe called the 'Internet.' There is no salvation in the Internet! There is no redemption in the Internet! There is no fellowship in the Internet! Do not waste your time on the Internet! Meet live, living, thoughtful, difficult, creative people face-to-face, and you'll never have to massage your machine again.

College is an unnatural place, if you think about it, and the years spent in college an unnatural time, for this is the last place and time when the best of all wisdom, of all arts and sciences, all human experience, is ordered and arranged for your convenience and consumption. We're like McDonald's, we do it all for you, everything here is arranged for your comfort, your consolation, and your instruction. We cater to your every need — we provide housing, we provide food, shelter, entertainment, protection, and now, thanks to Dean Lewis, soft toilet paper: we provide all of these things in order that you may become wise. We have created this place that you may become wise, and all you have to do is to turn up. Never again in your life will the world be so placed at your disposal, never again.....unless you get tenure and can stay here. So go to class: "If you see an intelligent person, rise early to visit him; let your foot wear out his doorstep."

The third thing that the text invites you to do if you would become wise and clever, is to think and remember. That is what it means when it says:

> *"Reflect on the statutes of the Lord, and meditate at all times on his commandments: It is he who will give insight to your mind, and your desire for wisdom will be granted."*

Think and remember. Some of you parents, and perhaps a few of you students, are of the view that the purpose of college, and especially of Harvard College, is to help you to get a job, and the very best job possible. We all hope that you do get a job: your parents certainly do, the Development Office certainly does, and you would be found with very little to do if you didn't have a job. That is not the purpose of Harvard College, however. This is *not* a trade school, nor is it a place for making what are commonly known as 'contacts.' The purpose of this College is to help you to cultivate those "durable values and satisfactions of life" that President Eliot mentioned, and they are cultivated by the fine art of thinking, which is what you do whether or not you have a job. To think is to contemplate appropriate judgements and actions in the absence of all of the evidence. Think about it. If you have all of the evidence and everything you need to know, of course you will be wise, of course you will be smart, of course you will be clever, but our text says: "Reflect on the statutes of the Lord..."

Now, even in these immodest and relativistic days most of you have been brought up with an acute sense of right and wrong. Your parents have tried as best as they can, with very little help from the culture, to instill in you some sense of moral purpose, some sense of judgement and discernment. The moral crisis of our time is not ignorance of the moral law, as is often thought, and the problem is not what we don't know but rather the will to act on what we do know. In a sermon to freshmen on a Sunday very much like this one fifty years ago, my predecessor, Dean Sperry, said from this very pulpit:

> "We are told that in times of crisis and opportunity our conduct is seldom determined by our surface conscious thought. The whole deeper stuff of the mind takes control then. The yield of our accumulated liv-

> ing over the years decides what we shall do at such times." ('The Desire of Discipline,' from *Sermons Preached at Harvard*; Sperry; Harper; 1953; P. 35)

Certainly in our national life, and probably in your personal lives, we are in such a time of crisis, and how we cope depends upon "the yield of our accumulated living over the years..." as Dean Sperry so ably put it.

Harvard, as is the world for which it is preparing you, is a place filled with temptations both subtle and blatant. You will be tempted to take short cuts. You will be tempted to plagiarize and to lie, to dissemble and to procrastinate, to cheat both yourself and others, and to find every excuse for your actions which will spare you responsibility and accountability. If you were not tempted in these ways you would not be human and yet you are very human, so in order to resist temptation the best in our tradition tells you to think about what it is that you are doing or not doing, and to remember the best of what you have been taught. Most moral lapses are not the result of ignorance, or even of evil, but of laziness and carelessness; and if you want to be more than another moral casualty in life's on-going soap opera you can be, but you will have to work at it harder than you ever have before. You will have to think, and you will have to remember.

Discipline is what it is all about. Those "durable values and satisfactions of life" are not possible without discipline, which is the application of steady habits to the uncertainties of this mortal life. The word 'discipline' comes from the same root as the word 'disciple,' which, as you Latinists know, means follower of a teacher. The example of such a teacher is Jesus, and the teachings that his disciples are meant to follow are what he says in the Beatitudes, which were read for us in our second lesson. To remember them is to be happy, to follow them is to be both disciplined and a disciple.

That is all well and good, but the problem with most of you is that you want to be leaders, not followers. For you, then, is the epitaph found on the walls of the village church in Sandwich, Kent, England, of a schoolmaster who taught an old friend of mine, who never forgot what the tablet said of his mentor:

> "In service he led; in leadership he served; and thus he set the feet of many upon the path of life."

His was a disciplined life that led to freedom for all who came under his care. That was true leadership, and who could aspire to an ambition greater than that? That is the kind of ambition that we aim to cultivate in this College, and if you are willing, that freedom and discipline can be yours. You can if you want to!

Now, a penultimate word to you parents and guardians who have entrusted to our care your most precious young. The rest of you, take a minute to wool-gather, I will be back to you in a minute. Parents and guardians, we will not fail you in the trust which you have placed here in this ancient College, but for our work to begin where yours has left off you must do one final and important thing: go home. Not right now, of course, but as soon as the work of today is over, kiss your children, check out their rooms and roommates once more, and leave. We cannot begin our work, nor can they theirs, until you are gone. God invented e-mail so that you can stay in touch without getting in the way. Trust us to do what you are paying us to do, and trust your children to do what you have taught them to do.

Freshmen, my dear young and bewildered friends, we have great hopes for you, we wish you God's blessing in what you are now about to begin. Remember that God who brought you through the worst day of your life is not about to abandon you in the best days that are ahead. If God will not give up on you, don't you dare give up on God, because together you can and will do great things.

"If you are willing, my child, you can be disciplined; and if you apply yourself you will become clever."

Let us pray:

> *Now, O gracious God, lift us up and send us out, ready for all that is ahead, secure in the knowledge that where we are, there too art Thou. Amen.*

September 6, 1998

GODLINESS AND GOOD LEARNING

The Fifteenth Sunday after Pentecost
Opening of Term

The Lesson

II Timothy 2:14-26 (KJV)

Of these things put them in remembrance, charging them before the Lord that they strive not about words to no profit, but to the subverting of the hearers. Study to show thyself approved unto God, a workman that needeth not to be ashamed, rightly dividing the word of truth. But shun profane and vain babblings, for they will increase unto more ungodliness. And their word will eat as doth a canker; of whom is Hymenaeus and Philetus, who concerning the truth have erred, saying that the resurrection is past already; and overthrow the faith of some.

Nevertheless the foundation of God standeth sure, having this seal, 'The Lord knoweth them that are his.' And, 'Let every one that nameth the name of Christ depart from iniquity.' But in a great house there are not only vessels of gold and of silver, but also of wood and of earth; and some to honour, and some to dishonour.

If a man therefore purge himself from these, he shall be a vessel unto honour, sanctified, and meet for the master's use, and prepared unto every good work.

Flee also youthful lusts, but follow righteousness, faith, charity, peace, with them that call on the Lord out of a pure heart. But foolish and unlearned questions avoid, knowing that they do gender strifes.

And the servant of the Lord must not strive but be gentle unto all men, apt to teach, patient, in meekness instructing those that oppose themselves if God peradventure will give them repentance to the acknowledging of the truth;

And that they may recover themselves out of the snare of the devil, who are taken captive by him at his will.

GODLINESS AND GOOD LEARNING

Text: Study to show thyself approved unto God, a workman that needeth not to be ashamed, rightly dividing the word of truth.

II Timothy 2:15 (KJV)

The text is advice from a seasoned and somewhat harried apostle of Jesus Christ to his young, nervous, slightly insecure apprentice. Not a bad text with which to begin an academic year, not a bad text with which to sum up a life, for I have chosen it for my tombstone, and have already instructed the cutter. "Study to show thyself approved unto God, a workman that needeth not to be ashamed, rightly dividing the word of truth."

Now, usually I do not mention denominational matters in this pulpit, but I am moved to do so this morning with particular reference to the great company of Methodists who, when they gather for their annual conference, in long tradition stemming from the eighteenth century open their proceedings by singing one of their founder's greatest hymns:

And are we yet alive, and see each other's face?
Glory and thanks to Jesus give, for his almighty grace.

What troubles have we seen, what mighty conflicts past?
Fightings without and fears within since we assembled last!

Charles Wesley, 1707-1788

Those are the great words of Charles Wesley, and they seem to me to be good words with which to renew our time together as the Christian Church at Harvard, for that is who and that is what we are. Not just a straggling group of intellectual voyeurs, not aesthetes come to get a whiff of very good music, not social climbers coming to the 'Harvard' church, we are the Christian church at Harvard, and it is good for us to be reminded of that and to remember it; and it is an act both of surprising and amazing grace that we are still here to say such things and to hear such things. People don't expect to find us at Harvard, even after three hundred sixty-two years, perhaps *especially* after three hundred sixty-two years. The other day I listened in on two tourists trying to explain Memorial Hall, out there on the delta. One, presuming to know more than she did, said, "Well, it used to be a church but now it's a dining hall. I guess they don't need a church at Harvard any more." Tempted as I was I did not interrupt, for this was clearly a heaven-sent illustration in search of a sermon, and this is that sermon.

When last spring I invited Billy Graham to preach for us this coming spring he replied affirmatively, and graciously accepted my invitation. Then, almost in an aside, he added somewhat wistfully that he wished that someone would write a book about the role that the Christian faith had played in the foundation of American higher education, for the religious origins of many of our colleges and universities are now a source of embarrassment rather than of pride. The story has been told but it is easily forgotten. Here at Harvard College we do our best to remember it, and it is never more important to remember those origins than to do so at the beginning of a new academic year.

The title of this sermon has a distinctly nineteenth century whiff to it, and rightly so. This phrase — godliness and good learning — was beloved of headmasters of English public schools in the nineteenth century who, following the inspiring example of Dr. Thomas Arnold of Rugby, rededicated their old foundations to the twin ideals of godliness and learning. They wanted their pupils to be both smart and good: brains and souls, or, as we might say today, hearts and minds, together constituted the civil, the educated, the moral person, and it was the duty of schools to inculcate these twin sets of virtues into the sometimes unwilling heads of their subjects. Their premise was that our duty to God would help us to better perform our duty to one another, our knowledge of God would help us to better appreciate all earthly and human knowledge, and our appreciation of earthly and human knowledge would help us to better understand the wondrous knowledge of God. We aspire, in their romantic vision, both to wisdom and to virtue.

The claim today seems naive. It sounds old-fashioned and impossible, and in some cases it may even sound self-indulgent. Colleges, as we know, are centers of research and teaching, indispensable arms of the secular order and the ever-expanding upward movement in our classless society. High culture looks upon religion through the gimlet eye of New Yorker cartoons and Saturday Night Live parodies, and religion is best kept private, for when it goes public it creates division and conflict. The surest way to ruin a cocktail party in Cambridge, or a lunch in the dining hall, is to speak of religion — except, of course, in the most abstract or deprecating way.

Here we are, though, here *you* are, for nobody has compelled you to come here this morning, no dividends are being given for your presence in The Memorial Church, no credits to students, no bonuses to the rest of you. Here you are, you have chosen freely of your own free will to attend here, for whatever reason, God only knows. Here we are in this great big church in the middle of this College, and despite the wishes of a few, we are not likely to go away. We nourish our inheritance, we nourish our historic claim to this patch of earth as ours by right — not by accident, not by condescension, but by right. Psalm 78, which we have just sung in paraphrase, and the Latin hymn through which you will struggle in a few minutes, affirm that we have been here before, and longer than anybody else. We claim unbroken succession to that bronze Puritan minister with the shiny toe who sits in front of University Hall, John Harvard.

Speaking of University Hall, many years ago when I was the very new young naive minister here, I determined to pay a pastoral call on all of the deans of the University. They hadn't invited me and they certainly didn't expect me, but they received me when I appeared at their doors. I went over to the Medical School, to the Law School, and I even called upon the dean of the Divinity School. I went hither and yon, and I saved the last moment for what was in many people's opinions, and still is, the grandest panjandrum of them all, the dean of the Faculty of Arts and Sciences. So I made my way over there to University Hall, and I climbed up the stairs, and I was received by his secretary, Miss Johnson, who intoned, "The dean will see you now." I was ushered into the presence, and a great and vast presence it was. He received me kindly, and we chatted about this, that, and the other, and after our chat he invited me to go around to his side of the desk, a huge desk with nothing on it — which I've learned is a sign of absolute power, a big desk with nothing on it: if you want to impress people, throw everything off your desk when they come to see you, because I was impressed. He said, "I want you to come around to my side of the desk and take a look at my view." So I went round his chair and we looked out of his window, and the only thing you could see from the dean's desk in University Hall in those days was the spire of The Memorial Church. He said, "I look at that every day, and I say to myself, 'What a beautiful church, what a lovely sight, though I suspect that if we were starting again we wouldn't put it just there...'" "There," however, or here it is, and we are not going to start again, and we're not going to pick it up and move it somewhere else, we are going to pick up where we have left off, and our predecessors and our ancestors before us. This church stands to remind all who pass by, as well as all who enter, that godliness and good learning still have something to do with one another, still are in an intimate relationship with one another, and never more so than right here, right now.

You might well be justified in thinking this a rather defensive justification of our existence by historic right, an argument that many of my English friends use in defending the anachronism of the House of Lords. You may well imagine my sympathies on that particular argument: I'm in favor of almost every anachronism one can possibly imagine for they protect us from the tyranny of the present, but I do not wish to argue simply from history or from tradition, important as they are. Let me give you two contemporary expressions of the point I'm trying to make.

Within the past year, within hailing distance of this College, two new secondary schools have been founded in a contemporary expression of commitment to godliness and good learning. The first of these is a new private Jewish preparatory school, The New Jewish High School, located not very far from Cambridge in Waltham, and the explicit ambition of its founders is to combine in one effort the rigorous traditions of Jewish piety, Jewish religious discipline, thought, and practice, and the great intellectual traditions of the west in which the Jewish intellect has played such an enormous part. Their ambition is to combine the rigor of the synagogue with the rigor of the academy in making a moral, social, and intellectual impact upon the youngest minds sent to them. This school is going against the tide of secular and assimilationist fashion, and its founders know it, and yet they are convinced that if they are an anachronism, they are a necessary anachronism. I learned of this new foundation through my old friend, the headmaster of Roxbury Latin School, himself a necessary anachronism; and the school, need I say, is oversubscribed, with people beating down the doors to get in, for they cherish for their young this now increasingly rare opportunity for godliness and good learning.

A second such venture is even more closely related to ourselves. A recent graduate of this College, a parishioner who as a student sat for four years in the pews of this church on Sundays and daily for Morning Prayers, a student now in our Divinity School, has risked all to found a new day school in Boston, The Epiphany School, which he means to be

— in a slightly infelicitous but perfectly understandable phrase — the 'Groton' of Roxbury. Very few people would put Groton and Roxbury in the same sentence but The Epiphany School is intending to do just that, and our student, our parishioner, my young friend John H. Finley IV, of the Class of 1992, is, as the founder of The Epiphany School, attempting to do just that, and to put to the test his Christian conviction that godliness and good learning are just what are required by the least benefitted and most marginalized youth in the city, for the salvation of their souls and for the redemption of our society. Plain living, high thinking, hard work, and a sense of the divine in the mundane are the lesson plans for this new school with a difference, and as you might expect, so risky a venture has elicited all sorts of criticisms and concerns. More than that, however, it has excited the imaginations of so many who have grown used to disappointment, despair, and defeat. 'Godliness and good learning.' This phrase, this ideal, is not just an appeal to some antique anachronistic thought, it is understood in our own time, in our own city, in our own neighborhood, as the formula for a renovated life, and, by God's grace, for a renovated society.

These are pithy illustrations, I know, of these two new schools, true and near at hand, but do we really expect them to have much impact upon the sordid world in which they are set? A little school in Waltham for Jewish piety and intellect; a little academy trying to bring godliness and good learning to Roxbury and Dorchester and the inner city of Boston? Are these not rather quixotic kinds of things, again indulgent luxuries? Because we cannot do everything, goes the argument, we should do nothing. We've all heard that one before. Might these newly-founded schools, in fact, appear even to be self-indulgent, romantic, perhaps whimsical efforts to spit in the cultural wind? Well, I can imagine sage Oxford and Cambridge men sitting before their college fires some three hundred sixty-odd years ago, sipping port and saying much the same thing about this up-start college of ours, this Harvard College, huddled as it was between the wilderness and the sea; and yet, here we are.

And are we not yet alive, and see each other's face?
Glory and thanks to Jesus give, for his almighty grace.

Do not despise the day of small things, nor the small expression of enormous adventure, for that is what the combination of godliness and good learning is all about.

I am very fond of a now little-read theologian who prospered in the first half of this century, William Ralph Inge, who made a point of saying that his name rhymed with 'sting,' not with 'cringe,' and was for many years known as the so-called "Gloomy Dean" of St. Paul's Cathedral in London. He was also a preacher of unusually apt philosophical analysis, and in an essay called 'Two Kinds of Knowledge,' the dean wrote:

> "There are two kinds of knowledge, of the things that are seen, and of the things that are not seen, or, as modern philosophy expresses it, of facts and of values. The supreme problem is to determine their relation to each other; the facile solution is to suppress one of the two terms in favor of the other."
>
> (*Things Old and New*; P. 71)

One would think that in a university there would be an easy division between these two kinds of knowledge. To secular learning we would give over everything having to do with things that are seen — "facts," as Dickens' Gradgrind did in his school — and to religion or to the speculative sciences would be left the matter of the things that are not seen, or "values."

Straightaway, though, we see the problem. Alone, the knowledge of the things that are seen, "true facts," as undergraduates like to call them, are superficial and often misleading, offering a false sense of accuracy, stability, and security. Look at our reliance on statistics and polls, for example. Yet the realm of pure values and speculative theory can be so heavenly that it is of no earthly good.

St. Paul casts the matter in terms of the relationship between the temporary and the permanent, and argues quite convincingly that the things that are unseen are eternal, while those that are seen are transient. No one in a university community needs to be reminded that we live in a mixed world and are forced to contend with both kinds of knowledge, with facts and with values, for godliness and good learning encompass both. Facts and values are our business, they are not mutually exclusive, and the believer is left to deal with his facts by the light of his values; and that relationship is an invitation both to imagination, the ability to see things that are not there, and to modesty, the capacity to cope with what we do not know and cannot do.

Our facts and our values in the context of Christian belief are acts of faith, articulate or not, which "begin as a longing to find some meaning in life, something permanent and solid behind the flowing stream of change and chance..." (Inge; P. 91), and end in our desire not just for knowledge but for goodness as well.

How do we take on this enterprise of godliness and good learning for ourselves? How do we go about this? Dean Epps gave us one clue when he read the first lesson, from Proverbs: "Cling to instruction and never let it go; guard it well, for it is your life." (Proverbs 4:13; REB). There is another clue. When the apostle Paul was determined to give some strong words of encouragement and advice to his young and nervous deputy, Timothy, about to start out on his own great adventure, he wrote to him: "Try hard to show yourself worthy of God's approval, as a worker with no cause for shame; keep strictly to the true gospel..." which is the Revised English Bible's translation of our text. (II Timothy 2:15; REB)

The object of our study here, my young, my old, my continuing friends, is to produce a work of which we need not be ashamed — not a book, not a career, not a masterpiece, but a life. Somehow we think of 'study' and 'work' as two quite different things, as: "I can't study right now, I have to go to work;" but what we are to take from the advice afforded Timothy is the notion that we are the work, we are the object of our own study which we offer for God's approval in the confidence that we have God's approval — for God's approval not of what we know or even of what we do, but of who we are and of who we are becoming.

My old friend David McCord, of the Class of 1921, once wrote of his Harvard experience: "The best thing I got out of College was myself." We know what he meant. The best can be even better when once we realize that it is our ambition to show before God our work, ourselves, by living and learning worthy of his approval, and without embarrassment.

It is a life's work, this business of godliness and good learning, and it is not over until it is over. It is the ancient work of this College, but even more to the point it is now our work, contemporary, immediate, existential and urgent, and begun anew today. Let us, by God's grace, get on with it.

Let us pray:

> *Direct us, O God, in all our endeavors, high and low, great and small, that we may prove ourselves worthy of the confidence Thou hast placed in us by Thy grace. Amen.*

September 13, 1998

WHO DO YOU THINK YOU ARE?

The Sixteenth Sunday after Pentecost

The Lesson

Romans 12:3-16 (NEB)

In virtue of the gift that God in his grace has given me I say to everyone among you: do not be conceited or think too highly of yourself; but think your way to a sober estimate based on the measure of faith that God has dealt to each of you. For just as in a single human body there are many limbs and organs, all with different functions, so all of us, united with Christ, form one body, serving individually as limbs and organs to one another.

The gifts we possess differ as they are allotted to us by God's grace, and must be exercised accordingly: the gift of inspired utterance, for example, in proportion to a man's faith; or the gift of administration, in administration. A teacher should employ his gift in teaching, and one who has the gift of stirring speech should use it to stir his hearers. If you give to charity, give with all your heart; if you are a leader, exert yourself to lead; if you are helping others in distress, do it cheerfully.

Love in all sincerity, loathing evil and clinging to the good. Let love for our brotherhood breed warmth of mutual affection. Give pride of place to one another in esteem.

With unflagging energy, in ardour of spirit, serve the Lord.

Let hope keep you joyful; in trouble stand firm; persist in prayer.

Contribute to the needs of God's people, and practise hospitality.

Call down blessings on your persecutors — blessings, not curses.

With the joyful be joyful, and mourn with the mourners.

Have equal regard for one another. Do not be haughty, but go about with humble folk. Do not keep thinking how wise you are.

WHO DO YOU THINK YOU ARE?

Text: Do not be conceited or think too highly of yourself...

Romans 12:3 (NEB)

The apostle Paul is usually thought of as having been possessed of an enormous ego, a huge sense of who he was and of what was expected of him, and certainly of a huge sense of what he expected of others; and in his letters he is constantly concerned with the question of identity. Who are we? Whose are we? How do we know in the world who we are? So, in the twelfth chapter of Romans, which I would argue is the greatest chapter in his greatest letter, he offers some significant pastoral advice on who we are and on how we are to behave. Now, not all of the advice is summarized in the words of my text this morning, but a very good place at which to begin, particularly in this place, is where he says, in the third verse of Romans 12, "Do not be conceited or think too highly of yourself."

For a few minutes on last Friday afternoon the eyes of the world literally were upon us in the Tercentenary Theatre, and for a minute or so — I hope you rejoiced as I did — it was wonderful to be able to escape the tawdry scandals in Washington and the tiresome malice of our public life, and for a moment to rise above it all, to be inspired, to be cleansed, to be moved in a direction we have not been in a very long time. The visit of President Mandela to Harvard will go down as one of the great moments in our history, not simply because he joins George Washington and Winston Churchill in having received an honorary doctorate degree from this university, but because for a moment one man was able to transform thousands in this place as he has been able to transform millions in his own country. The "angels of our better nature," to whom President Rudenstine alluded in his citation, were summoned, and were present. I watched all of us transformed: noisy, pushy, self-centered, conceited undergraduates and graduate students became quiet and calm, thinking absolutely about somebody else for a change; and my pompous, pushy, arrogant colleagues, all of whom are always fighting for every square inch of turf on that platform and elsewhere, were overwhelmed by the magnitude of the person in our midst, and for a moment we were all changed. We all went back to what we were by six o'clock, that can't be helped, but for an instant all reality was suspended in this wonderful kind of new reality, and for an instant we were able to associate ourselves with a man of such magnificent moral stature that the association elevated us all. It pleased me to realize that the young, raised on a diet of cheap and promiscuous celebrity, could at last recognize a hero when they were privileged to see one; and, unlike at Commencement, when the unrestrained and competitive egos of the candidates for degrees turn the Yard into a barnyard, on Friday we were all as one, and our only thought and care was to share something of this great man. If you want to know the difference between Friday and Commencement, it was that this was not about us, it was about him, and for that for which he stands. It was extraordinary, and those of us who were there will never forget it.

So, what is the secret? If you were the *People Magazine* reporter observing this phenomenon on Friday, you'd ask, "What is it that distinguishes Nelson Mandela from the rest of us?" Well, twenty-seven years in prison and a Nobel Peace Prize is a good place to begin. That distinguishes him from nearly everybody else in this room and in that vast audience, but my chief impression of what distinguishes Nelson Mandela and allows him to stand above and beyond so many of us, from having observed him from afar for many years and up close for a few precious minutes on Friday, is the very simple unsophisticated fact that this is a man who knows who he is. This is a man whose ideals are intact, but who does not necessarily live with the demons of his delusions. He has been neither seduced nor intimidated by what others think; rather, his authority, gravitas combined with grace, comes from that sense of knowing who he is and from being secure, stable, in his sense of worth and of being. As one of the old collects from the Book of Common Prayer tells us, "He does not stagger at the uneven motions of this world." He can laugh at himself and allow us to laugh at him and with him, and he can sustain himself and his moral purpose under the most dire of circumstances. It is his sense of secure self, I believe, that impressed and sustained his fellow prisoners on that bleak and barbarous Robben Island, the place of his imprisonment for so many years, and it was that same sense of self that charmed and inspired all of us who sat or stood within his presence on Friday afternoon. He knows who he is, and it is God's greatest gift, to allow us to know who we are.

Well, that's all well and good for Nelson Mandela, but how do you and how do I answer the question of who we think we are? Who do we think we are?

Our text from St. Paul's letter to the Romans warns Paul's hearers not to think too highly of themselves, not to be conceited, and at the start of another academic year here in Cambridge that is not a bad thought to keep in mind. If we Harvard people have one reputation with which we must contend in this world, it is that we think too highly of ourselves — at least, people think we think too highly of ourselves; however, as with so much conventional wisdom, I think there is something wrong with that analysis. It is not that we who are at Harvard think too highly of ourselves, for we are too smart for that; it is that others think too highly of us, and why should we be blamed for the misperceptions of others? We know one another well enough to know that we really aren't as great as everybody else thinks we are, but because they think we are, we have to take on the burden of greatness.

We are not the first people to find that knowledge and arrogance are intimately related. Our ancestors, Adam and Eve, discovered that, alas, in the garden, along with a host of other disagreeable facts which have since not gone away. The Jewish story tellers who gave us the story of Adam and Eve would have us believe that all was well when those two were barefoot and ignorant in the garden, and that their trouble came when they learned more than they could handle. They thought that they could become as gods, the creation story tells us, for that is what the tempter offered them in the apple, and yet when they ate they discovered that they were naked; in other words, they discovered that they really didn't know very much at all. In theory they, with that knowledge, then should have lived in a state of perpetual modesty and self-abnegation, with a certain amount of regret at having been so adventurous, but, as we know, they went off to rule the world and we, their children, are still trying to do so.

When St. Paul tells us not to think too highly of ourselves he is asking us to remember that record, to remember that inheritance which we bear with us every day. When he wants us not to be conceited, he wants us to know that we are not our identity.

Who do you think you are? Do you really believe in your heart of hearts, when the lights go down low, that you are in charge and have control, and that you are masters and mistresses of your destiny and of the universe? Do we really believe that we know much more than our ancestors? King Canute, you remember, thought he was so powerful that he could bid the tide not to come in: it did of course, and the hem of his garment got wet. Hitler thought he was so clever, so smart and so powerful that he could conquer and rule the world, and we see him in reruns on the History Channel. There are young men and women, many of whom are our own graduates, who think they can actually control the destinies of the world and rule the world and themselves through the power of Wall Street or of Washington. There are movie stars, moguls, and celebrities aplenty who actually believe that they are what their press agents say they are, and we know the folly of them because we know our own folly.

Conceit, however, is an easy target to hit — for we can always get a few cheap laughs and a few good rounds of applause in talking about the conceits of others — and a rather cheap shot at our question. You and I know that the posture of arrogance and conceit is usually a cover for a sense of insecurity, inferiority, and anxiety, and the posturing rather like whistling 'Dixie' out loud while passing through a graveyard at night. We are dealing with issues of identity, and ever since Adam and Eve we have been a little uncertain about what identity means.

I recall hearing my old friend and colleague, Dennis Campbell, then dean of the Duke University Divinity School, tell a story from this very pulpit of the funeral service of the last empress of Austria. The scene is wonderfully painted. Her splendid cortège arrived at the great west doors of St. Stephan's Cathedral in Vienna, with thousands in the streets watching its progress and thousands in the Cathedral awaiting its arrival. When it did arrive, her major domo took his great cane of office and banged on the cathedral door three times, demanding entrance for Zita, Empress of Austria, Princess of the House of Hapsburg, Mother of Sovereigns. There was a great silence, and the doors remained shut. He banged a second time, and repeated his words with even more force and fury in case those on the inside hadn't heard him. Again, a great silence. Finally, a third time, he knocked with his open palm on the great door, and said, "Please admit the earthly remains of Zita, a poor sinner who desires the mercy of God." Immediately the doors were flung open, and the service proceeded. Knowing who you are makes all the difference.

What, though, of that sense of identity that works in the other way, that moves in the opposite direction, which is not tearing down a false sense of ego and pride but is affirming a legitimate and justified sense of ego and pride? What about that sense of who we are? In 1896 a black man in Louisiana paid his fare and sat himself down in a railway car. He was asked to move because that particular car was reserved for white people and there was a perfectly adequate, perhaps even comparable, car elsewhere reserved for colored people, and all colored people were expected to sit in that car on the train. He refused to leave his place, and what is more, he sued. In answer to the surely asked question, "Who do you think you are?" he doubtless replied, "I am equal to anyone and everyone else on this train, and I insist upon being treated the same." He was of course to be denied and disappointed, and the famous case, 'Plessy vs Ferguson,' decided by the Supreme Court in 1896, provided the basis for legal segregation until Brown vs The Board of Education, and the modern Civil Rights Movement.

Surely, in the increasingly segregated world of the mid-twentieth century in South Africa, the young black Nelson Mandela must have been asked many times, "Who do you think you are?"

St. Paul tells us that we ought not to be conceited, and that is wise counsel, but we also ought to know who we are, and that is the essential counsel of our first lesson this morning, which Dean Lewis read for us. In the whole summary of the creation story the most important event in terms of you and of me occurs at the end of the sixth day, where Genesis 1:27 reads, "God created human beings in his own image; in the image of God he created them; male and female he created them." (REB)

This verse, Genesis 1:27, is the fundamental basis for our identity as human beings, and the particular basis for our identity as Christians. We are made in the image of God, and everything that we believe or do or that is done to us has to be understood in the light of that affirmation. We are made in the image of God, which means that there is that of God in every one of us, that every one of us bears the maker's mark, the maker's image; and it also means that there is that of every one of us in God. Now just think of the radical implications of that. If you would see who God is, first look in the mirror, but that's only a partial image, then look around; and it is the totality of what you see that gives you a clue of what it is that the creator had in mind in the first place. Any person who rejects another person rejects a part of God — that is the basis of the moral law — any person who rejects any other person rejects not just that person but a part of God, and anyone who rejects God rejects the image of God to be found in brother or in sister, or even in nature. Because we are created in God's image as human beings we are able to have fellowship both with one another and with God. Our identity stems not from what we do, or from whence we are, or from what we have, but from that and from whom we come. Our identity is not ourselves, our identity derives from the one from whom we come, and the beginning of all of that is God.

Perhaps you read, as I did, a marvelous short account in *The New Yorker* of a young boy who met his ancient grandfather and sat on the porch with the old man in darkest Appalachia, not surrounded by any of the sophisticated media of communication. It was clear through the story that the boy somehow wanted to communicate with his ancient grandfather and that the grandfather was more or less interested in communicating with the boy, and this is the exchange recorded. The grandfather said to the little boy, "Who are you?" and the little boy replied, "I'm so-and-so's son, so-and-so's grandson," and he made the obvious point that his identity was not in himself but in his relationship to these other people who in turn were related to this grand old patriarch; and he goes on to say, "I did not answer for myself, I answered for my people." We are related to all whom God has made and thus, while there are people we do not know, there are no strangers; while there may be people we do not like, there are no foreigners; while there may be people who live in other places, there are no exiles; and there is no one beneath contempt, no one beyond concern.

Such an obvious fact has always posed difficulties for thoughtful Christians, because once a thoughtful Christian has concluded that he or she is made in the image of God, he or she comes to almost the opposite rational conclusion that nobody else could possibly be; and hence our identity and our ego, instead of allowing us to share our relationships with other people, force us to become exclusive of other people, and somehow we become God's 'chosen' people, or in this community, perhaps God's 'frozen' people. Whatever we are we have no truck with others who do not share our race or our class or our ethnicity or our language or our sexuality, or any other of the distinguishing marks that make us so interesting. Even the white Christian slave owners in America in the nineteenth century understood this essential fact, that we are all created in the image of God and are therefore equal, and so they had to define their slaves as less than human beings, for if they were human beings they would have to be treated as spiritual equals, and if spiritual equals then the whole sordid system would begin to fall apart, as surely it did. We demonize and dehumanize others in order not to have to accept them as the same creatures of a creator God, and we learn our lessons only when we recognize in that diversity of human experience the presence and the image of that same God. God is not just nice to people other than ourselves, God *consists* of people other than ourselves, and so if you occupy a singularly unique place in the world you ought to recognize that not only is God there but that God is elsewhere as well. God is as foreign as the foreigner, as exiled as the exile, as different as the most different person can be. That is where the doctrine of God and the doctrine of human identity come together.

If you know this, if you understand this, if you realize in some moment of insight, of inspiration, that you are indeed a child of God, that you as you are now — with your thick lips, your yellow skin, your hooked nose, your life-giving breasts, your aging body, your youthful vigorous body — are a part of the image of God that God intended, then you are empowered, you are liberated, you are not merely born again, you are created again anew, bearing the image and the mark of the maker; and it is that which gives you power, it is that which gives you security and stability, it is that which allows you not to stagger at the uneven motions of this world. When you know this, when you realize this, no harm can come to you. Now that doesn't mean that you are immune from all of the terrible things of this life and this world, it means that no *harm* can come to you, because the only harm we need fear is the loss of the knowledge of who we are; and if we know that we are a child of God then nothing that this world can give or take away can harm us. We are secure in that knowledge. Nothing, nobody, can destroy you. They can lock you up for twenty-seven years, they can force you to hard labor, they can deprive you of music, they can humiliate you in a thousand countless artful ways, and yet you rule in the prison house and you walk out a prince, free on the outside because you have always been free on the inside. That is security, that is stability, and it comes from knowing that you are a child of God, you are created in the image of God, and that it is God's intention for you that you should represent God in the world.

Well, what an extraordinary week last week was, when you really sit down and think about it. I didn't know, for example, that George Corly Wallace had died, until Tuesday when I saw the picture in the paper of his funeral in Montgomery, the birthplace of the Confederacy, the capitol of Alabama. I knew that place very well indeed, for thirty years ago this month I began to teach at Tuskegee Institute in an Alabama that had been ruled ruthlessly by George C. Wallace. When I had arrived there his wife was serving as governor while he waited to return to overt power, and his malevolent spirit still brooded over the land even as I took my students to see the state capitol and the birthplace of the Confederacy. So, on Tuesday I looked at that photograph with keen interest. Did you notice what I noticed? Did you notice the sweet and delicious irony of Governor Wallace's coffin being borne up the capitol steps by white-gloved black state troopers who were hardly born when he was at his awful power? Here was a man who had done so much harm out of both ignorance and fear, but whose last years were marked by the growing sense that reconciliation of all of God's children, black and white, finally was what it was all about. He spent the last ten years of his life getting ready for last Tuesday morning. While he was free he was imprisoned by his own demon and his denial of God's creative power in other people; and while our Friday guest, Nelson Mandela, was in prison in almost exactly the same period of time, *his* spirit soared because he knew that he was God's child.

In the book of Proverbs there is a verse that reads, "For as [a man] thinketh in his heart, so is he." (Proverbs 23:7; KJV) The context is unhelpful, but the point is that it is from within that we form our sense of who we are; and that, alas, is where the self-esteem people start out well but get it wrong. They think that we should think well of ourselves in order to protect ourselves from criticism and difficulty, while the Bible's point is that we must think well of ourselves because we reflect the goodness of our creator, and that imposes a burden and not a liberty. Low self-esteem is not the issue but, rather, high expectation. We treat others well not because we are good but because they are created in the image of God, even as are we. We expect to be treated well not because we deserve it but because the God who created us all requires it. As Jesse Jackson might put it, "If you *think* you are somebody, you will act like somebody, and you will treat everybody like somebody." Somebody created in the very image of God.

Relationship and identity go hand-in-hand. We have no solitary identity, no being that is solely our own, the whole context of Romans 12 is corporate, cooperative, the parts of the body united in their specific duties for the well-being of the whole. Our image in Christ is a corporeal one, as St. Paul said, a unity in purpose, a difference in function, but an ultimate recreation of the unity of our original creation. We forget that at our peril.

Who do you think you are? What Nelson Mandela knows, what George Corly Wallace found out, you too can know, for when you know yourself to be a child of God made in the image of the divine, and that everybody else is made in that same image, you will not be content with anything less than that truth. If you understand and accept yourself as the image, the creation, of God, then everything else will take care of itself. You can bank on that.

Let us pray:

> *We praise Thee, O God, that Thou lovest us so much that Thou hast created us in Thine own image. Help us to love ourselves that we might better love Thee, and all of Thy creation. This we pray through Jesus Christ our Lord. Amen.*

September 20, 1998

WHAT KIND OF CHURCH IS THIS?

The Seventeenth Sunday after Pentecost

The Lesson

I Peter 2:1-10 (RSV)

So put away all malice and all guile and insincerity and envy and all slander. Like newborn babes, long for the pure spiritual milk, that by it you may grow up to salvation; for you have tasted the kindness of the Lord.

Come to him, to that living stone, rejected by men but in God's sight chosen and precious; and like living stones be yourselves built into a spiritual house, to be a holy priesthood, to offer spiritual sacrifices acceptable to God through Jesus Christ. For it stands in scripture:

> "Behold, I am laying in Zion a stone, a cornerstone chosen and precious, and he who believes in him will not be put to shame."

To you therefore who believe, he is precious, but for those who do not believe:

> "The very stone which the builders rejected has become the head of the corner,"
>
> and
>
> "A stone that will make men stumble, a rock that will make them fall;"

for they stumble because they disobey the word, as they were destined to do.

But you are a chosen race, a royal priesthood, a holy nation, God's own people, that you may declare the wonderful deeds of him who called you out of darkness into his marvelous light. Once you were no people but now you are God's people; once you had not received mercy but now you have received mercy.

WHAT KIND OF CHURCH IS THIS?

Text: Once you were no people but now you are God's people; once you had not received mercy but now you have received mercy.
I Peter 2:10

In Friday's *Harvard Crimson* I read on the editorial page an essay entitled *The 'R' Word*, with the intriguing box-quote question: "What does it mean to be a believer when believing is no longer in vogue?" The undergraduate author — whom I haven't met but certainly intend to — was musing, as seniors are wont to do, on the paradox that while his Roman Catholic faith means a great deal to him, he keeps it more or less under wraps here in college because of the pervasive sense that it is not too cool to be too hot about religion.

"In fact," he writes, "it would not be so far from the truth to describe the unspoken attitude toward religion in general and Christianity in particular as respectfully hostile." I like that phrase, "respectfully hostile," for it is redolent of a subtle accuracy; I like it, and will use it.

One of my colleagues told me recently that he had brought as his guest a distinguished French academic last week to the Special Convocation for Nelson Mandela, and that when I was announced to open the Exercises with prayer, the guest said to his host in some astonishment, "How is it that you would begin so important an occasion with an act of religion?"

Well. Religion in general, and Christianity in particular, have a bad name in the modern secular research university. Religion is suspect because it implies, indeed demands, a loyalty far greater than that which we ought to give to reason and to the Temple to Reason which the university has become. Christianity is also suspect because to many people it suggests a narrow and bigoted view of the world, it is contrary to reason, and it is socially devisive. It doesn't help, as my young essayist pointed out in the *Crimson*, that in contemporary America the term 'Christian' has been hijacked by a rather partisan and exclusive brand of zealots who seem to be in the exclusive business of putting people off and shutting people out.

Two weeks ago, in my Opening of Term sermon, *Godliness and Good Learning*, I did my best to make the case for the intimate and historic relationship between godliness and good learning; and last Sunday I tried to address your role in the process by asking *Who Do You Think You Are?* in a sermon by that title. Today I will address the particular identity and mission of this church as it seeks to minister in a community which more often than not seems "respectfully hostile" to the dimension of the sacred.

You will note, I am sure, the use of the two words 'identity' and 'mission,' one trendy and secular for everybody is "into" identity; and the other rather old-fashioned. People have objectives, tasks, and projects, but 'mission' has rather a dated, pious, ring to it. I have chosen it, as you might imagine, for this reason.

Let us consider 'identity' first. Next to the question concerning how the likes of me came to be minister here, and how much longer I expect to hang on, the most frequently asked question of me is, "Just what kind of church is this?" It is a good question. There are no signs on the outside of our building that would give away our identity, no red, white, and blue 'The Episcopal Church Welcomes You' sign, no cross outlined in lightbulbs suggesting a warm evangelical welcome inside, no cross, in fact, at all, for if you look closely you will see that we have at the top of our steeple a medieval pennant which has been familiarly known as 'King George's Underwear.' The building itself, however, make no mistake about it, has a churchy look: Sir Christopher Wren with an attitude, one might say, but what kind of church is it?

When you come inside the question becomes even more intense, for with all of its white paint and clear glass it looks like a big New England meetinghouse, but then there is the Georgian version of a medieval choir screen, and a very large pulpit. At the east end of the back space where the altar in any correctly-styled chancel ought to be, there is the organ.

Perhaps the service will give a clue? We begin our services in the way that for three hundred years most Protestant public worship began, which is with the singing of Old Hundred, a version of Psalm 100, and most churches haven't done that for years. The language is exalted, or stilted, as your tastes dictate, and since nobody knows the hymns, this must be an Episcopal church; the sermon is long and based on the Bible, so it must be nearer Presbyterian; we speak plainly about money, so it could be Baptist; and nobody shouts or is too demonstrative, so it cannot be Pentecostal. There are no guitars, praise songs, or children's stories, but instead a certain austerity, even the slightest hint of a chill, that is never broken by the 'kiss of peace.' The music is both exemplary and invisible, and people arrive as late as they possibly can and leave as early as they possibly can. *What kind of church is this?*

In the real estate trade, I am told, there are only three words that count: location, location, location. To adapt a philosophical concept to this vulgar iteration: location is destiny. Where you are tells much about who and what you are. When the Christians at Harvard in 1814 withdrew from the fellowship of the First Parish Church in Cambridge, they did so in order to form what they called a 'Church within the walls,' by which they meant a religious community unique to and uniquely situated within the precincts of Harvard College. To house their church they built University Hall, and until 1858 when Appleton Chapel was built, the present Faculty Room was the College Chapel and my predecessors sat where the dean now sits. Our church is still here within the precincts, and wonderfully if enigmatically situated between Widener Library and the Science Center. If those two places are dedicated to the *how* of things, we, between them, insist upon the *why*.

Our location, therefore, tells us that we are a church with a particular identity, meant to be a sacramental space in a secular and material world. Do you remember what a sacrament is? It is the outward and visible sign of an inward and spiritual grace, and buildings can be sacramental as well, and this one is particularly suited to that role, for what you see is meant to direct you toward that which you cannot see. It was a happy conceit of academic architecture in the nineteenth century to place the college library and the college chapel as two equal sides of the principal public space, and done to make a point now lost, alas, more often than not. Here, the point which might have been lost has been enhanced by placing the chapel quite by accident between the humanities and the sciences, related to each but beyond both.

It happens that on Thursday last I found myself in Mount Auburn Cemetery standing on Harvard Hill, the central bit of high ground that belongs to the Corporation of Harvard College, on the very spot where I had helped my old friend John Marquand to select his final resting place. As I looked east toward Cambridge through an artful opening in the trees I could get a clear and unimpeded view of the College with its towers, chief of which is the spire of this church. Ours is no longer the tallest piece of architecture, alas, William James Hall having intruded from that distance as our most visible mistake, but it is still by far the most beautiful.

The location of our church suggests our identity as a house of prayer in the midst of the life of the mind. Our location in Harvard Yard as opposed to in Harvard Square tells us, in the words of the poet Phillip Larkin, that we must be a "serious house on serious earth," a house whose very presence transcends its place, a place that is holy not because Harvard says it is holy but because, in the words of I Kings 8:29, "My name shall be there." This place is holy because it has been consecrated by generations of prayers and praises: God has been sought and found here, and extraordinary transactions have transpired. As Jacob, that most wily and shrewd of all the patriarchs, said of his encounter with a space not dissimilar to this one, "Surely the Lord is in this place; and I knew it not...this is none other but the house of God, and this is the gate of heaven." (Genesis 28:16&17). Our identity is the place where we have permission to meet God and God has an invitation to meet us, and certainly that can happen anywhere, but it must and does happen here. We express this identity in our worship, which is our chief work every day and especially on Sunday, for worship is not what we do while we are waiting to do more important things, worship is the most important thing that we can do, and that is why we work so hard at it, and take it so seriously.

It is this work that also translates our identity into our mission. That great document of reformed Protestant religion, the Westminster Confession, asks as the first question of the catechism, "What is the whole duty of man?" The answer is, famously, "To love God and to enjoy him forever." Now some of you are unaccustomed to the idea of "enjoying" God, and some may think that phrase ethically deficient: where, for example, are the admonishments to feed the hungry, clothe the naked, and save the whales? What our dour Presbyterian predecessors understood so much better than do so many of their descendants, however, is that all ethics and good works and high ideals and faithful living proceed only from the primary basis of the love and enjoyment of God. Because we enjoy, that is, celebrate, what God has done for us "in our creation, preservation, and all the blessings of this life," as we say in the General Thanksgiving, we are able both to love ourselves and to love others, and to withstand those who are at the very least "respectfully hostile" toward us.

This is the point that the epistle is trying to make this morning, where under the name of Peter is an encouragement to those early Christians who suffered at the hands of the Neronian persecution, not merely in "respectful hostility," but in ultimate hostility to the point of the sword. What should faithful people do? They should remember their identity.

"You are a chosen race, a royal priesthood..." "Once you were no people but now you are God's people..." and don't forget that, Peter tells them. Your mission? You have been set apart, he says in Chapter Two, in order that "you may declare the wonderful deeds of him who called you out of darkness into his marvelous light."

Let us put this another way. In the porch of Boston's Old South Church in Copley Square there is a wonderful tablet that summarizes the three hundred fifty year history of the third Church of Christ in Boston. It begins with the words, "Preserved of God..." The church to which Peter wrote, and the Old South Church, this church, and every church, has each been "preserved of God" in order that in every way possible we may "declare the wonderful deeds of him who called [us] out of darkness into his marvelous light."

Will this be easy? Of course not. The historical record is eloquent on the subject of the sufferings of the church in the world: we are not to be spared from suffering embarrassment, persecution, or even the respectful hostility of our colleagues, teachers, and friends. We have been preserved, "spared," as our ancestors delighted to say, both in spite of these and because of these, and rightly founded in the sure conviction that the gates of hell cannot prevail against us.

So, what is the bottom line? What kind of church is this?

We are a Christian church because we love Jesus and believe him to be the Christ.

We are a Protestant church because we cannot and will not deny our inheritance.

We are a Catholic church because we affirm the unbroken tradition from the apostles.

We are an orthodox church because we share in the great continuity.

We are an evangelical church because we share the good news.

We are a reformed church because we respect the integrity of the individual mind and soul.

> *We are an ecumenical church because we do not believe ourselves to be the exclusive objects of God's affection.*
>
> *We are a pilgrim church because we have not yet arrived at where we are going.*

We may no longer dominate the horizon but the horizon still dominates us, and we set our eyes, our minds, and our hearts on the realm beyond that which we can see.

Hear these words again, written to those who suffer at the hands of the respectfully hostile: "You are a chosen race, a royal priesthood, a holy nation, God's own people, that you may declare the wonderful deeds of him who called you out of darkness into his marvelous light. Once you were no people but now you are God's people; once you had not received mercy but now you have received mercy."

This is the kind of church which knows that to be true.

Let us pray:

> *We give Thee thanks, O God, for the Church — Thy Church and this Church. Where it is weak, strengthen it. Where it is fearful, encourage it. Where it is in error, correct it. Expunge from it all evil, malice, and small-mindedness; and make it large enough to receive all of Thy people, for Christ's sake Amen.*

September 27, 1998

HOW TO RUIN YOUR REPUTATION

The Twentieth Sunday after Pentecost

The Lesson

Luke 7:33-35;37-39;44-50 (RSV)

For John the Baptist has come eating no bread and drinking no wine; and you say, 'He has a demon.' The Son of man has come eating and drinking; and you say, 'Behold, a glutton and a drunkard, a friend of tax collectors and sinners!' Yet wisdom is justified by all her children.

And behold, a woman of the city, who was a sinner, when she learned that he was at table in the Pharisee's house, brought an alabaster flask of ointment, and standing behind him at his feet, weeping, she began to wet his feet with her tears, and wiped them with the hair of her head, and kissed his feet, and anointed them with the ointment. Now when the Pharisee who had invited him saw it, he said to himself, "If this man were a prophet, he would have known who and what sort of woman this is who is touching him, for she is a sinner."

Then turning toward the woman he said to Simon, "Do you see this woman? I entered your house, you gave me no water for my feet, but she has wet my feet with her tears and wiped them with her hair. You gave me no kiss, but from the time I came in she has not ceased to kiss my feet. You did not anoint my head with oil, but she has anointed my feet with ointment. Therefore I tell you, her sins, which are many, are forgiven, for she loved much; but he who is forgiven little, loves little." And he said to her, "Your sins are forgiven." Then those who were at table with him began to say among themselves, "Who is this, who even forgives sins?" And he said to the woman, "Your faith has saved you; go in peace."

HOW TO RUIN YOUR REPUTATION

Text: "The Son of man has come eating and drinking..."

Luke 7:34 (RSV)

The text this morning is the thirty-fourth verse of the seventh chapter of the gospel according to St. Luke, which, in the more vivid and archaic King James version, goes on to say that "The Son of man...is a gluttonous man, and a winebibber..."

As a rule I rarely advertise books from this pulpit, especially books writen by somebody else, but I make an exception this morning because a half-page advertisement in yesterday's *New York Times Book Review* caught my attention. It was for a new book, written by Donald Spoto, entitled *The Hidden Jesus: A New Life*, and the teaser to the ad, of enormous cost, asks, 'What Do We Really Know about Jesus?' The author is credited with the following conclusions:

- Nowhere in scripture is there anything against women becoming priests
- Sexual morality was not an issue of great concern to Jesus
- No true Christian can endorse capital punishment
- There are ancient anti-Semitic passages in the New Testament which Jesus himself would certainly have rejected

The book is endorsed by no less a spiritual writer than Thomas Moore, and I intend to get it to see if it follows through; and I hasten to add that I do not know nor have I ever heard of Donald Spoto, so we are not in league together.

Now, those of us in the business of talking and writing about Jesus might ask, "Does the world need yet another biography of Jesus?" Bookstore shelves are groaning with books about Jesus, and the world never seems to grow better for it, in fact it seems to get worse. Apparently we cannot get enough of Jesus, when all we need to know is contained in the four gospels, read out in church every Sunday, that tell his story but pale in weight and in number by the books about him. Is this another story about Jesus because we don't like the one we have? Perhaps the reason there has been such an industry in the life of Jesus is that we don't necessarily know or like what we find about him in the gospels, and are hoping for something better? If we keep working at it we just might come up with an agreeable, attractive, acceptable Jesus who is worthy of our literary efforts, and worthy of a half-page in *The New York Times Book Review*. If this new book pays any attention to the gospel portrait of Jesus and gives him back his life, then it will have justified its publication, it will be worthy of our efforts, and of a column in *The New York Times*. I intend to get it and read it, but I do wonder if this cynical and hypocritical age can endure the truth about Jesus, whom we have managed to neuter and recreate in our own image. If Donald Spoto's book tells the truth about Jesus, can you and I bear it?

Take today's lesson, for example, from the book of Proverbs, which Dean Kidd read for us, a book of wisdom with which our Lord as a good Jew would have been familiar, which justly sings out the praises of a good reputation: "A good name is to be chosen rather than great riches..." which is the same sentiment found in Ecclesiastes 7:1: "A good name is better than precious ointment..." This is the text inscribed on a memorial tablet in one of the St. Grottlesex school chapels which will go unmentioned, where in very large bronze letters is declared, 'Endicott Peabody Saltonstall: A Good Name is Better than Great Riches;' and if you can have both, why, all the better.

Well, this is a sermon about reputation and these are texts about reputation, and you are curious people who came here today to address the question of who we are, who people think we are, who we aspire to be, and to hear how to ruin your reputation. Reputation, we are told, is what both precedes and follows us, and, for better or for worse, a reputation is formed early and lasts long, and its image is hard to break. Here it may be useful as a helpful aside to offer a mild but pertinent distinction between 'reputation' and 'character.'

'Reputation,' I was told as a young man, is what people think of you; while 'character' is what God knows of you. I rather like that, for character, despite all of the talk by such virtue-mongers as Bill Bennett and his Republican friends, is ultimately rather elusive; God looketh upon the heart, man and woman looketh upon the outward appearance, and so it would appear that character is that which is ultimately known to God, while reputation is which passes in the meantime. Reputation is the stuff with which human beings work most of the time, the visible tip of the iceberg, the character of which is way below the surface. Whenever I see Charles Coulson on the television I know that I am meant to see a born-again Christian who now preaches virtue with the authority of a convicted and converted felon, but I still see, God help me, the arch-Watergate burglar. I try, but a reputation is a terrible thing not to be able to shake. Richard Nixon had more lives than a cat, but his reputation is still that of a crook: only God now knows the difference. Character is elusive, and I would be very suspicious of those who run on theirs, and you should be too: a 'good' character may simply mean either a lack of information or imagination, or of opportunity.

Reputations, however, are to be taken quite seriously, as we discover in today's second lesson, in which it is clear that Jesus is being compared with his cousin John the Baptist, at this moment a rival prophet of exceptional moral and ascetic qualities: John the Baptist, who would make Independent Counsel Ken Starr look like Johnny Rotten. We understand what the New Testament paints as a picture of John the Baptist: John the Baptist, prophet of righteousness, locusts, honey, wearing a hair shirt and wandering around without shoes all over the desert, who would certainly be no fun at a cocktail party — but, if you were looking for someone to save your soul, he is numero uno. "John the Baptist," says Jesus, "has come eating no bread and drinking no wine." He had a good reputation as a prophet.

At this point, though, Jesus, a rising new young prophet, was gaining a reputation as a healer of the sick, always a good way to gain such a reputation, for to take someone who is sick and make him well and allow him to testify about it is a very good and useful testimonial and endorsement. Earlier in today's gospel he goes beyond merely curing someone from the common cold, he raises from the dead the son of the widow of Nain, a remarkably sure way to establish a fine reputation. Passing through a village he comes upon a funeral procession of a widow who has lost her son and therefore the source of her support. Here is this dead boy on his bier, borne aloft by mourners and pallbearers, and Jesus confronts the scene, and, as Luke tells it, says to the young man, dead as a doornail on the bier, "'Young man, I say to you, arise;' and the dead man sat up and began to speak." Now that is a remarkable occurrence, even you would be impressed if that happened here in The Memorial Church at some memorial service, and we said to one of our colleagues presumed to be safely and finally dead, "Get up!" and he did, and more than that, began to talk. What does the gospel say? "Fear seized them all," reports Luke, "and they glorified God, saying, 'A great prophet has risen among us!' and 'God has visited his people!'" Now I know that some of you don't know the Bible and think that I am making all this up, but I am not, it is all there, read it, it's in Luke 7:16, and it's an incredible story. "And this report concerning him," Luke continues, "spread through the whole of Judea and all the surrounding country." He was gaining a reputation, he was building up credits, people heard about him and wanted to see and to hear him.

So Jesus's reputation began to grow so fast and so remarkably that even John the Baptist wondered, "Are you he who is to come, or shall we look for another?" Jesus refuses a direct answer, an annoying characteristic of his throughout the gospels, but he praises John, saying, "I tell you, among those born of women none is greater than John; yet he who is least in the kingdom of God is greater than he" — the sting in the tail.

This is the context of that famous scene of hospitality where in Simon the Pharisee's house — not Simon Peter, don't confuse them — Jesus creates a scandal by accepting the intimate ministrations of a woman of the streets, of low repute. What did she do? She crashed the party, she wasn't invited, she was a gate-crasher as probably so many at crashed parties around here last night at the Head of the Charles, popping in to a party saying they know Fred when they've never heard of Fred. So, the woman crashed the party, she stood behind Jesus trying not to be noticed, and she washed his feet with her tears, wiped them with her hair, and anointed them with precious ointment.

Now, even the dullest of you knows that this is pretty intimate stuff, playing with feet, weeping, washing, anointing; it's very tactile, this is not a metaphor, this woman was all over him, or at least all over his feet — and who was she to be doing this in the first place? For her to be there at all was little short of scandalous, for who was she, to be in the presence of the prophet? That is scandal of the first order, for a woman to be in the same room as the great prophet when she was supposed to be outside or in the kitchen, or anywhere but near the scene of the great visitation. That raises other questions. Where did she get the precious ointment? What did she do to get the money to pay for the ointment? Maybe it's best not to ask, not to inquire too closely. By what right did she presume the intimacies of a friend, a host, even of a lover? Only the most intimate of relations allows somebody to do this to somebody else; it is only a host who washes the feet of a guest in his house, only a lover who washes the feet of his or her spouse or companion. Who is she to do this, and what was she trying to advertise? What was her game? What was she up to?

She was well known in the town, she had a reputation, we might say, and so the criticism falls on Jesus, for, when the Pharisee Simon, who had invited Jesus home, saw this, he said to himself, "If this man were a prophet [meaning a true prophet], he would have known who and what sort of woman this is who is touching him, for she is a sinner." (Luke 7:39) The assumption is that if Jesus were a real prophet he would have known who she was, and if he had known that she was a sinner he would have had nothing to do with her. Those two assumptions hold this story together.

Here was a situation in which the woman had nothing to lose, and Jesus, it would appear, had everything to lose: his rising credentials as a prophet with a deep knowledge of people, his moral purity which should be preserved against the contamination of sinners, and most of all, his simple good judgement and *gravitas*. If he didn't value his own reputation, at least he should have valued the reputation of his host, in whose house these intimacies were publicly and unashamedly displayed. Had he no sense of place? No judgement? No sense of pride? He embarrassed his host, yet he rebukes the host and not the woman, saying to Simon, "Do you see this woman? I entered your house, you gave me no water for my feet, but she has wet my feet with her tears and wiped them with her hair. You gave me no kiss, but from the time I came in she has not ceased to kiss my feet. You did not anoint my head with oil, but she has anointed my feet with ointment. Therefore I tell you, her sins, which are many, are forgiven, for she loved much; but he who is forgiven little, loves little." (Luke 7:44-47)

One cannot imagine such behavior from John the Baptist, or even, for that matter, from anyone whose job it is to varnish one's reputation for probity and morality. Virtue, as we all know, is keeping a conspicuous distance from vice; but, as our text puts it so clearly and unambiguously, "The Son of man has come eating and drinking;" and, as is also very clear, the son of man consorts with people of low degree. Eating and drinking, consorting with people whom you and I would either raise an eyebrow about, or spend very little time with.

The King James version of the Bible is wonderfully vivid here, translating Luke 7:34, "Behold a gluttonous man, and a winebibber;" and the only other time that that word, 'winebibber,' is found in scripture is in Proverbs 23:20, where in good advice to the would-be moral Jew, it is written, "Be not among winebibbers; among riotous eaters of flesh — a direct prohibition against the very thing that Luke describes our Lord as being. Both St. Luke in his description, and Jesus in his action, knew what they were doing: this is no accident, no editorial slip of the tongue, no casual mistake, for Jesus does not conform to the moral dictatorship of the many, he accepts neither the conventional wisdom nor the conventional virtue, and in this he makes some formidable enemies — and isn't it often said that we should be known by the enemies we make? Who are your enemies? Who really doesn't like you? Who would seek to do you in? Then you have to ask if it is worth it. To be known by one's enemies is to have a catalogue of those things against which many might well object.

Pharisees, for example, do not like to be rebuked, especially publicly, and particularly in their own houses. Jesus's grandstanding in the house of Simon, taking the part of the fallen and brazen woman and later more notoriously drinking with publicans, tax collectors, and those outside of the chosen few, would earn him the enmity of those who had better reputations than his to maintain, and they would succeed; we know that they succeeded: they would see him on the cross, and it doesn't get any better than that if you wish to put your enemy out of business.

Jesus's greatest crime was that he disturbed the balance of power and destroyed the serenity of those who believed in the immutability of the social order and in the superiority of their own moral vision; and he makes them, and us, all nervous and upset. Our lesson from Luke is just one of dozens of examples in which he does this, all with an eye not to what is apparent to the human sensibility — reputation — but to what is known to and loved by God — dare we call it character? In this way he ruined his reputation for classic prophethood, which usually means the absence of vice, and replaced it with an affirmation of virtue, which consists in the nature of one's own heart and its relationship to God; and if that is described in Donald Spoto's book, it's a good book; and if it is not described in Donald Spoto's book, it is a wicked book and not worth the paper it is printed on. It is this consistent, vivid, and confrontational system of morality that characterizes the life and the teachings of Jesus and makes him so fundamentally unacceptable to us, to all of us, his followers.

Most of the time we do not worship the Jesus of the gospels but rather a pale construction, a pale imitation who reflects the rather weak virtues of our culture. We like his healing of the sick — who would be against the healing of the sick? — but we do not like his condemnation of the righteous. We think his parables interesting and perhaps worthy of study in the Divinity School or the English Department, but we do not like his judgements about money. We are sorry that he ends up on the cross, a tragic ending to a noble life, but we cannot accept that his resurrection is for the sinful, and not for the virtuous.

I hope that Mr. Spoto, in his book, spends a great deal of time on Jesus's social teachings on wealth and money — those who have it and those who want it, which just about covers everybody in this congregation — for if he does he will learn that Jesus is much more interested in the burden of money than he is, for example, in the vices of sex; and this is only one instance in which we edit out what we know of Jesus. We, on the other hand, are much more interested in sex, and we define our virtue in terms of it but leave our money, and discussion about it, alone.

Jesus spends his time with and risks his reputation for those noticeably different and cast out from conventional polite society. We segregate those different from ourselves, and in the terrible logic of a climate that permits this, we kill them, as was done to that poor gay boy in Wyoming, news of whom cannot have escaped any of us.

If we tame the social conscience of Jesus we allow the savage in every one of us to escape, to run rampant, and there is nothing in this world more dangerous or destructive than savagery done in the name of religion. Did you notice that the funeral of Matthew Shepard was picketed by members of a fundamentalist Christian Church that bears the name of Baptist — God spare us identity with such wicked people — and that they had signs saying, "God Hates Fags," presuming to quote from the epistle to the Romans? This was done in the name of the gospel. There can be no moral cover for either such a belief, or for such a behavior; you cannot hide under the cushion, 'I feel sincerely and strongly on this point of view.' You may try to hide, but you are wrong.

The week's news was not all bad, however, thank God. On Wednesday, *The Boston Globe* reported that the Dutch Reformed Church in South Africa publicly repudiated its old racist theology and its reading of the Bible in order to support apartheid. It adopted a "resolution rejecting apartheid as wrong and sinful not simply in its effects and operations but in its fundamental nature." The resolution called apartheid "a travesty of the gospel," and apologized for what it called "sinful." It took the Southern Baptist Convention one hundred thirty-five years after the end of the War Between the States, as they delight to call it, to apologize for the same sins.

Thank God it is never too late to repent, that is, until Jesus comes, but where will we be when the Church at last repents of its destructive treatment of homosexuals and its reading of scripture which allows society permission to act upon its innate savagery? Where will we be when the apology is written? The moral equivalent of the scene in Simon's house in today's gospel would be cast in gay terms, and if that distresses you it should, and so should the gospel.

A good reputation is a terrible thing to lose, a better reputation a glorious thing to gain. Jesus was a winebibber: "Behold, a glutton and a drunkard, a friend of tax collectors and sinners!" That means that in Jesus's fallen circle of friends there may yet be room for you and for me. His ruined reputation may just help us to rehabilitate ours, and for that we should say "Praise God!" and "Amen."

Let us pray:

> *O God, we give Thee thanks that Jesus came among us, and dwelt within us, and rehabilitated the worst of us that the best in us might come forth. Now send us out into the world to do our daily task inspired, and moved, and provoked by the power of the holy spirit. Amen*

October 18, 1998

SURPLUS AND SUBSTANCE

The Twenty-first Sunday after Pentecost

The Lesson

Luke 21:1-9 (KJV)

And he looked up, and saw the rich men casting their gifts into the treasury. And he saw also a certain poor widow casting in thither two mites. And he said, "Of a truth, I say unto you that this poor widow hath cast in more than they all: for all these have of their abundance cast in unto the offerings of God, but she of her penury hath cast in all the living that she had."

And as some spake of the temple, how it was adorned with goodly stones and gifts, he said, "As for these things which ye behold, the days will come in the which there shall not be left one stone upon another, that shall not be thrown down;" and they asked him, saying, "Master, but when shall these things be? and what sign will there be when these things shall come to pass?"

And he said, "Take heed that ye be not deceived: for many shall come in my name, saying, 'I am Christ;' and the time draweth near: go ye not therefore after them."

But when ye shall hear of wars and commotions, be not terrified: for these things must first come to pass; but the end is not by and by.

SURPLUS AND SUBSTANCE

Text: "For all these have of their abundance cast in unto the offerings of God; but she of her penury hath cast in all the living that she had." *Luke 21:4 (KJV)*

My text is the fourth verse of the twenty-first chapter of the gospel according to St. Luke, where our Lord makes a comparative statement and an absolute judgement.

Those of you who were here last Sunday know that I spoke of that nameless, infamous woman in the gospel who anointed Jesus's feet and washed them with her tears, and if you wanted to, you could say that that sermon was about sex. Next Sunday, on All Saints' and All Souls' day, we will speak of the faithful departed, and you might think that that sermon will be about death. Today, in the account of the widow's mite from which our text is taken, it is obvious that we are speaking about money, or so it would seem. If we had Madison Avenue values here, or even the sensibilities of talk radio, we could advertise this as a series entitled 'All You Need to Know about Sex, Money, and Death;' but then, there is more to each of these sermons than any of those.

We have heard many times this story of our Lord in the gospel of Luke:

> "He looked up and saw the rich putting their gifts into the treasury; and he saw a poor widow put in two copper coins. And he said, 'Truly I tell you, this poor widow has put in more than all of them; for they all contributed out of their abundance, but she out of her poverty put in all the living that she had.'" (Luke 21:1-4 (RSV))

or, as the King James version puts it:

> "And he looked up, and saw the rich men casting their gifts into the treasury. And he saw also a certain poor widow casting in thither two mites. And he said, 'Of

> a truth I say unto you, that this poor widow hath cast in more than they all: for all these have of their abundance cast in unto the offerings of God; but she of her penury hath cast in all the living that she had.'"
>
> (Luke 21:1-4 (KJV))

Most of us have grown up with the story of the widow's *mite*, and we know that it means a small denomination of ancient money, but as children we hear before we read or spell, and so I thought that the story was about the widow's *might* — a modest, but useful preaching point. Our Lord said, "This poor widow has put in more than all of them; for they all contributed out of their abundance, but she out of her poverty put in all the living that she had." Now the context for this, in the preceding chapter, is Jesus's criticism of the rich and visible believers, the Pharisees, the rich, the powerful, who liked to wear long robes and stand in public places, and made much of their piety and of their philanthropy and good works; and in one sense this is just more of the same, criticizing the establishment, those people for whom doing good works and giving good gifts doesn't cut anywhere into the substance of their being. People give who can afford to give. Here, the story contrasts with one who in Jesus's eyes cannot afford to give, and therefore gives everything that she has.

There are times, I think, and this may be one of them, when we wish that the text were less clear and more ambiguous. It would be helpful in this text, for example, to discover that there are several nuanced hidden levels of meaning whereby it does not say what we think it says. It was Mark Twain, more cynical than devout, who said, "It is not what I don't understand in the Bible that troubles me, it is what I do understand." This is one of those texts: we get it. We can and we do understand the text about the widow's mite, and that is the trouble; and it troubles us, I suggest, on two counts, with the first in the context of a much larger anxiety that we Christians have, which is that we are troubled when we talk about money.

There! I caught you, I can see you already frowning and freezing up, already grabbing for that part of you which is most important to you, holding on, thinking, "Here we go again." We don't like to discuss money in relationship to our church or to our faith or to our religion, although we will talk about it as far as the national debt is concerned, we will talk about it as far as taxes are concerned, we will talk about it as far public expenditure is concerned — but we don't want to talk about it in terms of our religion or our church or our faith because somehow, somewhere, somebody has told us one of the few religious principles that we remember, which is that religion is 'spiritual' and money is 'material,' and that never the twain should meet — especially in church. Hence ministers, particularly those of the more respectable 'mainline' churches, those churches from whom most of you have fled for the time being in order to come here on Sunday morning, are usually embarrassed to speak of money; and at best devote a few minutes on one Sunday a year, supported by a phalanx of sympathetic lay people, to little homilies on 'stewardship.' Very subtle, artfully produced letters and cards are given which, if you are lucky, will not mention money or need or giving at all, and most congregations are equally embarrassed and annoyed by even these little subtleties. You should be grateful to me that I am not going to preach about money on Stewardship Sunday in November, because I am speaking about it today; and you don't have to stay at home on Stewardship Sunday, because the sermon for that day is the one that I am giving you right now.

It is not that combination of the spiritual and the material that is the source of our chief discomfort, I would argue, and not so much that we dislike or even distrust the mixing of the spiritual and the material. The honest reason that we are dissatisfied is that in most cases we are very much attached to the material and do not wish to be persuaded to part with it either by Jesus or by a preacher. Our text this morning permits us to talk about money apart from that annual Sunday on which we appeal for a lot from a lot of you, to defang the subject, if you will, and to express your legitimate fears about your claim on your money and your money's claim on you, and to do so in the context of what the gospel teaches and what Jesus preaches.

I have said that our first anxiety about this text has to do with the subject of money and the mixing of the material and the spiritual, and we will come back to that later. The second anxiety has to do with what we know the moral of the text to be, and its obvious conclusion that Jesus approves of those who give more than we think they can afford. The rich, according to the parable, give out of their abundance, their surplus, their disposable income that they can dispose of in charitable benevolent philanthropic ways, Jesus says, but the widow gave all that she had. Non-disposable income is what we can't get along without; and no one can give too much. So, when we hear the story of the widow's mite our first sympathy goes out to that the poor widow who had no idea what she was doing and gave it all away, and now she will be an even greater burden upon the state, and those rich Pharisees will have to give even more to sustain her who could have sustained herself had she given only one copper coin instead of two. The rich give out of their surplus, says Jesus, but the widow gave out of her substance, that is, the essence of who she was. She gave all that she had and, not simply content to describe the transaction, Jesus says that that is the better way: she has given more than all of them; in other words, no one is too poor or too constrained to give, and no one may give too much. We may not understand the principle behind this, but we certainly understand that it is this of which Jesus approves, and because of that, you and I are obliged to take it seriously.

Now, we may not understand the principle demonstrated here by the widow, we may not understand the notion that no one is too poor or too constrained to give, but the poor have no problem with this principle and perhaps we can learn from them. By no means was my family wealthy when I was growing up, although they worked very hard to conceal from me the facts of just how poor we were. For my parents, poverty of means was an attitude to be overcome by wealth of spirit, and so we were rich but just didn't have very much money. I remember as an absolute principle of our household that when the monthly accounting of the family income came around, before the bills were considered — the mortgage, heat, food, and clothing addressed — the church money was first set aside, taken out of the file, sealed up in envelopes to be given in church, and put in the drawer so that we would not be tempted to raid it for necessities as the month went along. In the piety of my shrewd and very Yankee family God's money was taken out first, for of course it was God's money and not ours, and only after that was given were the needs considered for which my father and my mother, and eventually I, had worked so hard.

It was not through pride that my parents did this, it was just their lifelong practice, for it was what Christians did, and somehow, with so economically unsound a practice, they nevertheless managed week after week, month after month, and year after year. They were not by nature charitable or philanthropic, it was not their habit to look down the list of appeals in the newspapers, or on the radio and eventually on television, to decide where they were going to spread their resources, but they did make that point of first setting aside God's money out of their money; and they didn't think of themselves as doing a great thing but rather as doing the right thing as they understood the gospel to teach it to them, and the least that they could do. They understood and were not frightened, though I cannot say for certain that they never suffered, for I saw very little evidence of it. Nor can I say that they were openly rewarded, with showers of blessings pouring down upon them through the open windows of heaven, as is promised by so many television and radio evangelists in the gospel of wealth. I saw not much effect at all. They weren't impoverished, and they weren't overly endowed with worldly riches, they simply had an honest relationship with money and knew that a significant portion of it did not belong to them but to God, and so, being basically honest people, they gave it back to God.

While my parents were not tithers, many were, and I grew up in a church where lots of people tithed. Now, probably among you this morning are some M.B.A.s and even some Ph.D.s who have never heard of tithing, and perhaps a few others of you as well do not know what it is, either as a theological or a biblical or an economic principle, and so I will explain it to you. The tithe is a tenth, and tithing is the old biblical principle much approved of under the law of Moses, that ten percent of what you have belongs to the Lord, and the first tenth is holy unto the Lord. The principle is that one hundred percent comes from God, God wants you to keep and enjoy and multiply ninety percent, but ten percent belongs to God. So, for every dollar you have, ten cents belongs to the Lord, before taxes — in the days before taxes. The tithe, in fact, may be thought of as the first tax. As all things come from God, according to the theory, all things belong to God, but God claims only ten percent of it, for God's own work — basic, elemental economy.

In early Christian times, and in the early church, it was out of the tithes of the faithful that the charitable work of the community of believers was performed. It was the tithe that founded and funded medical care and hospitals, funded schools, and provided for the sick, the afflicted, orphans, and widows, and for children and others unable to care for themselves. Social welfare, in which the church has always been concerned, was run on the principle of mutual responsibility, of which the tithe was the minimal expression. You could, and were frequently encouraged to, give more: you could not give less.

Perhaps it is because of the example of the charity of the poor that I witnessed as a young man that I believe that these principles still work today. I think it is easy to eavesdrop in this community upon the charity of the rich, for all the buildings around us are monuments to the charity of the rich. You know that old saying, 'Old Harvard graduates never die, they just turn into dormitories;' and it is true that we see the charity of Mrs. Widener and Mr. Canaday and Thomas Hollis and all of those people around us; but I grew up instructed by the charity of the poor, which is all the more compelling because they had so little to give.

In the little Bethel AME church to which my family belonged, along with the few other colored families of Plymouth, Massachusetts, in those days fifty years ago, in addition to their morning churches, it was the custom — and I have written about this elsewhere — to take up the offering not as we do it here in The Memorial Church or in most churches, but by having the people proceed to the communion table at the front of the church to present their monetary gifts before the stewards, who counted the money as the gifts were put down. This would be done during much singing and greeting — it would be sort of a combination of the offering and the kiss of peace, if we had the kiss of peace here. You'd come down the center aisle, there would be a table there, there would be stewards there, you'd be greeting them, they'd be greeting you, the church would be filled with singing and joyous music, you'd go back greeting people on their way up, and the stewards would be doing a running tally. Then the music would stop and they would announce what the total was, saying, "We need fourteen dollars and forty-four cents, and we're going to do this again;" and they would do it again and again and again, calling the people forward until the day's goal had been met — and no one could leave until it had been met or even exceeded. Only then, when there was reason to do so, would we sing the Doxology. These were people who had next to nothing, poor people giving out of their substance and not out of their surplus, giving that which was essential to them, who had enough confidence in themselves, in their church, and in their God to place the material at the disposal of the spiritual, and it worked: the church is still there.

In the matter of our text, all the biblical scholarship tells us that widows in biblical times were among the most vulnerable and marginal members of society. In that age of a patriarchal society, where a woman's status depended upon her relationship to a man — father, husband, or son — a widow often had fewer rights than a male child, and less freedom than a female child. Her source of protection and security was gone, and so too such financial independence as she might once have enjoyed. Surely there were rich widows, but not many, and not often do they play a role in scripture. Widows in the New Testament are vulnerable and poor, and Jesus and St. Paul both specifically enjoin believers in the early Christian communities to look after widows and orphans, to visit them and take care of their needs, for they had no safety net but the community.

So, when our Lord invokes the example of the poor widow in St. Luke's gospel, it is of the same moral effect as his commendation of the woman who crashed the party in last Sunday's gospel: he again uses the marginal to drive a point to the center. He takes people on the outside edges of society and culture and social and economic security, and he uses them to drive the point that is central to his understanding of his gospel, and to what he wants you and me to understand about the gospel. The point is, if she, the poor widow, can do so much with so little, what more then can be expected of you who have so much? That is the point which cannot be evaded or avoided in this lesson about surplus and substance.

Our Lord is worried here not so much about financial formulae or 'scales of gifts,' as they like to say in the Development Office: he is speaking, rather, of the place in which one places one's ultimate trust, and of the means of expressing that ultimate trust, which is what we call faith. In other words, the woman who gave two coppers out of her poverty decided that she was not going to be defined by her poverty, or limited, but rather that by her total generosity she would be defined by her confidence in God's work and her total gratitude for God's grace. She who had received all was going to give all. She is an example of the expression that 'those who have suffered most have most reason to be both grateful and generous.' She thought in terms not of what she did not have, or even of what she lost, but of what she had; and out of a sense of gratitude disproportionate to all of her means she gave it all to God, thus attracting Jesus's attention, and ours.

We might be able to take this text more seriously if we knew what happened to her, but we don't know what happened to this poor widow, whether blessings attended her way, or whether she was thrown further upon the mercy of others. Did she win the lottery? Bingo! — a million coppers for you, my dear, as long as you live? Did a rich man marry her and provide economic security for the rest of her days? Did somebody say, "You can't be allowed to do this, let us replenish your supply of this world's goods." It would be helpful for us to know if it all turned out well, that there is no risk to giving it all away, and that you don't have to hold on to just a little bit against a rainy day. Alas, we don't know what happened to her, there is no secret text to tell us, and there is no reassurance that she did not suffer for her extravagant act of generosity.

This is not an essay in sociology, this is not a *quid pro quo*, this is a moral tale whose details are meant to point up a larger principle and a larger issue, and if you think that the moral is that the poor should give even more than they do now then you have missed the point, for this is not so much about those who can't, as it is about those who can and yet do not give in proportion to what has been given to them. Those who do not give in proportion to their substance have every reason to be worried about this particular story. The widow is used to cast a light upon the rest of us, rich and not so rich alike, to consider by the light of her example and of Jesus's commendation just what we ought to be doing with our money, and what ought to be our relationship between our money and our faith. If money talks, what does it say about you and about your faith?

For most of us looking for a way out it is easy to be lost, and convenient to be lost in the obvious extremes of this parable. Few of us are as poor as the widow, and few of us classify ourselves among the mighty rich, although among you there are both rich and poor. Most of us see ourselves in neither category, we just try to get along, to do the right thing with as little impact upon our pleasures and our resources as possible. Ambrose Bierce said that a "Christian is somebody who lives a life of virtue insofar as it is not incompatible with a life of pleasure." I know many who say, "I will be charitable when I am rich.....or richer;" or, "I cannot afford to act upon my more generous impulses." Often I see seniors in the College who are asked to contribute something to the annual College Fund as they make their way out of Harvard, students who have received far more than they deserved both from the living and from the dead, and many of these young people have already crafted the artful questions and answers of their elders, saying that on a cost benefit analysis of the situation they don't feel that they are yet in a position to pay a portion back to Harvard because they've already paid so much in to Harvard. It starts in this sort of stingy charity that says, "When I make my pile then I will consider giving something from it." This story is meant to shame those kinds of stingy impulses, and to say that giving comes not out of surplus and convenience but out of substance and opportunity. I spend a great deal of time asking people for money, and I have heard all of these excuses, some of them even from some of you.

What our Lord wishes us to understand is that giving is not so much concerned with the size of the gift as it is with an attitude toward life, toward self, and toward God. If you understand that life itself is a gift from God, if you understand that you are meant to express God's self-giving life in the world, and if you are confident and hopeful that God will sustain you in wealth and in poverty and in everything in between, then you will see life as giving and not as holding. You remember what Churchill said, himself always worried about money and not famous for his charity? "We make a living by what we save, but we make a life by what we give." When in three weeks' time we commemorate our benefactors and our war dead we will not remember what they saved — whether it was their money or their lives — we will remember what, and that, they gave.

Now, let me not flatter you by suggesting that you don't know what this is about, for I know that you know all of this and that there is not a new thought or a new syllable here; you have heard it all before. The first lesson, from Micah 6, says it all: "He has showed you what is good." God has already made clear to believers what is expected of us in our attitude toward life, toward self, toward God, and toward others. You know this. What then is the proper response to all of this? Do I want you to sit down and write out a new cheque or a new will, or both? Do I want you to come forward as Dr. Meyer and I receive and count your contributions to the work of this church?

No, not at all, we don't want as simplistic a response as that. I want you to think about the gospel. I want you to think about the life that you have been given by God through his great mercy, and about what is most fearful to you, and what is most precious to you, and about those things in this world for which you are most grateful. I want you to think about your fair share of your material responsibility in God's world, to this church, and to other agencies of good work. I want you to consider — not just today or tomorrow, but as a part of your thinking — your giving not in proportion to what you have but in proportion to what you have been given; and I want you to conduct this little spiritual audit in the quiet and odd moments of your lives over the next coming weeks and days. If you begin, my good friends, to reconsider how to live your life with these concerns in mind, I would be willing to speculate that you will find your life increasingly worth living; and that is exactly what our Lord has in mind for you.

Let us pray:

> *We thank Thee, Lord Jesus, for the gift of Thyself that allows us life. Through living and giving may we give out of our substance glory to Thy name. This we pray in that name. Amen.*

October 25, 1998

THE WORK OF THE SAINTS

The Commemoration of All Saints and All Souls

The Lesson

Ecclesiasticus 38:31-34 (REB)

All those rely on their hands, and each is skilful at his own craft. Without them a city would have no inhabitants; no settlers or travellers would come to it. Yet they are not in demand at public discussions, nor do they attain to high office in the assembly. They do not sit on the judge's bench or understand the decisions of the courts. They cannot expound moral or legal principles and are not ready with maxims. But they maintain the fabric of this world, and the practice of their craft is their prayer.

THE WORK OF THE SAINTS

Text: But they maintain the fabric of this world, and the practice of their craft is their prayer. *Ecclesiasticus 38:34*

My text is from the final verse of the thirty-eighth chapter of the book of Ecclesiasticus, and if you are a remotely curious listener of lessons and texts, you will want to know who 'they' are who will maintain the fabric of the world. It is the business of the Feast of All Saints and All Souls to answer that question and to describe them.

'They,' in the first instance, are those of whom we read in the lesson, and it speaks to the fact that the scribe, or scholar, gets his wisdom because he has the leisure to pursue it. It is the theory of the University that it is our, the academics', business to get smart. What about those who do real work for a living, however, those who do not have time to contemplate the deep things of life? What about the farmer, whose discourse is of the stock of bulls? What about the blacksmith, who sweats in the heat of his furnace? What about the potter, who applies the heat to finish his glaze? 'They' are the people who work, who "put their trust in their hands; and each becometh wise in his own work." (Ecclesiasticus 38:32)

Like these ancient workers you, too, are terribly busy, worn out, frightened, and as a result of too much to-ing and fro-ing you may think that you have no time at all to think, let alone to maintain the fabric of the world, but you have, you have an essential link. You may not 'have it together' for yourself but you hold it together for everybody else, and that is what the lesson means when it says "'They,' (meaning you) maintain the fabric of the world; and in the handiwork of their craft is their prayer." 'They' do ordinary things not necessarily exceptionally well but faithfully in good times and in bad, and that is what it means to "maintain the fabric of the world:" prayer is to do your job.

Now some of you will be disappointed to hear this. You freshman parents, for example, have returned this weekend to check up on your considerable investment, for you are not spending all of your money to see that your son or your daughter becomes ordinary: everyone has a constitutional right to be exceptional, and you do not expect them to maintain the fabric of the world, you expect them to rule the world, or at least to work closely with those who do.

Others of you will be disappointed because you know that this is All Saints Day, and you believe that you have a right to hear about some exceptional people, some heroic people who are remembered for the incredibly impressive things they did for God. There were those early Chrisitan martyrs who willingly gave up their lives for the gospel and shamed their tormentors: St. Sebastian who took the arrow, and St. Lawrence, who was put to death on a barbecue and when he was done on one side, asked to be turned over. In our own time we recall the heroic lives of such martyrs as Dietrich Bonhoeffer and Mother Teresa, who cast enormous shadows.

It is true that Holy Mother Church takes very seriously those who suffer for the truth and give their lives for it, martyrs and heroes; and it is also true that we are meant to hold in admiring remembrance those who do heroic and godly things and who serve both to inspire and to intimidate us as well, but on All Saints Day we, like God, are meant to embrace all, all the saints, the ordinary with the extraordinary, the exceptional with the unexceptional, even those like us who are carrying on God's work. While all of the great saints of the faith have their own days, as any devout believer knows, this day, All Saints Day, is for everybody else, for all of us who, exceptional or not, carry on as best we can the work that God has given us to do.

Thus, All Saints Day celebrates in the first instance those who keep on keeping on, who have not given up, who have not grown weary in well-doing, who have not given in to cynicism or despair. The saints are those who simply show up, who do what they can where they are with what they have; or, in other words, "The most heroic thing you can do is what you can." Somebody told me that Newt Gingrich said that and it's so good that I can't believe it, but if he did, God bless him, and if he didn't, well, I just did.

The saints of God are those who do what they can, and who did what they could. We are reminded of this when we cast our eyes over the list of names of saints and souls whom we have commended to God today by our prayers of remembrance. This being Harvard some of the names will be familiar for their earthly distinctions and accomplishments, but for most of us most of them are very ordinary men and women whose twin claims are that we loved them, and that we believe that they are loved by God. They did not heroic things but they did what they could where they were, with what they had. We remember them today.

That is good, but it is not all there is to it, not at all! We do not simply remember the saints, we participate in the communion of the saints. Present, past, and future blend as one, and perhaps the most extraordinary claim of the Christian faith is the conviction that in God's economy and in Christ's love the living and the dead continue in fellowship with one another, friends above and friends below, and that both communities, those on earth and those in heaven, have fellowship with each other and with God, who cherishes each and both. If we believe God to be with us now, what is to prevent us from believing in the conviction that when we die we grow nearer to God, and not more distant? Out of our sight does not mean out of God's sight.

The ancient formula was elegantly simple: we remember the saints and the saints remember us, for we are united in a common memory, and in the mind and heart of God. This, I know, will seem implausible if not impossible. As our Noble Lecturer recently reminded us, Freud would say, "Grow up," while C.S. Lewis would say, "Wake up;" and so we should. How silly, self-indulgent, and even egotistical it is for us to think that God is interested only in those of us who happen still to be walking around.

When the Apostles' Creed bids us affirm our belief in the communion of saints, when we gather around the holy table and invoke the saints, when we remember our dead and bid them remember us we affirm our membership, our participation in a fellowship that is above and beyond time and place. If this is too hard a concept for you to contemplate right now you have the rest of your life to do so, but remember — as Cardinal Newman reminded us — "Life is short, death is certain, and the world to come is everlasting."

To remember this, and them, then, is our work. The African poet and novelist Chinua Achebe put it well for us when he said, "There is no better time to talk about the living than when we remember the dead;" and by this I take him to mean that to remember the dead is to continue their work among the living. In that sense they still live among us while we make their unfinished work our own, and we are to carry on in our place as they once did, and to realize that their work is now ours. Neither the living nor the dead can rest until all of God's work is done on earth as it is in heaven, and death, we must remind ourselves, does not interrupt our continuity but affirms that continuity in God. St. Paul said, "Whether we live or die we are the Lord's."

Every year around Commencement I participate in memorial services for classes celebrating their fifth to their seventy-fifth reunions, and I tell them that to remember is to be reformed, re-created, made anew. Without communion with our dead we cannot be fully human, and through art, as the poet Auden reminds us, "We are able to break bread with the dead." Mozart, that musical artist, helps us to do that today in this service of remembrance.

Thus, once again we take up the glorious work of the saints, theirs and ours, and for it and for all those who share with us in it, both the living and the dead, we say only one thing, "Alleluia! Alleluia!"

Let us pray:

> *Our Father in heaven, we give Thee thanks for all those near to us and dear, who walked in Thy light, in whose lives we have seen that light, and at whose hands we have received the mysteries of Thy goodness and Thy grace. Make us glad in all those whom Thou hast given us out of the world, who have faithfully lived and at the last have quietly died, who are now gone before us into the heavenly places. Amen.*

November 1, 1998

PART TWO

Sermons for Advent, Christmas, and Epiphany

IT'S ABOUT TIME

The First Sunday in Advent

The Lesson

Romans 13:7-14 (NEB)

Discharge your obligations to all men; pay tax and toll, reverence and respect, to those to whom they are due. Leave no claim outstanding against you, except that of mutual love. He who loves his neighbour has satisfied every claim of the law. For the commandments, 'Thou shalt not commit adultery, thou shalt not kill, thou shalt not steal, thou shalt not covet,' and any other commandment there may be, are all summed up in the one rule, 'Love your neighbour as yourself.' Love cannot wrong a neighbour; therefore the whole law is summed up in love.

In all this, remember how critical the moment is. It is time for you to wake out of sleep, for deliverance is nearer to us now than it was when first we believed. It is far on in the night; day is near. Let us therefore throw off the deeds of darkness and put on our armour as soldiers of the light. Let us behave with decency as befits the day: no revelling or drunkenness, no debauchery or vice, no quarrels or jealousies! Let Christ Jesus himself be the armour that you wear; give no more thought to satisfying the bodily appetites.

IT'S ABOUT TIME

Text: In all this, remember how critical the moment is. *Romans 13:11*

Perhaps you remember, as I do with a certain combination of annoyance and relief, that old proverb, "If at first you don't succeed, try, try, again." That was usually applied to mistakes in the piano lessons of my youth, to a renewed effort to climb the unclimbable rope in the boys' gym class, to identify a chemical unknown, or to an effort to solve a problem in algebra which also remained unknown. I can hear my mother, my teacher, my coach, who all said to us at one time or another: "If at first you don't succeed, try, try, again."

If we hear this phrase less and less today it does not mean that we are getting better and better, it may rather mean that "If at first you don't succeed, there is something wrong with the test." Despite the culture of self-esteem, self-delusion, self-indulgence, and self-enhancement, however, most of us do not believe that we are roaring successes, that all of our efforts work, and that we get it right the first time. Most of us with an ounce of self-analysis know that we do not get it right, and in our private moments we know, in the words of the General Confession, that "we have left undone those things which we ought to have done, and we have done those things that we ought not to have done, and there is no health in us." We know the truth of that.

Advent Sunday is the Christian new year, we have passed fifty-two Sundays since we last celebrated the Advent of our Lord and the beginning again of the whole liturgy of redemption, and I ask you if you are any better than you were at this time last year. The politicians would say, "Are you any better *off*?" — and the answer for most of you would be that you are better *off*, but that's not the question at the moment. The question is whether you are any *better*, and the answer to the question is probably "no." You might say, "I wish I were, I really tried, I really worked, I really hoped, I made some ambitious plans for my spiritual, my moral, my intellectual, my social life, but if you really want to know the answer now I would have to say that no, I'm not much better than I was at this time last year."

If that were all there was to it, 'it' would be all over, too bad, you had your shot, you messed it up, you blew it, you are the same stingy mean-minded parochial, provincial, narrow little soul you were on Advent Sunday 1997, and what is God going to do with you? Some of you have been at this for threescore years and ten plus, and you still haven't got it right; and there's not much promise for those bright young things behind the choir screen, either. If that were all there was to it, one final reckoning, one final audit, one final summing-up, there it would be, guilty as charged, take me away; but the glory of the Christian faith, the good news of the gospel, the essential kernel of goodness that is proclaimed to us in word and sacrament over and over again, is that this isn't all there is to it. We do get to try again because we have not succeeded at first. Remember all of the resolutions of the last year, all of those good intentions, all of that moral resolve? They remain for us to revive, revise, and attempt again. Only you know how far short of your own mark you have come but you do know, as do I, and thus we come to Advent Sunday, the beginning of the church's new year, more or less where we were last year. At Advent, Holy Mother Church says that we may start again, we may begin anew, we may cast off the works of darkness, in the words of the Collect and of Paul's letter, get rid of that burden of gloom and doom that we have been carrying all year long, and start afresh. Put on the armor of light, now. That means that we are meant to look forward, to take up another chance, to embrace another opportunity, to try and try again.

Now when you take an audit of this sort at the end of the liturgical year or at the end of the calendar year or at the end of your birthday, more often than not the emphasis is upon what didn't get done, the promises broken, the failures embraced, the opportunities lost. We beat up on ourselves, we do this all of the time. Advent does call us to recollect our sins and those failures and those missed opportunities, but the Advent message is not upon failure; the Advent message is about opportunity and expectation, about what we might attempt, and each year in our pilgrimage we come a little closer to the light and the light comes a little closer to us. God gives us this time, this focused Advent time, to get our act together; in fact, 'salvation' and 'redemption,' those great Christian and Advent words, are about time, time that God has now made available for us to try and try again. It is *all* about time, and it's about time we understood this and embraced this time not as the delay of the Lord, which is what worried the early Christians, but as the patience of the Lord saying that he wants to give us time so that we might put on the armor of light and cast away the works of darkness. Think about the patience of God. How many opportunities have we been given to seize the light, yet we have preferred the darkness? Here is one more chance, one more time, one more moment in which you can affirm God's intention for you. It's about time, it's about God' time, it's about your time, it's about this time.

This is St. Paul's point in our second lesson, where in Romans 13 he writes vividly, using the metaphor of sleep and wakefulness, that it is time for the believers to wake up — he didn't say, "and smell the coffee," but that is what he meant — and realize that salvation is nearer now than when we first believed. Now, some will read this as Paul's view that Jesus's physical return to earth in glory is nearer to his return to earth than at any other point in the life of the Roman Christians, and I have no doubt that that reading is substantially correct in the Pauline context. There will be many of our brothers and sisters in these pre-millennial days who will say the same thing, the radios and the televisions and eventually the newspapers will be full up with it, but there is another way of looking at it, which is that we grow now nearer to Christ than at any previous time in our own existence. Think of it: it is not that we are constant and Christ moves toward us until we two finally meet, which is a kind of popular and populous notion, that we stand here waiting for him to come along, and he will, but that's not it; it is rather that you and I as believers, as brothers and sisters in the faith, are not static but dynamic and we move toward him and grow in our relationship toward Christ. It's not just the second coming, it's the third and the fourth and the fifth and the sixth as we grow and move in our relationship toward Christ in the time that God gives us, renewing time, Advent time, in which to do it; and he says, "Wake up! You're still here, you're on the move, you haven't failed yet and you haven't achieved yet, so get on with it."

All of the historic emphasis on the second coming of our Lord places all the burden upon him and on what he does and when he does it, and I think that that's wrong because the gospel places the burden of expectation not upon Christ, who will come when and if he pleases, but upon us. We are the ones who move in the Advent drama, we are the ones who are meant to move, we are the ones who are meant to grow and to be dynamic, we are not waiting for Jesus to sort it all out, we are growing into Christ, moving toward him even as he comes toward us. Think of the prodigal and the father. The father didn't stay in the doorway waiting for the boy to arrive, the boy didn't stay where he was, waiting for the father to pick him up, they met each other on the way, remember that? That is what Advent time is about: we meet Christ on the way. He comes to us as we grow toward him. Paul wants us to understand that the responsibility is upon us to fulfill the law and he is very clear about this in Romans 13, first telling us to obey the laws, pay our taxes, and do the work of good responsible citizenship. Read it again for yourselves. He does not tell the Christians to shun the world, abstain from corrupting responsibility, hie to the mountaintop and in white robes wait for Jesus to come and carry us on up in some heavenly 'Beam me up, Scottie' vision of the next life to come. Paul doesn't have anything to do with that nonsense. No, Paul says that you have things to do and you must do them. The law, both civil and moral, still abides: "You shall love your neighbor as yourself." Love does no wrong to a neighbor, therefore love is the fulfilling of the law. The ethics of the Christian citizen are in no way eliminated by the nearness of the Lord's return.

Furthermore, as Paul tells us, there is now more expected of us than mere waiting and whining, "When is he coming? Why not now? Am I ready? Is he ready?" There is more for us to do than that: "Let us conduct ourselves becomingly as in the day," he says, "not in reveling and drunkenness, not in debauchery and licentiousness, not in quarreling and jealousy." Let us try again to do the works of righteousness, let us pick up once again those high ambitions, those persistent patient acts of kindness, that is; let us try again to get things right with God and with our neighbor. Now is the time to do it, Advent is the time of renewal; all of it's about time, however much of it you still have, how well you use it, and how quickly it passes. Christians are people who are not supposed to be diminished in mind or spirit by the fact that time is our most valuable and our least containable resource. I could tell you that should you die within the next hour you should rejoice to go, but if I tell you that you'll all be terribly nervous, for you didn't come to The Memorial Church to be told that your hours, your days, are numbered, although they are, and that you have less time now than when I began. You should consider the fewness of our days not as God's threat or punishment but as the precious time that you have — we have — in which to try, try, again.

There may be something that you have been meaning to do but have put off; perhaps there is someone with whom you mean to be reconciled; perhaps there is some act of kindness that needs to be acknowledged, some letter to be written, some wrong to be put right. I don't know what it is but you know what it is, for we are all filled up with unfinished business. The curse of this life is to leave it with unfinished business, to miss the opportunity to say and to do the things that need saying and doing, and the blessing of this life is to have time, one more time, in order to do what needs to be done. It's about time, it really is. Casting off the works of darkness means taking on the duties of the day, a critical moment, and, as our Puritan ancestors used to say, to live each day, including this day, as if it were your last, because it could be. You need to face that, and I do too.

God's greatest gift to us, apart from himself in Jesus Christ, is the gift of time — time, as we pray, for the amendment of life, time to start again, time for renewal, time to try, try, again — and Advent reminds us that now is that time and that we must not look backward to some historical pageant far away and long ago but forward as children of the light, people of the day in faith of the dawn. God wants you to get it right, which is why he has spared you to this moment; God wills you to succeed, and not to fail. God rejoices in your accomplishments, not in your frustrations. It is T.S. Eliot who calls us undefeated only because we have gone on trying. It's all about time, and it's about time that we accept the grace of time renewed for life renewed. Don't forget how critical this moment is for you: it's about time, my friends, it really is.

Let us pray:

> *We give Thee praise, O God, for the renewal of life and the renewal of time. Help us to use both wisely, for the sake of the kingdom of Jesus Christ, through whom we pray. Amen.*

November 29, 1998

THE COURAGE TO HOPE

The Second Sunday in Advent

The Lesson

Romans 15:4-13 (RSV)

For whatever was written in former days was written for our instruction, that by steadfastness and by the encouragement of the scriptures we might have hope. May the God of steadfastness and encouragement grant you to live in such harmony with one another, in accord with Christ Jesus, that together you may with one voice glorify the God and Father of our Lord Jesus Christ.

Welcome one another, therefore, as Christ has welcomed you, for the glory of God. For I tell you that Christ became a servant to the circumcised to show God's truthfulness, in order to confirm the promises given to the patriarchs, and in order that the Gentiles might glorify God for his mercy. As it is written,

> "Therefore I will praise thee among the Gentiles,
> And sing to thy name;"
> And again it is said,
> "Rejoice, O Gentiles, with his people;"
> And again,
> "Praise the Lord, all Gentiles,
> And let all the peoples praise him;"
> And further Isaiah says,
> "The root of Jesse shall come,
> He who rises to rule the Gentiles;
> In him shall the Gentiles hope."

May the God of hope fill you with all joy and peace in believing, so that by the power of the Holy Spirit you may abound in hope. I myself am satisfied about you, my brethren, that you yourselves are full of goodness, filled with all knowledge, and able to instruct one another.

THE COURAGE TO HOPE

Text: For whatever was written in former days was written for our instruction, that by steadfastness and by the encouragement of the scriptures we might have hope. *Romans 15:4*

Advent is the season of hope, and we worship the God of things that are not yet, the God of things that are to be. That is both true and easy to say, and I have just done so; but hope, real hope, Christian hope, is not quite so easy to come by. Sometimes our hope fails us for lack of imagination, lack of courage, or for not thinking or hoping 'big' enough — cheap and inadequate hope. Let me illustrate.

Our good friend, Lord Runcie of Cuddesdon, the one hundred second Archbishop of Canterbury, told a marvelous story a few weeks ago in London of his friend, the British ambassador to the United States, Sir Nicholas Henderson, who at the height of the Cold War was interviewed at just about this time of year by a features reporter from *The Washington Post*. The question, a features sort of question, was, "Mr. Ambassador, what do you want for Christmas?" Sir Nicholas, a master of British reserve and understatement, and not wanting to appear greedy but wanting also to be truthful, replied to the reporter that all he really wanted for Christmas was a jar of fruit preserved in ginger, such as you could get at Harrod's or in Fortnum and Mason's. Apparently he liked that and that was what he would like for Christmas, and he hoped that Lady Henderson or somebody would give him such a jar. A few days later *The Washington Post*'s Christmas feature article described in detail what the diplomatic corps hoped for for Christmas: the Russian ambassador hoped for peace and good will; the Swiss ambassador hoped for genuine disarmament around the world; the Spanish ambassador hoped for Gibraltar to be given back; the Israeli ambassador hoped for peace in the middle east, and so on and so on and so forth. Sir Nicholas, the British ambassador, was recorded as hoping for a jar of preserved fruit. Now, obviously of all those things hoped for, Sir Nicholas's hope was the most obtainable, and he was doubtless the only one who got what he wanted for Christmas; but by comparison, as Lord Runcie pointed out, his hope seemed to lack a little in imagination or courage. Sometimes we do not hope enough.

Sometimes, however, our hope seems doomed and we dare not ask for more than we can see amid the bitter reality in which we live. Let me illustrate again. Yesterday I got my Christmas letter from an old friend and colleague, formerly Episcopal chaplain here in the University, now twenty years ago. You here I know are all also experiencing these fat, reproduced letters on colored paper, badly printed up with all sorts of news you are not really interested in receiving. I dutifully read through mine, and I came to his penultimate paragraph, which reads as follows:

> "As the holiday season once again approaches, I want to wish you all the joy and happiness possible in a world so filled with poverty, hunger, and violence, and in a country so rife with anger and hatred that a black man is dragged to his death behind a truck, a gay man is hung on a fence like a scarecrow, and a doctor is shot for performing a legal procedure. While the Congress and the press and many ordinary citizens are preoccupied with petty matters, major issues of foreign policy and domestic consequence go unattended, or at best are given short shrift. My hope is that somehow this tide can be turned.....I must confess, however, that I have little, if any, confidence in this occurring."

Sometimes, particularly at this time of year, hope seems shabby and miserable, inadequate, when we are surrounded by the mendacity and the mediocrity of this world. I think, in part, this is why more of us applaud rather than deplore Thomas Johnson, who is fast becoming one of my heroes, the man who for ten years lived underground in a hole on Nantucket undiscovered and undisturbed, living in the bowels of the most expensive real estate in the world until his hideaway was discovered this past week — we've all been reading about this in the papers. "How nice it would be," thought I, "to scamper into the ground like Thomas Johnson, and to pull the earth over me like a character in *Wind in the Willows*;" but now poor old Johnson is forced to join the rest of us, while some of us say, "Why should he enjoy those dark and private comforts while the rest of us have to contend with Christmas and our noisy, difficult neighbors?" We haven't heard the end of his saga but, alas, I think we all know how it is likely to end.

Hope, you see, is not an act of will so much as it is an act of imagination and of courage. Hope, it strikes me, is not that word that we utter at the bedside of the dying when we say unthinkingly, "I hope that this will all end well," and what we mean is that we hope that the apparent direction in which this life is going will not go in that direction. That is not hope but a kind of mindless optimism, of which we shall say more a little later. The substance of hope is that somehow we will get through and go through this inevitable direction, because on the other side is that hope into which we believe we have been called and for which and by which we have been prepared all our lives. It is that kind of hope that the doctors simply do not understand at the bedsides of the dying, it is that kind of hope which is the ultimate resource available to the faithful, an act of imagination and courage; and imagination and courage are required, for hope deals with what has not yet happened. Hope allows us to see beyond what is and to imagine, to see with our inner eye, what might and what ought to be. When we say, as we often do, that hope triumphs over experience, that is precisely what we mean. Left alone to a life of experience, where we deal with nothing but the facts, where we are content to address only the tangible, the material, the really real, the mundane, we are doomed to the accumulation, the sum total, of that experience. Experience tells us only where we have been, like driving a car by the light of the rearview mirror; and there can be no ultimate satisfaction in the accumulation of that experience. Christian hope is meant to guide you into the place where you have not yet been, and into becoming the person you have not yet become.

That is the radical dimension of the Christian faith, and it is not content with the notion of Christianity celebrating the things that are, or worse still, of Christianity celebrating things as we imagine them once to have been. There is no good place in history to which Christians can turn; I defy any of you to show me a Christian time better than this one. This is as good as it gets, and that is always the case, and it is never good enough. Those who live by the faith of nostalgia or some sentimental history, some imagination of the good old days or the good old times, or some time, any time other than this time, clearly are not seeing clearly. They are seeing only a partial picture, and refuse to see that the gospel is not interested in either the confirmations of the past or the confirmations of the present.

The Christian faith is, and has always been, prophetic, speaking of the time to come, of things that are not yet, of places we have not yet been to, of people we have not yet become. That is the image: none of us, and no place, and no time, is good enough, not yet. No past and no present is superior to the future that is yet to be. That is not just any old future, not just what happens at the end of divine service, or at the end of your undergraduate career, or even at the end of your life. It's not just any future, it is God's particular future where certain things are meant to happen, and we know what those are. We know what they are because the Bible tells us what they are, and in Advent we are reminded of the content of God's future. You heard it twice this morning, first in Isaiah's old prophesy, "The wolf shall dwell with the lamb, and the leopard shall lie down with the kid, and the calf and the lion and the fatling together, and a little child shall lead them." (Isaiah 11:6) You heard it all, and some of you have seen it in that marvelous painting by the Quaker, Edward Hicks, called 'The Peaceable Kingdom.' Many of us have sung it, even, in the marvelous setting of 'The Peaceable Kingdom' by Randall Thompson, who wrote our second anthem this morning. We have all seen and heard, routinely, that vision of what the content of God's future is meant to be.

We are too smart, though, for that: been there, done that, it doesn't work, we're too shrewd, too realistic, to take this image of the peaceable kingdom too seriously, for we know better. Our bitter experience of the past has taught us to expect little of the present, and even less of the future, and so we have substituted a shallow optimism for a deep hope. Basically, way down deep, we are very shallow indeed. Maybe it's a national characteristic, but we Americans describe ourselves and are often described by others as optimists, natural-born optimists. We are a people carved out of the failures and disappointments of the rest of the world, and our cultural and political isolationism is meant to protect us from the negativity of the rest of the world. That is why we have always been suspicious of immigration in this country, of course after our own ancestors made it here, and why we are suspicious of people who don't look like ourselves or talk like ourselves, or who come from different places, because they will spoil our optimism. We like to walk on the sunny side of the street, we like to wear a sunny face, and to wish everyone a happy and nice day. We want our movies to have happy endings, as in *It's a Wonderful Life*; we want our Broadway musicals to be upbeat, and that is why every Broadway musical sounds the same and certainly ends the same; and we know that the the air around this time of year is filled with "Tidings of comfort and joy, comfort and joy; O, tidings of comfort and joy..."

Our optimism, however, characterized by these attitudes and habits, doesn't square with our perception of reality. We know that there is no genuine peace on earth, we know that there is no fundamental lasting good will to those with whom he is well pleased. We know that the holiday season tends to bring out the worst, not the best, in people, particularly in our own families. I know, and I know you know, how much we dread Christmas day, because we are living with the paradox of great expectation on the one hand and grim reality on the other. We know that for ourselves constant good cheer is hard to manufacture and even harder to maintain. It is this contrast between our hyped expectations, aided and abetted by the sales people and the ads of *The Boston Globe* and *The Boston Herald* and all of the media outlets, by all of the window designers in all of the shops, by places like the Coop and every department store that you can imagine, jingling and jangling for weeks: it is these hyped expectations of this season on the one hand, and their inevitable capacity to disappoint us on the other, that creates the well-known seasonal depression for which for many people alcohol, or some other stimulant, alas, is the only solution.

Advent hope, my friends, is meant to be the sobering antidote to false Christmas cheer. That is why the church drags you kicking and screaming through Advent, that is why it forces you to confront the promises and their lack of apparent deliverance now, that is why the church requires that you look ahead and not back to the manger of Bethlehem, that is why we light these Advent candles: to lighten the darkness and not simply to allow you a better rearview window view. That is why it is my job, and that of every preacher and priest in Christendom on these four Sundays in Advent, to place these facts and these promises and these hopes before you, and it is your duty as the faithful in Christ to consider them. You have no choice. This you must do. Advent is not celebration, it is not the moment for dancing around the light pole; Advent hope is not an exercise in nostalgia or seasonal optimism; Advent is not celebration but fortification against the very forces that would drive us to despair and drag us downward; Advent is an exercise in endurance, in preparation for the long journey to a time and a place where we have not yet been, and for which all of the past and all of the present are mere preparation. This is what Paul, the apostle to the Gentiles — that is, to us — means to suggest when he writes in Romans, "For whatever was written in former days was written for our instruction, that by steadfastness and by the encouragement of the scriptures we might have hope." In other words, the Bible is not a record of human achievement, nor even of divine achievement, but a record of divine promises and a constant tale of human folly. We are meant to learn from these instructions and these experiences, not to reenter 'Bibleland,' as Krister Stendahl once described it, but to be encouraged and prepared for that time which has not yet been. These things were written for our instruction, that by steadfastness, holding on, by the encouragement of the examples within the scriptures, both positive and negative, we might have hope.

Paul was writing to a people who knew the promises, and he cites them in this chapter when in verse twelve he recalls Isaiah's vision of the lamb and the wolf. He was writing to a people who knew the promises but who also knew the bitter experience of disappointment, of "hope deferred," in that marvelous phrase of the playwright, Lorraine Hansbury: "Hope deferred, which is like a raisin in the sun; it dries up and turns hard." These people knew the experiences of a world not yet ready for God's prime time, and that is still our world, not yet ready for God's prime time. He was writing to a world in which black men and gay men and others are still murdered by Christians, he was writing to a world in which violence flourishes in the name of the pro-life movement, and he was writing to a world in which the Christian faith is used so often to consecrate the *status quo* of the favored and the privileged, a people like you, and like me. He understood that the optimist among us says that this is the best of all possible worlds, and the pessimist agrees.

Optimism — I'm prepared to be quoted on this — simply doesn't cut it: it cannot stand the sharp ray of experience or disappointment. Optimism alone drives people into fantasy, and sometimes into terrible rage and disappointment.

Sometimes it is difficult even for me to remember anything other than happiness and the bright promise that lay ahead for me in the Plymouth, Massachusetts, of the 1940s and early 1950s. There were very few black families living in town, maybe four or five of us and most of us were related in one way or another, and we were colored then, not black, and we'd all lived there for a very long time. We were totally socialized, totally adapted, black Yankees, Afro-Saxons, if you will, every one of us, and they all talked as I do and I talk as they did, if that helps to explain anything for any of you. Once a month, on Sunday morning after church when my mother and father and I left to get into our car to drive home for Sunday dinner, there would have been placed on the front seat, through the open window, a brown paper bag, carefully sealed and tied up, and when we got home we would find in that parcel a modest treasure trove of magazines, the only copies in the entire town of Plymouth of the newly-founded *Ebony* magazine, its down-market offspring, *Jet*, and well-thumbed copies of *The Pittsburgh Courier*, the nation's then-leading black daily newspaper. These periodicals, kind of black *Life* magazines, were subscribed to under cover of darkness it seemed, by only one of our families, and circulated quietly among the colored families. We read them quietly and faithfully and passed them on until we all had read them, and in addition to their stories of uplift and achievement in the black America of fifty years ago, they also contained gruesomely vivid accounts of murders, rapes, lynchings, and race wars in far-off places like Detroit and Atlanta. They contained a vivid chronicle, a vivid account of a segregated America, and of most of America's desire to keep it that way.

It was almost an embarrassment to read such things in the "land of the free and the home of the brave," the "land of the Pilgrim's pride," and it was hard to take when my parents, in an understandable desire to protect me from the consequences of a false optimism, reminded me that this was the real world, and that the world in which I was living was a world of illusions. Contrary to how it may appear, and to what some of you may think, I have never forgotten that. Not for one minute, as your pastor these many years, have I forgotten that. Black people in America have never been optimistic for we know better, but we have always been hopeful, full of hope. That is why we continue to sing James Weldon Johnson's *Lift Ev'ry Voice*, and respond particularly to the words:

Stony the road we trod,
Bitter the chast'ning rod
Felt in the days when hope unborn had died;
Yet with a steady beat,
Have not our weary feet
Come to the place for which our fathers sighed?

That, my friends, is not a statement but a question, and for the faithful in Christ the answer must continue to be a resolute "No, we have not!" We have not yet come to the place for which our fathers and mothers sighed and neither have you, not even the most well-off of you, not even the brightest of you, not even the best of you; and to think that we have is to be sadly deluded. The Advent hope reminds us that this is true, and the Advent hope reminds us that it takes courage to hope in spite of circumstances, courage to persevere beyond the apparent and the convenient, courage not to be satisfied or dissuaded with our circumstances, not to take for granted who we are, or where where we are, or what we do. There must be amongst us all a divine discontent, a constant irritant that can never be satisfied until we are where we are meant to be, and this is not that place.

To imagine Isaiah's peaceable kingdom as still possible, still expectant, still desirable, is to have the courage not of our conviction but of our imagination and our hope; and perhaps the most courageous thing to do in desperate, disappointing times such as these is to affirm a steadfast hope out of all proportion to what passes for reality. Let me illustrate for the final time.

Over the west door of an English country church, in the county of Leicestershire, is an inscription written in the seventeenth century at the time of the English civil war between the Royalists and Puritans, a nasty, unpleasant confrontation:

> "When all things sacred were throughout the nation either demolished or profaned, Sir Robert Shirley, Baronet, founded this church: whose singular praise it is to have done the best things in the worst times and hoped them in the most calamitous."

"To have done the best things in the worst times and hoped them in the most calamitous." Sir Robert built a house of prayer in the middle of the carnage of a brutal civil war, and, except in the minds of the historians, that war is long over, long forgotten, yet the church at Staunton Harold in Leicestershire still stands, you can see it today, a monument to the courage to hope, to have done the best of things in the worst of times.

Our war with our world, our spiritual war and the war for our souls, is no less serious than that one, with the stakes even higher; and to wage it, especially in these Advent days, "May the God of hope fill you with joy and peace in believing, so that by the power of the Holy Spirit you may abound in hope."

Let us pray:

> *Blessed Lord, who hast caused all holy Scriptures to be written for our learning: Grant that we may in such wise hear them, read, mark, learn, and inwardly digest them, that by patience and comfort of Thy holy Word, we may embrace and ever hold fast the blessed hope of everlasting life, which Thou hast given us in our Saviour Jesus Christ. Amen.*

December 6, 1998

NEVER GIVE UP!

The Third Sunday in Advent

The Lesson

Matthew 11:1-11 (RSV)

And when Jesus had finished instructing his twelve disciples, he went on from there to teach and preach in their cities.

Now when John heard in prison about the deeds of the Christ, he sent word by his disciples and said to him, "Are you he who is to come, or shall we look for another?" And Jesus answered them, "Go and tell John what you hear and see: the blind receive their sight and the lame walk, lepers are cleansed and the deaf hear, and the dead are raised up, and the poor have good news preached to them. And blessed is he who takes no offense at me."

As they went away, Jesus began to speak to the crowds concerning John: "What did you go out into the wilderness to behold? A reed shaken by the wind? Why then did you go out? To see a man clothed in soft raiment? Behold, those who wear soft raiment are in kings' houses. Why then did you go out? To see a prophet? Yes, I tell you, and more than a prophet. This is he of whom it is written,

> 'Behold, I send my messenger before thy face,
> who shall prepare thy way before thee.'

Truly, I say to you, among those born of women there has risen no one greater than John the Baptist; yet he who is least in the kingdom of heaven is greater than he."

NEVER GIVE UP!

Text: Blessed is he who takes no offense at me. *Matthew 11:6*

My text is the sixth verse of the eleventh chapter of Matthew's gospel, which might be better translated, "Happy is the one who does not give up on me."

My colleagues who visit and preach from this pulpit, both from this country and from abroad, all remark on what a listening congregation you are. I just had a letter from Carl Scovel, of King's Chapel, Boston, who preached here two or three weeks ago, who said, "What a treat, what a delight it is to preach to a congregation of such obvious listeners." I thought you ought to hear that. You have a reputation out there, and I think it is well earned, well deserved, and I want to make sure it is well earned and well deserved by hoping that you have listened carefully to what I have tried to do with you and for you over these Advent Sundays, because a good listening congregation is also a good remembering congregation, and if it listens and remembers well it might just make a difference. I hope that you listened on Advent I, two Sundays ago, when I said that the first word for Advent was 'time,' and taking time seriously. I hope that you listened last Sunday, when I said that the second word for Advent was 'hope,' and having the courage to hope with imagination and to take it seriously. Today the word I give for Advent III is 'perseverance,' and knowing when not to give in despite the odds against keeping on. Advent is the beginning of our Christian cycle, and this is basic teaching, basic instruction in the things which you need to know to survive, to endure, to persevere in yet another Christian year. Time, hope, perseverance: thus our text.

When Jesus says, in our text for this morning, "Blessed" — or 'happy' — "is the one who does not give up on me," he acknowledges with an unusual candor that it is very easy to give up on Jesus. It is easy to wonder if there is anything to all of the promises that we hear over and over again, that we read, and nourish in our bosoms. He understands that we will easily be tempted to ask where is the proof of the pudding. Where is the sign of his coming? Where are the evidences that all of these things that we have listened to so carefully for so long are true? My old and dear friend Professor Mason Hammond used to say, after attending the daily services of Morning Prayers regularly since 1921 without exception, "I've been saying The Lord's Prayer for seventy years and things have only got worse." So, you may well wonder where the signs are of his coming, why, as Erma Bombeck once said, "If life is a bowl of cherries, what am I doing in the pits?"

Why do all of these great experiences, such as they are, always happen to somebody else and not to me? I am as faithful, I am as persevering, I am as courageous and imaginative and hopeful as the next person, but my story is not even tragedy, my story is farce! Somebody else manages to pull out the victory. "Blessed is the one who does not give up on me...." in spite of the evidence, or maybe in spite of the lack of evidence. Somebody once asked whether if being a Christian were a crime there would be enough evidence to convict any of you here this morning. I know that that probably depends upon the definition of what crime is, but nevertheless we probably have enough stories of our half-empty glasses rather than of our half-full glasses.

That is the Advent question and there is nothing wrong with it, one shouldn't feel guilty about asking for a little proof, a little demonstration. The Advent question is that question that the disciples of John the Baptist ask Jesus in our lesson: "Are you the one who is to come, or shall we look for another?" John the Baptist had been preaching the coming of the Lord, he had been in prison, but now he had heard of another prophet out there and he wished to know if this Jesus, of whom much now had been heard, was the real thing. He had a right to know, he had invested all of his life in the promise of his coming, in the prophecies of better times and better things, and there had been many people promising many things over a long period of time, and nobody had delivered the goods. Things were as badly off as ever they had been, and so it was a fair question of Jesus. "Are you the one who is to come?" Jesus is asked; "or should we look for and wait for and invest in somebody else?"

Jesus answers the question, but in his doing so we are not quite so certain that he is 'the one.' The answer that he gives is enigmatic. First he answers the question not with a definite 'yes' or a definite 'no,' in the way that lawyers prefer, but rather he demonstrates what he wants them to understand by his answer. How does he do so? He doesn't say, "I am the prophet, or I am not the prophet." He says, "The blind now see, the lame now walk, the lepers now are clean, and the poor have good rather than bad news preached to them, the dead are raised." Those are meant to be pretty convincing proofs; John's people had waited for so long and had been so often disappointed in their hopes. Here, Jesus answers their impatient question with a demonstration of results: all of these things that represent what is wrong in this life — blindness, lameness, leprosy, despair, and death — have been put right. In Charles Wesley's great hymn, 'O for a thousand tongues to sing...,' he writes almost lyrically in the fourth verse:

Hear him, ye deaf; his praise, ye dumb,
Your loosened tongues employ;
Ye blind, behold your Saviour come;
And leap, ye lame, for joy!

He gives all of these verbal qualities to infirmities, to disabilities. What could be a clearer representation of the presence of the promises, the presence of God, than when these afflictions, these difficulties, these disabilities over which we have no control, have suddenly been dissipated? Who would not readily believe if indeed these wondrous healings could be both seen and experienced? If we all could witness miracles, if we all could experience miracles, belief would be easy and sermons would be unnecessary, if miracles worked. Think about that. At the bedside of the dying we have all heard, or perhaps uttered, a version of the prayer which reads: "I pray to that in which I don't believe for that which I do not believe to be possible, and hope to be proven wrong." We have all done it, we have all heard it, and in most cases our worst expectations have been confirmed.

What does it mean, though, when Jesus says at the end of this remarkable list of demonstrable proofs of the dead being called to life and the blind being given sight and the lame being able to leap about; what does he mean when he says, "Blessed is he who takes no offense at me?" That seems a strange thing to say to conclude this list of extraordinary proofs.

Well, to get some sense of the answer to that question, we have to turn to the preceding chapters in Matthew, where Jesus's teachings are summarized not in their usually rosy optimistic formula easily paraphrased as 'when good things happen to good people' — like us. Here in the chapters just before our lesson in Matthew this morning there are some hard sayings, some things not so easily digested as the Golden Rule and the Beatitudes. Take, for example, in the closing verses of Matthew 10, where Jesus says, "He who finds his life will lose it, and he who loses it for my sake will find it." That seems a high risk strategy. Then there is an uncomfortably enigmatic phrase when he goes to assault the family, and family values, which should give serious pause to so many Christians who have made a fetish of the family. This is what our Lord says: "For I have come to set a man against his father, and a daughter against her mother, and a daughter-in-law against her mother-in-law; and a man's foes will be those of his own household." That should give you all comfort as you look at your families around the Christmas table.

What about those words in the same chapter that make the easy maximizers and the social justice types rightfully squirm in their seats, when Jesus says, "Do not think that I have come to bring peace on earth; I have not come to bring peace, but a sword."

We can follow, we can even worship the one who produces healing miracles at the drop of a hat, but what about the one who promises nothing but, in the words of Sir Winston Churchill, "Blood, toil, tears, and sweat"? We might add to that, "and sacrifice and disappointiment." Can we continue to hope in such a one? Is this the one we have sought or should we look for another, a better, an easier, a more confirming prophet? Ought we not to invest our fragile and limited resources in somebody else? Jesus understands our anxieties, and that is why Jesus understands that the test of faith is this: are you with me when there is no apparent reason to be with me? That, my friends, is the hard question of faith. Are you with me when there is no readily demonstrable apparent reason to be with me? Are you with me because I feed you with the loaves and fishes? Are you with me simply because I can turn water into wine? Are you with me because I can bring your friends back from the dead? Are you with me because I can make the rain turn into the sun? That's easy, who wouldn't be with somebody who could do that? That's a no-brainer, that takes no courage, no imagination, no risk at all. The great test of faith is always this: are you with me when there is no apparent reason to be with me? Are you with me when I appear to have run out of miracles with your name on them? Are you with me when I have failed to address your immediate set of problems in the way you want them addressed, and on your timetable? That is the test of faith.

I would like to propose to you that our greatest temptation is not to sin, although that temptation is great, but we are not so easily evil as we are easily discouraged, and discouragement is our greatest temptation. It is through our discouragement, and not through our sin, I would argue, that Satan enters in. It is not when we are blatantly evil that Satan marches in and lays claim to the territory of our heart and our soul; it is when we are prepared to give up or to give in that we have lost the game, and it is at that point of despair that we need to hang on the most.

Think of the sliding scale of discouragement in which we have all taken part. First we begin to doubt ourselves — we begin to say, "I'm just not up to it, I used to be good at this sort of thing but maybe my talents have been over-rated, maybe I have overestimated my own skill, I got through yesterday, I don't think I'm going to get through today, and I'm sure I won't get through tomorrow:" we begin to doubt ourselves. We doubt our motivation, imagination, intelligence, creativity, and we do it when we look in the mirror in the morning, and we do it when we brush our teeth at night. The first sign of discouragement is a lack of confidence in ourselves. Then we begin to doubt others because we know that if we're not up to the mark, we're absolutely certain that they are not up to the mark. "I used to be able to depend upon her, she's let me down;" we think, or "I used to be able to trust him but he's done me in; I don't know if I am prepared to cast my fate in with that group of people, I don't trust them, I don't want to rely on them..." Our own sense of self-doubt creeps into our sense of our doubting others, and the ultimate way down is our ultimate discouragement in God. We doubt ourselves, we doubt our neighbors, and then we doubt God. We say, "I know you created the heavens and the earth, I can read about it, I've heard it many times, that's a very impressive thing that you did; and I know you saved the children of Israel, and that's wonderful too, good for them, good for you; and I know you've done various bits and pieces hither and yon and that's lovely, but what have you done for *me* lately, God? Don't you see me here, turning slowly in the breeze? Have you forgotten me? Have you failed to look at what direction my tired, tortured little life is taking? I'm glad you're over there working in Africa, and I'm glad you're helping out in Bosnia, and it's very good that you're tending to things in Northern Ireland, but where are you now when I need you?" Doubt of self, doubt of neighbor, doubt of God. Are you the one who is to come? Are you the one who is to deliver the goods, or shall we look for another? Discouragement is the door through which Satan enters, and when Satan is there, that is when and where sin flourishes.

Advent is the season for such sharp questions. We have a right to ask these questions here and now. If not now, when? If not here, where? We look around and see nothing really changed or even changing. Clerks are still rude, trains are still late, the Middle East is still a mess, sickness still flourishes, and this whole Advent season is as brittle as ever it was, brittle as old holly.

I was sick this week with the full force of what remains of this cold, and I took the liberty of staying at home; and I thought that for a little consolation I would watch a little mindless television. It couldn't be more mindless than what I discovered, for I watched the impeachment hearings over the course of the week. I watched them on Monday, I watched them on Tuesday, I watched them on Wednesday, and thank God I was well on Thursday, because I couldn't bear it any more. I have never felt more helpless or hopeless than I did watching that tawdry soap opera unfold itself as all those bit players played their bits; and the fact that I know that I am not alone in that sense of great frustration gives me no comfort whatsoever. "Happy is the man who does not lose faith in me," Jesus says, "even when there is no evidence of faith around me." I thought about that, and I thought that the fact that Jesus warns us of this at the end of his list of miracles comes not as a surprise or an incongruity, but strangely as a word of encouragement. What is the spin on that? When we are most tempted to give up, when it is easiest to throw in the towel, to give up on ourselves, on our neighbors, on God, on the whole system, that is when we must hold on for dear life. When it is darkest we must wait for the light, when we are most tempted to give up is when we must never give up. Just because you've heard it before, just because your mother said it to you, doesn't mean it isn't true. At the most delicate, difficult, frantic, frustrating moment of our experience when we are tempted to give it all in, that is the one moment when we must never give up and never give in.

Perhaps you have been reading over the last few days, as I have, of the work and now, alas, the death of Henry Hampton. Henry Hampton was our neighbor over in Boston who produced the PBS special, *Eyes on the Prize*, the great television epic, I regard it, of the history of the civil rights movement. I got the whole set because I was once a trustee of the Public Broadcasting Service, and one of the chief benefits, the only benefit, I should say, that I got out of my trusteeship was being given some wonderful series. I got *Eyes on the Prize* because I had missed it when it was on the tube, and I sat down last winter and decided to get my money's worth. It was in eleven volumes. This was an extrordinary experience, this was my time, this wasn't ancient history, this is my lifetime, these are my people, this is my experience, this is my history, and this was so powerfully new and transforming that I couldn't stop watching the tapes.

When Henry Hampton was asked what he hoped he had accomplished in his magnificent series, he said that he wanted to capture the perseverance of the people as an essay not simply in law or in political strategy or as a social movement, but as the sure conviction nourished in discouragement. I love that phrase, "The sure conviction nourished in discouragement." For too many of us, certainly for too many of you, the civil rights movement is the 'I Have a Dream' speech in front of the Lincoln Memorial, or maybe it's the occasional bad footage of Bull Connor and his dogs and his fire hoses, but Henry Hampton wanted to prove to us that when you watch the footage and hear the testimony and, more importantly, look in the faces and listen to the voices of the anonymous black men and women and children praying and singing to a God who seemingly had forgotten them, and a nation that seemingly was willing to do the same, you come away with the sense that these black folk made both God and the nation finally do the right thing. Why? They never gave up. They kept on keeping on, and they never lost their faith in either God, who might appear to be absent and distant, nor in the United States, which can so easily be perceived as indifferent, destructive, and hypocritical.

This is one of the convictions that should rise out of our Advent consciousness, that it is discouragement, not success, which is the mother of conviction. That is a hard lesson to learn and to teach in this place, in this college of ours, this university of ours, this environment of ours which bows down before the tin-pot god of success. Even your problems must be better than other peoples' problems, even your neuroses and psychoses must be more interesting than those at Leslie, or at BU or MIT. I hear them all the time, I see them all the time, I walk and listen and work among you, I know that this notion of success is both stimulating and corrosive, and that is why it is important to understand that in the gospel of Jesus Christ it is discouragement which produces and sustains conviction. The Bible is not a book about success, it is a book about conviction arising out of discouragement.

That is something of the view once put forward by Dr. George Washington Carver, the famous wizard of Tuskegee who singlehandedly saved southern agriculture by his experiments with the soil, and with the peanut and with the sweet potato and with cotton, and with the ordinary things of the earth. He said that he learned more from his failures than from his successes because it was his failures that kept him going; and that is a scientific insight that we easy-going, cuddly humanists often fail to remember. It is the failures over there in the Mallenkrodt Chemical lab and in the biological laboratories that produce the Nobel prizes, not the successes; it is the failures that keep those characters going over and over and over and over again 'til eventually, maybe even after their deaths, their work is got right. It's the easy humanists over there in the Barker Center who figure they've got the last possible meaning out of a Shakespeare sonnet, and then go on to deconstruct it as fast as they possibly can. Give me an honest scientist any day, who cultivates the art of failure out of which conviction rises. I'm not a good scientist at all but I'd rather be a bad scientist, in some respects, than a successful humanist by the human definition of success. Dr. Carver knew what the novelist F. Scott Fitzgerald once said of the creative urge: "Vitality shows in not only the ability to persevere, but in the ability to start over." That too is the lesson of Advent, and that is what the great Advent prophet Isaiah wants us to remember as well.

Today's gospel states the problem: "Are you the one who is to come?" Jesus's answer after the miracles is not at all clear, but Isaiah leaves us in no doubt when he asks why they doubt the Lord. "Why do you say, O Jacob, and speak, O Israel, 'My way is hid from the Lord, and my right is disregarded by my God'?" Then, in one of the most powerful, poetic constructions in all of scripture, he thunders out, "Have you not known? Have you not heard? Has it not been told you from the beginning? Have you not understood from the foundations of the earth?" (Isaiah 40:27;21)

The writer doubts, the prophet reminds, the believer is faithless, but God is faithful. The Lord does not grow weary or faint or lose patience with us. We grow weary, we are easily intimidated, easily diverted, easily driven to doubt; we look at every disappointment as God's personal referendum against us. Think of it, the God who has created the heavens and the earth has taken time out from his very busy schedule just to frustrate you! What an ego trip that must be. Isaiah goes on to say, absolutely directed to a congregation in a university church: "Even young people full of energy and promise, people for whom everything is possible, even you at the peak of your powers doubt yourselves, doubt each other, and doubt God." Even with everything you have — looks, brains, options — on your own you have nothing. You know this: "Even youths shall faint and be weary, and young men shall fall exhausted." (Isaiah 40:30)

God, however, gives power to the faint, who know that they have God's power only when their own fails them: out of discouragement, not out of success, comes conviction. Thus says the prophet, "They who wait for the Lord shall renew their strength." What will happen to them? "They shall mount up with wings like eagles, they shall run and not be weary, they shall walk and not faint." (Isaiah 40:31) Why? Because they rely not upon their own strength but upon the provident strength of God, and you wouldn't know that there was any provident strength of God until you found that your own strength had been exhausted. Conviction comes out of discouragement and not out of success.

Now, what's the bottom line? We should never give up on God because God never gives up on us. It is as simple as that. We speak so easily of the perseverance of the saints, but it is God who perseveres after us, it is God who pursues us like the hounds of heaven, it is God whose patience does not run out, it is God's love that will not let us go, and which continues to say age after age, "Come unto me all ye who are weary" — and laden and troubled and discouraged— "and I will give you rest." It is God who comes into our lives over and over and over again, encouraging us to never give up because God never gives up on us.

When Jesus says, "Blessed" — or 'happy' — "is the one who never gives up on me," he wants us to know that the one constant, the one eternal truth, the one sustaining fact in all creation is neither life nor death, but God's love for us. That is the only constant that there is. We should never give up that sure conviction, for it is both our history and our promise. It is all that we have, and it is all that we need.

Let us pray:

> *O God, we praise Thee for Thy constant love toward us. Help us to never give up that sure conviction. Through Jesus Christ, our Lord. Amen.*

December 13, 1998

UNITED WITH CHRIST
The First Sunday after Christmas

The Lesson

Colossians 2:6-15 (NEB)

Therefore, since Jesus was delivered to you as Christ and Lord, live your lives in union with him. Be rooted in him; be built in him; be consolidated in the faith you were taught; let your hearts overflow with thankfulness. Be on your guard; do not let your minds be captured by hollow and delusive speculations, based on traditions of man-made teaching and centred on the elemental spirits of the world and not on Christ.

For it is in Christ that the complete being of the Godhead dwells embodied, and in him you have been brought to completion. Every power and authority in the universe is subject to him as Head. In him also you were circumcised, not in a physical sense, but by being divested of the lower nature; this is Christ's way of circumcision. For in baptism you were buried with him, in baptism also you were raised to life with him through your faith in the active power of God who raised him from the dead. And although you were dead because of your sins and because you were morally uncircumcised, he has made you alive with Christ. For he has forgiven us all our sins; he has cancelled the bond which pledged us to the decrees of the law. It stood against us, but he has set it aside, nailing it to the cross. On that cross he discarded the cosmic powers and authorities like a garment; he made a public spectacle of them and led them as captives in his triumphal procession.

UNITED WITH CHRIST

Text: Therefore, since Jesus was delivered to you as Christ and Lord, live your lives in union with him. *Colossians 2:6*

We had a splendid pageant here on Christmas Eve. As they say in Lake Wobegone, all the children were exceptional, and we all saw the

...old, old story of unseen things above,
Of Jesus and his glory, of Jesus and his love.

Most of us remember the pageants of our youth, and when we watch the children we are transported back to that youth, that innocence. My old friend Forrester Church, minister of New York's very urbane All Souls Unitarian Church, advertised his parish's Christmas pageant to rootless New Yorkers as the kind they would remember from "back home," wherever that home was.

We would linger there, but we dare not. Christmas nostalgia can do positive damage to Christian faith, and we must not let the narrative get in the way of the message that Christ makes a difference in the life of the believer. Notice that I did not say that Christ makes a difference in the life of the *world*, but rather that Christ makes a difference in the life of the *believer*. This is the same place it was before the miracle of Christmas and the glories of Christmas Eve. People are the same as they were before, by and large, even you, even I; and the same as we were before we knelt in adoration before the manger. Remember too the context of the holy birth, the birth at Bethlehem which occurred in a world that took little positive notice of it, where taxes were and are still collected, innocent children were and are still slaughtered, shepherds still have to work for a living, and those most exotic of all visitors, the heavenly host of angels and the earthly sages, the wise men, all go back to where they came from. The world did not stop on its axis on Christmas Eve, and Christ did not stand up and confront the malefactors of great wealth or the engines of earthly principalities and dominions in the way that we would expect.

It is not sufficient for Christians to say that they believe in Christmas, whatever that means. It is imperative for Christians to say that they believe in Christ, and that that belief makes a difference in their lives, in your lives, in our lives.

This is the message that St. Paul wants to communicate to his correspondents in the Colossian city to whom he writes. He is in prison, and it is from prison that he writes to try to straighten out some fundamental confusions in the church of the Colossians, and to try to encourage them to establish some priorities of belief and of action. It should be a reassuring thought to realize that St. Paul had never heard of Christmas, that St. Paul did not celebrate the birth of the Savior, or that the Colossians would not have known Advent or Christmas, for these are not people caught up in the narration of the Christmas story but people caught up in the experience of Jesus Christ and the difference it ought to make in their lives. The Colossians were not sure who Jesus was — a wise teacher, a good man, a failed prophet in league with the various philosophical systems that were at work? They were not sure what claims he had upon them or they upon him. Paul, as he writes, is eager to correct any misconceptions, and he wants his listeners, his young Christians — this is written some fifty years after the death of Jesus, so the church is very young, very forming, very fluid — to grow and mature in their understanding of and relationship to Jesus. Nostalgia would not do for these young, new, and shaky Christians: a clear, stable relationship was what was called for. In the first chapter of his letter he wants them to understand that Jesus is God's son not just in metaphor but in fact, and as such, that "he is the image of the invisible God, the first-born of all creation; for in him all things were created, in heaven and on earth, visible and invisible, whether thrones or dominions or principalities or authorities — all things were created through him and for him... For in him all the fulness of God was pleased to dwell, and through him to reconcile to himself all things, whether on earth or in heaven, making peace by the blood of his cross." (Colossians 1:15-20)

Paul does not see Jesus as some sweet and weak baby in a manger, some interesting narration about which we will hear further as we go along. Paul sees Jesus as the full expression of God himself: if you would see God, you will see Jesus. That is the message.

Now these are pretty strong claims and the passage may seem to some of you rather heavy theological sledding, especially on this not-very-important Sunday after Christmas when you have done God the favor of coming to church. It is Paul's point, however, to remind the Colossians that God's work in Jesus Christ is no casual thing, no accidental thing, no incidental thing, no little bit of stage-crafting or mimicry or dramaturgy. This is the work of God in creation, even more important than creation. Jesus is serious business, God's work done in human flesh with divine power and authority.

This is the audacious claim of the Christian gospel — that God himself chooses to do the work of human salvation in the form, in the flesh, of his own son. That is the outrageous claim by which we are known and defined, and it is a scary claim, which is why people are less and less inclined to make it. It is a scary claim because it means that God has taken us so seriously that we must take ourselves seriously and God seriously — and that claim is too much for this world to take, or at least for it to take as seriously as it ought. That is why at Christmas we do everything possible to diminish this audacious, astonishing claim upon us, everything possible to trivialize this extraordinary interruption of the cosmic order, and we do it by trivializing the great mystery of the incarnation so that it becomes just another winter's tale, like the *Nutcracker* or a well-dressed department store window, or a particularly correct performance of the *Messiah*, or some opera star warbling *O Holy Night*. We consciously allow these trivializing things to dominate at this time of year because we cannot bear to face that astonishing, audacious claim. We actually like the harmless baby and the silly sheep, we have turned a tin ear to the carols and sing them as so much background noise to holiday-making, and we are surprised when anyone takes offense at any of the signs and symbols with which we are so familiar.

Why should anybody be concerned about nativity scenes on the courthouse lawn, or stars, or Christmas carols, or even Christmas music? Everybody understands, including Christians, that they are all just so much cultural paraphernalia; in fact, I have even heard Christians saying to their Jewish friends, "Don't worry about all this, it doesn't mean anything, it's right up there with Santa Claus." Why should Jews and Muslims be offended by the empty signs and rituals of Christians who themselves no longer take them seriously, and no longer believe that they do in fact make a difference, and that they are designed to confront as well as to embrace?

The editors of *The New York Times* try to find 'soft' stories for Christmas Day, instances of warm fuzzy occurrences in the city, of people actually saying 'please' and 'thank you,' and not shooting one another, and so on. They had a story of a rabbi who went to visit a vibrant black church and in essence said that the theology didn't make much sense to him, the religious ecstasy didn't make much sense, but it was a wonderful experience. He said, "Can't we just have the spirituality without the theology?" which is what probably about eighty per cent of the Christmas Eve congregations in Christendom say: "Can't we just have the spirituality, the nice smell of incense, the greenery, the flickering candlelight, the obnoxious children, can't we just take all of that in and not worry about all of that theological stuff?" This is the reasonable plea of a lot of reasonable people such as yourselves, at this time of year. Well, the answer is no. No, you can't have the spirituality without the theology; no, you can't, you are writing cheques on an empty account if you try to do that, you cannot have that, not here at least, not in a Christian church where we celebrate as the only truth we can own God's reunion with his creation, where we believe with the first and last article of our creed that the divine is made human and the human divine in the image of God. If you cannot sign on to that, then you cannot sign on to very much in this place.

St. Paul was not concerned with trying to make sense of Christmas, thank goodness; he had a much easier job to do than have all of his succeeding Christian preachers. He was not concerned with Christmas because there was no such thing as Christmas for St. Paul to be concerned about. What he wanted his listeners in the Colossian church to understand is that we are meant to be united with Christ, we are not meant to stand afar off at a distance and admire a pageant as somebody else's play in which other people's children are taking starring roles. No, we are meant to be in the pageant, we are meant to be united with Christ because the pageant is about Christ and about us. The most important truth in the whole world is that it is God's intention that we be united with Christ, and that to know that truth makes a difference in how we live in and cope with the world. There are practical consequences to this. This is what Paul means when he says, in the words of our text, "As therefore you received Christ Jesus the Lord"— "as you have welcomed him into the world," we might say — "so live in him, rooted and built up in him and established in the faith, just as you were taught..." or, "Therefore, since Jesus was delivered to you as Christ and Lord, live in union with him."

Christ shares our destiny, and we are meant to share his. It is a transaction, and the fundamental building-block of the Christian faith is that God is involved in this transaction with us. Christ shares our destiny and we are meant to share his. We are at one with him. That is as simply put as it can be. Christ was born of a woman that we might be born of the spirit, Christ lived that we might have abundant life, Christ suffered that we might not have to fear suffering, Christ died that we might not fear death, and Christ arose that we might not fear life. Knowing all of this, knowing that there is no place where we can go where Christ has not been before us, knowing that there is no place where we can go where Christ is not already there with us, knowing all of this, what can possibly trouble us? What can possibly get under your skin or get into your mind or turn you inside out or put you in turmoil. That is the question that Paul puts to the Romans in perhaps his most famous chapter: "If God be for us, who [or what] can be against us?" Translate that in the context of our lesson: "If Christ is with us and we are with Christ, what can possibly be done to us that will hurt or harm or threaten or intimidate us?"

What, then, are the practical consequences of this bold claim of union with Christ, this essential message that Paul speaks over and over and over again in all of his letters, but most clearly in this particular letter to the Colossians? He answers that question, and my advice to you — I know that I have less to do now than I ordinarily would do, and you have little to do this afternoon but to clear up some clutter under the tree, pack off some relations, polish off some left-overs, so you have time this afternoon to read the book of Colossians, I just know you do. My suggestion is that you do so, and you'll see what he's talking about. I can only abstract it, but you should sit down, it will take you only ten minutes, if that, and will be much more edifying than any editorial page in the country. Consider it. What Paul wants you to know is that union with Christ does make a difference. Are you worried about how you are going to face the world tomorrow after too long a Christmas interruption? Are you worried that things are going to be just as they were before the office party, or, worse, just like the office party, a kind of Groundhog Day with Christmas tinsel over and over and over again?

What does union with Christ mean? What does Christ do for you and for me? Paul tells us, at verse 15: "He disarmed the principalities and powers and made a public example of them, triumphing over them in him."

In other words, to disarm the principalities and powers is to acknowledge that you are no longer in bondage to those terrors and fears that intimidate and control you. Now remember, Jesus did not disarm the

Roman Empire, he did not confront Caesar Augustus and his successors and the *status quo* of the world as it was, he didn't disarm them by doing them in but by refusing to be intimidated by their power, and that was the secret of his power. You're not going to be able to walk into the office tomorrow and disarm the boss, unless you "go postal" as they say, and I wouldn't advise that, but you have the power in your own hands to decide that you will not be held bondage, hostage, to circumstances. Say to yourself that you cannot change the circumstances but you will change how you will deal with them. How can you do that? Very simply. Name your fears! Put a name and a face and a lantern on your demons. What are those terrible controlling forces, those dark demons which hold you in spiritual blackmail, hovering over you even now? What are those old and unresolved sins that burden you still and weigh you down after many years? Is there some unresolved conflict, some terrible thing that you once said or did or wrote or thought, some hurtful thing that you are thinking about even now, some wound you are nursing, some wound inflicted upon you? What is it that keeps you from the truth when you do not really wish to lie? What is it that makes you weak when you want to be strong? What is it that makes you arrogant when you want to be modest? What is it that makes you hateful when you want to be loving? Name these things: guilt, anger, fear, frustration, trying too hard, trying too little, doubting God, doubting self, doubting everybody? Are you like that famous hog on ice, not able to walk off and not willing to be pushed? What are those things? I'm not on a fishing expedition here, my friends, I speak from experience. I know not all but many of my demons, and the few that I don't know you will tell me about, I can rely on that. What are those things which keep us in bondage to an invisible realm from which we would like to escape but we don't dare?

Union with Christ, Paul reminds us, means that we no longer have to fight those old battles as though every day were a referendum for our souls, a battle and vote we are likely to lose on our own. This is what he means when he says, "See to it that you are not easily deceived, easily intimidated by human quackery." That is essentially what he says at verse 8. "Remember that you have been buried with Christ and your sins and demons and fears with you, and raised to newness of life," he says at verse 12. "You who were dead in your debts and trespasses, those sins of omission and of commission, those terrible things that you remember in the quiet watches of the night and early in the morning, you whom sin kills,

God in Christ has forgiven you..." You are carrying burdens you no longer need to carry: leave them in the grave, you have been baptized in Christ to newness of life. You don't have to die, as we say at Easter, to live. That is what Christ wants us to know, that is what Paul wants us to know, that is what union with Christ means. God has made us alive again and he invites us to new life, and in a very vivid legalistic image at the end of this chapter Paul says that Christ has cancelled the bond, cancelled the mortgage with its legal demands, and instead of letting that mortgage, that indictment, that list of sins burden you and crucify you, what Christ does is crucify your burdens and sins on the cross. Instead of you hanging up there, it is your sins, your burdens, your anxieties, your torments, that are hung up there for all to see. That is what he says at verses 13 and 14, and that is what he means when at verse 15 he proclaims, "He disarmed the principalities and powers and made a public example of them, triumphing over them in him." By naming your demons, by naming those principalities and fears, you are halfway down the road to being free of them.

To be united with Christ means, then, that we neither face nor fight our demons alone, and to realize this is a sign of growth. This is the point that Paul wants to make to the Colossians, and that I want to make to you. This is a sign of maturity and of stability, and without this knowledge we cannot hope to cope in this world. It's as simple as that.

A few weeks ago I was speaking with a priest who spends most of her time ministering in nursing homes — not an easy assignment. She conducts daily services in a very large nursing home in the Philadelphia area, and I asked her what it was like having to cope in an environment where depression, illness, medication, and the sense of the end of the line are very much in the air. She said that from that experience she has learned that her captive audience, living in an ever-shrinking world, wants three things from her sermons. First, the people want to laugh because laughter proves that they are still alive; there is something very important about laughter as a means by which God enters in and all fears and anxieties are temporarily suspended, and they want to laugh even though perhaps there was not a lot to laugh about. Secondly, they want to hear of her experiences in life so that they can check them against their own; her witness ignited their memory, so that too was another sign of being alive and alert; and thirdly, they want a word of hope so that they will realize that no matter how lonely they might be, they are not alone, and would not be alone.

Life is funny, and I believe that God does slip in through the laughter, for he's done so many times in this church. We share our stories because life is really all one tale, and the most important affirmation we can make is that we are not alone or on our own but are in fact united with Christ; and that is what the angel meant when he said that the little one, this little babe so few days old who would come to save us, would be known as 'Emmanuel,' which interpreted is 'God with us' — here, now, and forever. That is our claim to fame, the only claim we have, the only claim worth making.

"Therefore, since Jesus was delivered to you as Christ and Lord, live in union with him."

That is all you need to do, all you need to know; and everything else will fall into place.

Let us pray:

> *O God, for the gift of Thyself in coming into the world among us as one of us, for the blessed assurance that we are Thine and Thou art ours, we give Thee thanks. Joy to the world! Amen.*

December 27, 1998

PLENTY GOOD ROOM

The Second Sunday after the Epiphany

The Lesson

Matthew 8:5-13 (RSV)

As he entered Capernaum, a centurion came forward to him, beseeching him and saying, "Lord, my servant is lying paralyzed at home, in terrible distress." And he said to him, "I will come and heal him." But the centurion answered him, "Lord, I am not worthy to have you come under my roof; but only say the word, and my servant will be healed. For I am a man under authority, with soldiers under me; and I say to one, 'Go,' and he goes, and to another, 'Come,' and he comes, and to my slave, 'Do this,' and he does it." When Jesus heard him, he marveled, and said to those who followed him, "Truly I say to you, not even in Israel have I found such faith. I tell you, many will come from east and west and sit at table with Abraham, Isaac, and Jacob in the kingdom of heaven, while the sons of the kingdom will be thrown into the outer darkness; there men will weep and gnash their teeth." And to the centurion Jesus said, "Go; be it done for you as you have believed." And the servant was healed at that very moment.

PLENTY GOOD ROOM

Text: "Many will come from east and west and sit at table with Abraham, Isaac, and Jacob in the kingdom of heaven..."

Matthew 8:11

You will have noted that we have had two lessons about healing this morning, two wonder-working stories, if you will, two miracle stories, two medical stories. In the first lesson, from the second book of the Kings, we heard the story of Naaman, the man who nearly wasn't healed because he didn't believe in the power of the possible. He declined to believe that what he could do was sufficient, he declined to believe in what was readily available to him as a simple home remedy, a basic cure, and he declined to believe that anything so simple, so available, and so free could possibly be the real thing for the healing of his leprosy; and so he stormed off in a rage. He had heard of the prophet in Israel, he had made a great journey from a foreign land to be healed and, simply put, he was insulted, he was dissed when, when he sent his servants inside to announce to the great physician that he was there, the servants came out with a message from the doctor telling him to go dip himself seven times in the River Jordan, and that that was all he had to do.

It was as if you or I spent a fortune in very expensive referrals to some high-priced clinician on the top floor of the Massachusetts General Hospital and the doctor sent out a nurse practitioner to tell us to take a dip in the Charles River and go home, and call him in the morning. First our dignity would be insulted and we would think to ourselves that we had come to see the doctor, not an intern, not a medical student, not a nurse, and not a nurse practitioner; and then our confidence would be assaulted because if the cure was this simple, this cheap, and not expensive, painful, or exotic, it could not be worth the doing of it. This is what Naaman means when he says, "Are not Abana and Pharpar" — wonderful words — "the rivers of Damascus, better than all the waters of Israel?" In other words, "I could have stayed at home and done this, for all of this trouble."

The day is saved by his servants who, probably tired of their master's complaining and kvetching time and time again, say to him in these very useful words, "If the prophet had commanded you to do some great thing, would you not have done it? How much rather, then, when he says to you, 'Wash, and be clean'?" Deciding to act upon the counsel of his servants Naaman did the possible, if you will: he dipped himself seven times in the River Jordan and he was made clean, with his leprosy vanished and his skin taking on the texture of a baby's.

This important man of significance nearly lost his opportunity to be saved because he did not trust the act that was possible for him to do, which is a footnote that I often use to Harvard students at Commencement time. This church is filled with seniors whose first efforts will be to save the world, to find a cure for cancer, a cure for inflation, a cure for the common cold. They will document and patent it all, they think, and they will do it before their fifth reunion; and then when they find that they can't do it all they give up and by and large do nothing, or they go to law school. Rather than setting their hands to the possible they seek the impossible, and they neglect the opportunity that is right before them. The lesson, at its most obvious, is clear: God does not set before us impossible tasks. He may set difficult tasks, or tasks which we would rather not do or which test and challenge and confront us, but the old aphorism is true: 'God enables what God requires;' and sometimes what God requires is surprisingly simple and obvious — love your neighbor as you love yourself, do unto others as you would have them do unto you — not complex, for the problems are usually with ourselves.

Enough of that for now: in the second lesson we encounter the second healing story. Here we have another worldly man, another non-Jew, who requires help. This time, however, it is not for himself that he seeks help but for his servant, in a nice reversal of the Naaman story of the first lesson for those of you who are interested in textual criticism: someone can make a dissertation of this, I have no doubt. The hero of this lesson is the Roman centurion, Cornelius, and we know that he is an important man because like many important men he tells us just how important he is: "For I am a man under authority, with soldiers under me; and I say to one, 'Go,' and he goes, and to another, 'Come,' and he comes, and to my slave, 'Do this,' and he does it." Here is a man who understood not only the theory of power but the authority and the exercise of power: he doesn't shrink from power, he's not ashamed of it, he's not embarrassed by it, he doesn't boast about it, he simply knows what it is and how to use it. He was the best sort of Roman functionary, yet this man of power and influence, this man accustomed to running the show, could not command his servant to be healed, could not snap his fingers and have his servant, who lay at home paralyzed and in great torment, rise up and walk. He had reached the limit of his power, and more importantly, he knew that he had reached it.

So, Cornelius seeks out Jesus. In the verses just preceding our lesson today, if you want to check the context, Jesus has gone around already healing people of leprosy and other diseases and has acquired quite a reputation, so Cornelius did not have to go to the Yellow Pages to find out who was available as a miracle worker for he knew about Jesus, and when Jesus entered into his town he sought him out. In the words of the New Testament he "beseeches" Jesus, a word that is quite the opposite of command: he asks, he entreats, he solicits, he begs, he does what it takes to get Jesus's attention — and these are not too strong words here. Then something quite remarkable happens: Jesus says, "Okay, fine, I'll come to your house, I'll heal your servant," without any great theological dialogue at all; but Cornelius says, "No, no, I am not worthy to have you come under my roof, but only say the word, and my servant will be healed." For Cornelius it couldn't be simpler: "Just say the word, right where you are, and I know that my servant will be healed. You don't have to come into the house, you don't have to touch him, you don't have to ask him any questions, you don't have to examine him, you don't even have to see him, you are so great and so good, only say the word now, and I know that this servant of mine at home on his bed of pain will be healed;" and that stuns Jesus.

Jesus is not easily or often surprised but here he is stunned and impressed, and we know that he is because he says to those who are with him, "Truly, I say to you, not even in Israel have I found such faith." Of course he didn't find such faith in Israel, they were always testing and prodding him, asking him by what authority he did this, or who was worthy to receive that healing, or what was the theological precondition of all of this — all of these grids, all of these questions, all of these interrogatories, and here is this Gentile centurion who says, "All you have to do is stand where you are and say the word, and my man will be right as rain." Jesus was impressed.

How do we know this? By what means would Cornelius have this understanding? Perhaps he was so desperate that he was ready to believe anybody at any time? Clearly he was not as picky or as prickly as

Naaman; he didn't have to think twice about what needed to be done.

In the words of our text, Jesus says, "Truly, I say to you, not even in Israel have I found such faith;" and in expanding upon that remarkable conundrum, that in the land of the faith such faith could not be found, he says, "I tell you, many will come from east and west and sit at table with Abraham, Isaac, and Jacob in the kingdom of heaven, while the sons of the kingdom will be thrown into the outer darkness; there men will weep and gnash their teeth." What an extraordinary statement! Here this Jew says to this Gentile, "You, and many others like you will sit with the great patriarchs of Israel enjoying God's favor and presence while those who believe that they have a right to sit in God's presence, that they have a permanent reservation on the seat, will be cast into the outer darkness where there will be crying and gnashing of teeth." Then, almost as an incidental detail to the story, Jesus says to the centurion, "Go; be it done for you as you have believed;" and the servant was healed at that very moment.

Now Naaman and Cornelius are marvelous examples of healing miracles, medical tales, wonder-works where the sick are made well and God is glorified. To some, even to many, and perhaps even to some of you, that is sufficient, for God makes the impossible possible, and that is why God is God. For that reason alone we should believe, we should be quiet, we should be grateful, and we should go home. There is something else at work here, however, which is useful for us to consider at this time of year when we celebrate the feast of the Epiphany, the Manifestation of Christ to the Gentiles, the public display of the identity of God in the world. This is no private little manger event, this no secret private parochial God; here at Epiphany we celebrate God writ large, made live, abroad and stalking the earth. Epiphany is the Manifestation of Christ to the Gentiles — which is the formal title of the Epiphany season — to the non-Jewish world, and hence to the whole world. Both Naaman and Cornelius are Gentiles, both healings are made possible by the intercessions and interests of Gentiles, and all of the major figures except for Elisha and Jesus are Gentiles. Remember, it is Naaman's servants who push him toward the river and his healing, perhaps even pushing him in, hoping he would stay in; and it is Cornelius, that Roman under authority, who beseeches Jesus to heal his own servant, sight unseen.

Perhaps we might say, in language popular a generation ago in theological circles, that these are 'tales of liberation.' Easy to say, for surely both Naaman and the healed servant were liberated from their diseases and healed from their afflictions. I wish to use liberation in a much larger context, however, and will argue that it is God who is being liberated from the parochial captivity of those who regard him exclusively as their own, of those who think it unimaginable that God would have any activity, interest, or care for anybody outside their — or our — gilded circle. God, by these two tales, is freed to be God not just of the Jews, whom he never forsakes, but of everybody, everywhere, under every other possible claim. God is freed to be God. The message that God means to communicate to the world through Jesus Christ at Epiphany is that God has compassion, concern, and connection with and for the whole world and not just for our particular tiny familiar corner of it. The Manifestation of Christ to the Gentiles means literally that God so loved the world that he did not confine himself to a tiny portion of it. Indeed: "Many will come from east and west and sit at table with Abraham, Isaac, and Jacob in the kingdom of heaven;" or, as the spiritual, so gloriously sung by the choir this morning, puts it:

Plenty good room! Plenty good room!
Plenty good room in my Father's kingdom:
Plenty good room! Plenty good room!
So choose your seat and sit down.

It is important to realize that neither of these two healings is subject to conventional theological testing. Naaman is not asked whether he believes in the God of Israel, and the servant of Cornelius is not asked if he believes in Jesus Christ as his personal Lord and Savior. While it is the faith, unspecified and unconfessed, of others that brought them there, they, these two healings, are the objects of a benevolent God who heals them because they belong to him, they are a part of his creation, his kingdom. God heals them because God made them and loves them, and God claims them as his own. To the Jew or to us they may appear to be the 'foreigner,' the 'other,' the 'stranger,' but to God they are his own, even as we are his own.

Why is that so hard, so impossible, so difficult to believe and to accept? Why is it that the most committed Christians find this notion of an inclusive God so difficult to take seriously? Why is it that those who believe the least among us at least believe that God is capacious enough to take it and us all in? Have you ever thought of that conundrum?

Last week I was in Florida to give a book talk to a large and attentive audience on Tuesday evening in the Coral Gables Church. At the question period, as I have found to be the case over and over again in my travels across the country during the last two or three years, the very first question went something like this: "If in this world Hinduism is true, Islam is true, Judaism is true, then how can Christianity be true? Isn't Christianity the only way, and hence the best way?" You can fill in the appropriate biblical verses cited to support that point of view.

This was not meant, as it frequently is, as a hostile question; the woman who asked it was genuinely perplexed. As I discovered later, she had been brought up in a warm evangelical faith, and even though she had lived all of her life in rural, parochial, Protestant poverty in the deep south, she knew that she was better off than most of the people on the globe because while she didn't have much, she had Jesus and they hadn't, and that meant that, as the old spiritual said, "She had a title to a mansion on high." Now that her consciousness had been expanded and the world was a much smaller and more cosmopolitan place than she could have possibly imagined, connected by the telephone, the telegraph, the telegram, the Internet, C-span — all of the things that bring the world into our households in an instant — she wondered what God really had in mind for those millions and millions of people who quite happily are not Christians, and are not even Protestants. I replied, at first obliquely, by reminding her of J.B. Phillips's small book of many years ago, *Your God is Too Small*, in which he says, in essence, "If you think your God is only your God, and hence the only God, then your God is too small."

Today's healing stories are tales of a large God, a capacious God, an enormous God whose love encompasses not just those who believe in him in just the same way that we do, but whose love is expressed for all of his creatures and for all of his creation in languages, in ways, and in customs that they best can understand. It would be a careless and a callous God indeed who would create the world and want the credit for the whole system, and then leave out of his compassion and consideration vast quantities of his own creation. That strains credulity, and pushes the envelope. We who bear the name of Christ must never shrink from proclaiming and celebrating what he means to us as a manifestation of God in the world, but we must also never be so arrogant or ignorant as to suggest that we are the only and exclusive means by which God is at work healing and redeeming his creation. This is a particularly American sin, since there are some among us who actually believe that we are God's best and final laboratory in the world, and that the best argument for

Christianity in the world is us. I pray God that that is not so, and you had better pray God too, that that is not so.

This past summer, as I found myself in Hawaii, I recalled in horror that we were the ones, particularly from New England, who took Mother Hubbard dresses to the Hawaiian Islands and dressed the natives up in them, stole land from them, and left them with our neurotic version of the gospel, thinking that a subservient Christian was better than a healthy and prosperous heathen. There were many native Hawaiians at the wedding of which I was a part, and one said, "I wouldn't tell people that you're from New England." I asked, "Why? I'm so proud of being from New England;" and he replied, "They regard New Englanders as the source of all of their troubles;" and we were, and are.

Remember also that ours is the country whose southern slave-holding Christians believed that they were doing God's will by whipping and branding their human property into submission for the salvation of their souls while their bodies, their children, their wives, husbands, fathers and mothers were sold off as real estate and chattel, all in the name of the gospel. We cannot hide from it, we cannot duck from it, it will plague us to the end of time. A God small enough to be reconciled to that kind of moral schizophrenia is a God too small for this creation, a God too small for the gospel, and a God too small for me, and he ought to be too small for you, too.

It is hard for me to believe that were Dr. Martin Luther King, Jr., alive today he would be seventy years old; and even harder to believe that Duke Ellington would be one hundred years old: these anniversaries are overwhelming. We should note, though, that on this seventieth anniversary of the birth of Dr. King, the chief characteristic that we ought to call to mind from his example and ministry is his large-hearted image of a God who was big enough and gracious enough to forestall justifiable vengeance upon professing white American Christians who behaved so badly, a God of compelling and forgiving love by which we all, oppressor and oppressed, would be bound together and sit down together not only in heaven but right here on earth. That was the substance of his dream, that God would envision and enable our vision of our neighbors and ourselves as enlarged: "plenty good room" both here and now for us all.

My mother told me of her grandmother, Minerva Spratley Williams, a devout Christian, who had lived in the closing days of slavery in Virginia. She was once asked by her daughter, my mother's mother, if she thought that white people would be in heaven — an interesting question. Apparently Great-Grandmother replied with something to the effect that she hoped not but that if they were, she hoped that she would not have much to do with them. Not for her was our anthem, *Plenty Good Room*: there should be separate rooms to pay for the terrible oppression of her people at the hands of white people.

If there is any reason at all to remember Dr. King it is to remember that he did not invoke what this country truly deserved, divine retribution, a vengeance from on high, but rather that he invoked a generous, hospitable God in whose kingdom in heaven there was "plenty good room," and that so too on earth there ought to be as well. Dr. King caused us to look into the deep pit of our own self-destruction, he forced us to take a good look at it, then he helped us to step back; and for that we should be grateful.

A large God, then, one who is not restricted to our parochial, peripheral vision, should make us both glad and modest: glad that we are a part of God's economy, that we figure in God's plan, that God cared enough to send the very best, Jesus Christ; and glad that in Jesus we have seen "the brightest and best of the sons of the morning," and have a human example as to what that plan is — and modest because we cannot presume to speak for God, or to speak for those to whom God speaks in ways different from the ways in which he speaks to us. Modesty means assuming that God knows more about the business of human salvation than we do, which is a very hard lesson for us to understand, but understand it we must.

Who do you suppose goes to heaven? Who do you suppose is up there? What do you suppose are the demographics of the great white city in the sky? Only Republicans? Only 'real' Americans? Only Protestants? Only straight people? Only white people? There are people who actually do believe that that is so but that, of course, is a description of hell and not of heaven.

Remember the famous guided tour of heaven, where God takes a newcomer around? In one room there are a lot of people dancing and drinking. "Who are they?" asks the visitor. "Oh, those are the Southern Baptists, making up for lost time." In another room there is loud, noisy conversation, rackety-rack, clackety-clack: "Who are they?" is the question. "Those are the Quakers, also making up for lost time." In yet another room there is a group of people just beginning to have a good time. "Those are the Presbyterians," says God; "they are learning how to have fun." As they turn the corner, at the end of the corridor there is a room in which a lot of people are looking very serious. "We must be very quiet here," God says; "we mustn't disturb them, for these are the Catholics and they think that they are the only ones up here."

In these days of ecumenical sensitivities, in this month of prayer for Christian unity, we recognize how silly and, we hope, how dated such a story now is; and we should be stimulated to realize that the God who can comprehend in one breath Protestants and Catholics, Christians and Jews, also does the same for all of the believers of the world, and has already done so. This should not make us think any less of our own revelation, but rather it should make us modest, and glad that the God who created the world and everybody in it has "plenty good room" for us all. If God can love them, so too can and must we, for God's sake and our own.

Let us pray:

> *"Many will come from east and west and sit at table with*
> *Abraham, Isaac, and Jacob in the kingdom of heaven..."*
> *For that we say, "Thanks be to God." Amen.*

January 17, 1999

FOOLISH WISDOM FOR TIMID PEOPLE

The Fifth Sunday after the Epiphany

The Lesson

I Corinthians 1:18-31 (RSV)

For the word of the cross is folly to those who are perishing, but to us who are being saved it is the power of God. For it is written, "I will destroy the wisdom of the wise, and the cleverness of the clever I will thwart."

Where is the wise man? Where is the scribe? Where is the debater of this age? Has not God made foolish the wisdom of the world? For since, in the wisdom of God, the world did not know God through wisdom, it pleased God through the folly of what we preach to save those who believe. For Jews demand signs and Greeks seek wisdom, but we preach Christ crucified, a stumbling block to Jews and folly to Gentiles, but to those who are called, both Jews and Greeks, Christ the power of God and the wisdom of God. For the foolishness of God is wiser than men, and the weakness of God is stronger than men.

For consider your call, brethren; not many of you were wise according to worldly standards, not many were powerful, not many were of noble birth; but God chose what is foolish in the world to shame the wise, God chose what is weak in the world to shame the strong, God chose what is low and despised in the world, even things that are not, to bring to nothing things that are, so that no human being might boast in the presence of God. He is the source of your life in Christ Jesus, whom God made our wisdom, our righteousness, and sanctification and redemption; therefore, as it is written, "Let him who boasts, boast of the Lord."

FOOLISH WISDOM FOR TIMID PEOPLE

Text: "...but God chose what is foolish in the world to shame the wise, God chose what is weak in the world to shame the strong..."
I Corinthians 1:27

That cynic, that humorist, Mark Twain, was not noted for his piety, his religious devotion, his spiritual sensibility, but he once wrote a telling remark that I think will allow us to consider this morning's text. Mark Twain said that it was not what he didn't understand in the Bible that troubled him; what troubled him was what he *did* understand. Where we would like the Bible to be wonderfully ambiguous and vividly vague, alas, more often than not it is painfully clear. Take, for example, this morning's lesson from the epistle, which is as clear to us today as it was to the Corinthians to whom it was first written by St. Paul. In describing those first hearers of his word, the Corinthians, Paul says to them, "Consider your own calling: not many of you were wise by human standards, not many were powerful, not many were of noble birth." This is hardly a way to flatter an audience or to win its attention or affection, and it was probably as difficult to have heard then as it may be for some of you to hear now. He reminds them in no uncertain terms that by the standards of this world they — you, we — count for little, and they bring very little to the table, very little that will last and endure, very little to cause the world to say, "Look at these Christians, look what they bring! Such beauty, such intelligence, such wisdom, such power, such wealth..." Not at all. You don't have very much to offer, you're not a very attractive bunch of people, most of you are very uninteresting: you know that, and if you don't, ask the person in the pew next to you. We bring very little to the table, and in a candid phrase we might call the New Testament a 'Loser's Charter,' and the New Testament community a hospital for the walking wounded.

Remember the old exchange where someone says to the local preacher, "The church is full of hypocrites;" and the minister answers, "You're right, and there is room for one more, so why don't you come join us?" Substitute the word 'loser' for the word 'hypocrite,' and you understand at least a part of the point that St. Paul is trying to make.

Now that's a very interesting analysis of a congregation long gone, long dead and far away, but how does this text, how does this concept play in a place and a time when it is unacceptable to lose and, indeed, where the gospel of success and ambition is the only gospel that counts? What happens when, in hearing this lesson, you think that it is about 'them,' 'those other people out there,' whoever they are, and not about you? Would St. Paul write the same letter to the Christians gathered in The Memorial Church this morning?

By worldly standards we are thought here, of all places, to be among the wise and the powerful, the great and the good of the land. We're not great and good of ourselves: one of the benefits of being at Harvard is to rub up against somebody who *might* be great or good. We call this networking. Someday, somehow, somewhere, that casual conversation in Annenburg Hall will lead to something, somebody, somewhere. There is no point in paying $32,000.00 *per annum* if we are not to be guaranteed some assumptions about our goodness and our greatness, and the goodness and greatness of our place: it has even been said that around the world the two universal truths known about the United States are Harvard and Coca-Cola. We, of course, know that only one-half of that claim is valid, and that is why our motto is *Veritas*.

Some of you may remember that some years ago the dean of Marsh Chapel at Boston University and I engaged in an exchange of pulpits. I took our choir and went over there across the river to Marsh Chapel on a Sunday morning, and Dean Thornburgh brought his choir and came here, and we conducted services in each other's place. Quite naturally, since we each considered the day a bit of a day of rest for both our congregations and ourselves, we each quite naturally took a sermon out of the sermon barrel to take along with us, on the assumption that we could each preach the good news to the other's congregation, and who would be the wiser. Neither of us knew what the other was doing, and we were mildly amused when we each looked at the Orders of Service and discovered the other's title. The sermon that Bob Thornburgh chose to bring to The Memorial Church was entitled 'God and the Know-it-All;' and mine for Boston University was 'Ordinary People.' I hasten to say that our congregations were more charitable than annoyed, and we were grateful for it; but we do have a sense of where we are and who we are and what we are about, and we rather do think of ourselves as quite extraordinary people.

It goes against the conventional wisdom in this country, saturated with the signs of apparently successful religion, that God has a primary interest in people who in fact do not represent wisdom, or power, or success, or earthly fame but are called to be God's people in spite of themselves and not because of themselves. If we are extraordinary people it is not because we are so extraordinary that God notices us; we are extraordingary people — if we are — because God has *chosen* to notice us as we are.

The conventional wisdom tells us that if we can get only the bright people, the right people, the powerful people, the successful people, the ambitious people to believe and to come to church, then we will have given pleasure to God and assurance to ourselves. The conventional wisdom also says that if you go to church and say your prayers you will be healthy, wealthy, and wise. Either way, we tend to associate the church of God and the people of God with power, wisdom, influence, and success. Job would be a terrible person to interview on any of the televangelist shows that we have today. Here is a man who suffered, here is a man who was abused, here is a man who lost everything of value, of importance, here was a just man who was treated unjustly. We don't like to hear that, we want to race to the bottom line — "I prayed for a new pair of shoes and I got stock in the shoe company." We want all those kinds of success-oriented values to confirm our piety, and the deal is this: "God, I will pay some attention to you if you pay a lot of attention to me, and let everybody know that you have done it." Here we are in a culture where we have made spectator sports a religion, and religion a spectator sport, and it is not surprising that there is no alternative to winning.

Paul calls the Corinthians losers, however, and says that God has a special purpose for losers, a vocation for losers, if you will, and that is to shame the wise and the strong so that if we dare boast of anything we boast not of ourselves but of the Lord. Perhaps that is too clear for some of you, but it is an essential truth for all of us. We all know, at least in our innermost secret hearts, that although we want to walk among the winners, we really are honest-to-goodness losers ourselves. We are those losers to whom the epistle is written, and for whom the gospel is preached. If we had all of the answers and all of the influence necessary to make our way from one victory to another, from one triumph to another, why would we waste our time in coming here? If we had all of the assurances that we want people to think we have, the knowledge that we hope we have, we would have chosen the wiser course this morning, which is to be with those over there in Canaday Hall, who are just about rising. They don't need to worry about all of these things and that is why they are not here but you are; and you and I know our basic need even if we don't want that need to be advertised.

Most of us know that we are neither fully what we appear to be, nor sufficient in what we are, and church is one of the few places in which we can confess to the truth about ourselves and not lose face according to the conventional wisdom. You go to your shrink and pay God knows how many dollars for the fifty-minute hour, and you say to your shrink, "I am a terrible, wretched person..." and the shrink will stroke his or her chin and ask you how long you have felt that way about yourself, and off you go — but when you come here and say, "I am a terrible, wretched person," we say, "Yes, we know you are! So am I, and so is everybody here, and that's why we're here." God has chosen the weak, the poor, the foolish, the needy, the ineffectual, the losers in this world to confound the wise so that we do not take pride or glory in our own achievements or in our own accomplisments, but we glory in the Lord.

One of the reasons people have always found solace in religion is the firm conviction that even though we are uncertain about coming as we are, that God accepts us just as we are. We live in terror that if our neighbors, our colleagues, our friends, our teachers, our roommates, our parents, our spouses, really knew us as we really are before we put our face on, as it were, they would not like us, they would reject us, they would despise us, they would find some reason to turn away from us and, perhaps worst of all, they might laugh at us. So, we put on our faces, our facades, whatever they may be, our costumes, our degrees, our credentials, our ambitions, our hauteur, our humor; we put on our pious faces for church, our smart faces for school, our tough faces for business, our sensual faces for love, our brave faces for conflict, and so on and so forth. Only God sees us as we really are behind all of these masks, and only God accepts us as we really are, and that knowledge is the saving knowledge that is the source of our help and our hope. Somebody loves me as I am. What a reassurance that must be for those of us who cannot love ourselves as we are.

We all associate Billy Graham with the splendid hymn of that pious, dull, and ailing nineteenth century female hypochondriac, Charlotte Elliott:

Just as I am — without one plea,
But that thy blood was shed for me,

And that thou bidd'st me come to thee —
O Lamb of God, I come.

How many times have you watched that hymn being sung as thousands and thousands of people across the *stadia* of the world make their way down from the bleachers to the anxious band in front of the cross and Billy Graham in the pulpit? What draws them there? Even Billy Graham would say that it is not his preaching, it is not his *persona*, it is not his style, it is not his star-appeal or charisma. What draws them there is the notion that somebody loves them just as they are, without one plea, without one credential, without one thing to offer in the face of who they really are. It is that notion that has opened the doors of the church to millions across the millennium. The operative line that has caused people to consider God's invitation to them is the first one: "Just as I am..." Sitting here, just as I am, without any preconditions, without any presumptions, without any claim to credentials or authority or influence or power or piety or glory or righteousness — without any of that, but:

Just as I am — though tossed about
With many a conflict, many a doubt,
Fightings and fears within, without —
O Lamb of God, I come.

It's a magnificent bearing of powerful witnessing, and this powerful affirmation has opened the doors of Christian faith to so many, and perhaps to some of you here this very morning. The conventional wisdom says that somehow we must prove ourselves worthy to God as we try to daily prove ourselves worthy to the world and to one another. So, when I get a little smarter I'll spend some time thinking about God; when I get a little richer I'll give a little more money to God; when I get a little older I will share some wisdom about God; when I get a little wiser, when I understand more, when I can do more, when I can say more, when I can see more, then I will be worthy of my Harvard degree, and of God's attention. Just a little more of all of these things, and God just might notice me and pay some attention to me.

The conventional wisdom tells us that this is so, and we are ruled by nothing if not by the conventional wisdom. They talk about the Doctrine of Original Sin, and many of us Protestants know about the Doctrine of Original Sin, but there's nothing original about any of the sins that I know you have committed or that I have committed, for they're dull, boring, and conventional sins because we are driven by the conventional wisdom. Yet, says the annoyingly unambiguous apostle Paul: "For consider your call, brethren; not many of you were wise according to human standards, not many were powerful, not many were of noble birth; but God chose what is foolish" — that's you, and me — "in the world to shame the wise, God chose what is weak in the world" — that's us — "to shame the strong, God chose what is low and despised in the world" — that's also us — "even things that are not, to bring to nothing things that are, so that no human being might boast in the presence of God." It could not be more plain, nor more clear. Remember when Eubie Blake, the old black piano player, the godfather of ragtime, came here to give a concert in Sanders Theatre? He was ninety-nine years old and he tore up the place, just tore up the keys, unbelievable, and he gave a little talk afterward which he began by saying, "If I had known I was going to live so long I'd have taken better care of myself."

By the conventional wisdom the Christian church should have expired a long time ago; it should have gone under at the crucifixion, it should have gone under the first time the Lord failed to meet his appointment to return, it should have gone under the first moment a Roman emperor stamped his foot, or a pagan horde overran the outposts of civilization, or some obnoxious secular with a superior argument smashed some pious Christian in the halls of rhetoric. It should have gone a long time ago, and yet it — we — are still here. The weak and the despised design to confront the smart and the powerful. It's all true.

We, though, are a timid people, you and I: timid, timorous. Now I don't mean by this that we are weak in the face of obvious danger, I don't mean that we retreat in the face of adversity, for we all come from strong pioneer stock. We will never back down in a confrontation, we will give as good as we get: just try insulting us or impugning our identity, or our integrity, whatever it might be; but beneath all of that bluster, all of that posturing and sticking out of the chest, all of that ruffling of the feathers, we are timid, especially as Christians. Some of us are timid because we're not sure that the gospel is true, some of us are timid because we hope that the gospel is not true. We can take the heat, most of us, but it is not 'heat' that the gospel requires of us. We are timid because while we know the gospel to be good, good enough even for us, we know also that it is too good.......to be true.

I am always reminded of how too-good-to-be-true the gospel is when we read out the Beatitudes in church as we did this morning. You should see yourselves when the Beatitudes are read, it's a wonderful sight, for a soft glaze like that on a honey-dipped doughnut begins to creep over over the faces of the congregation, there's a certain sort of "Been there, done that, heard it all before," look, as the lists of 'Blesseds' rolls on over you like a mantra from a simpler, earlier, more naive past.

> "Blessed are the poor in spirit..." You can almost hear, "Right."
> "Blessed are the peace-makers..." "Okay, if you say so."
> "Blessed are those who mourn..." "Uh-huh."
> "Blessed are you when men shall revile you, and persecute you, and say all manner of evil against you falsely, for my sake, for so persecuted they the prophets who were before you..." and that produces a colossal yawn.

The conventional wisdom tells us that the peace-makers are given prizes in Oslo but that the great prize of peace usually eludes them and us; conventional wisdom tells us that mourning the loss of a loved one will break our heart, and there is nothing happy about that. If you have ever been trashed by your enemies or abandoned in the pinch by your friends; if you have ever had nasty letters sent to you, either anonymously or known; if somebody has ever confronted you in an argument; if somebody has ever dealt with you cruelly and rudely for the sake of the gospel, you know that you don't simply roll over and say, "Well, so persecuted they the prophets who were before me." It hurts. It is nasty, and when the meek inherit the earth, then it's time to get out of here as fast as possible.

Yet, if you want to know what is the content, the essence of this foolish wisdom that God promises to the timid people of Corinth through the gospel of St. Matthew and the powerful writing of Paul, that content is here in this teaching of Jesus from the Sermon on the Mount known as the Beatitudes. If you want to know what Jesus thinks about important things, there it is in Matthew 5, and on. How strange these concerns of Jesus seem to us in the Beatitudes, because in our culture we are obsessed by politics, by sex, and by money and almost any combination of the above; and yet none of these three subjects, my dearly beloved friends, feature in the essential teachings of our Lord and Savior Jesus Christ. None of those three is there. Somehow we have got this conventional wisdom mixed up with the foolish wisdom which offers us quite a different, quite a compelling, point of view.

Perhaps we can make this contrast more clear. I live off of the books of dead preachers, thumbing through them to try to derive some wisdom, as I hope that my successors will live off of my books; and some years ago in a used book store I picked up a clatch of books that belonged to the late Theodore Parker Ferris, Rector of Trinity Church in Copley Square. I was a great admirer of Ted Ferris, and I actually knew him in my early days here and his latter days at Trinity Church. I began to read a book of his, and it was wonderfully underlined: it's interesting to see what somebody else thinks is important in a book and, as it happened, everything that Dr. Ferris thought was important I too thought important. It was a great, saving thing, and in the back of the book I found this piece of paper in Ted Ferris's own distinctive hand — I think you can see it here.

The scrap of paper addressed the problem of the Beatitudes, and he had two columns summarizing the conventional wisdom of the world and the foolish wisdom of the gospel. The first column, using language which was then not a problem, he heads 'Our Man,' and the second column 'His Man,' meaning Jesus. 'Our Man' is meant to be prosperous; 'His Man' is meant to be poor, unpossessed, and unpossessable. Dr. Ferris writes: "The conventional wisdom says that we should be unconcerned and uninvolved; the foolish wisdom says that we should be concerned and involved. The conventional wisdom says that we should be go-getters; the foolish wisdom says that we should be 'waiters.' The conventional wisdom says that we should be satisfied, our needs must be satisfied; the foolish wisdom says we should be unsatisfied until we reach the kingdom of heaven. The conventional wisdom says, "Be kind when it's convenient;" the foolish wisdom is that we are kind when it is inconvenient. The conventional wisdom says that we must be flexible, versatile, able to respond to our options; the foolish wisdom says we must be disciplined and focused. The conventional wisdom says we must be money-makers; the foolish wisdom says we must be peace-makers. The conventional wisdom says that we must direct our whole life toward being popular; the foolish wisdom says we must be prepared to be persecuted." Nowhere in these definitive statements does Dr. Ferris spend any time whatsoever on politics, sex, or money, the three things that obsess most American Christians today. Here is the way his list reads:

Our Man	His Man
poor	poor — unpossessed and unpossessable
unconcerned and uninvolved	concerned and involved
a go-getter	a waiter
satisfied	unsatisfied
kind when it's convenient	kind when it's inconvenient
versatile	disciplined
money-maker	peace-maker
popular	persecuted

Well, conventional wisdoms come, and they go, and the church of Jesus Christ continues until the end of the age. Here we are. Is it a credit to our own ingenuity, our own cleverness, our own genius, our own brightness? Is it perhaps an act of instutional management on our part that we are still here, a credit to the quality of our own lives, to the brightness of our own imaginations? Well, think again. This is what it says: "The quality of God is wiser than human wisdom and the weakness of God stronger than human strength." He has chosen things without rank or standing in the world, mere nothing, to overthrow the existing order, so no place is left with any human pride in the presence of God. By God's act you are in Christ Jesus, God has made him our wisdom and in him we have our righteousness, our holiness, our liberation, our freedom. Therefore, in the words of scripture, "God chose what is foolish in the world to condemn the wise, what is weak to shame the strong, so that if anyone boasts, let him boast in the Lord." Foolish wisdom for timid people? Take it: you'll be the stronger for it.

Let us pray:

> *O God, we praise and thank Thee that Thou hast taken us nobodies and turned us into somebodies by the grace and power of Thy holy Spirit. So set us up on high and lofty places that we may ever give praise and glory to Thee and to Thy name. This we pray through Jesus Christ our Lord. Amen.*

February 7, 1999

PART THREE

Sermons for Lent and Easter

THE LENTEN LIFE

TEMPTATION AND THE VULNERABLE BELIEVER

The First Sunday in Lent

The Lesson

I Corinthians 10:1-13 (RSV)

I want you to know, brethren, that our fathers were all under the cloud, and all passed through the sea. and all were baptized into Moses in the cloud and in the sea; and all ate the same supernatural food and all drank the same supernatural drink. For they drank from the supernatural Rock which followed them; and the Rock was Christ. Nevertheless with most of them God was not pleased; for they were overthrown in the wilderness.

Now these things are warnings for us, not to desire evil as they did. Do not be idolaters as some of them were; as it is written, "The people sat down to eat and drink and rose up to dance." We must not indulge in immorality as some of them did, and twenty-three thousand fell in a single day. We must not put the Lord to the test, as some of them did and were destroyed by serpents; nor grumble, as some of them did and were destroyed by the Destroyer. Now these things happened to them as a warning, but they were written down for our instruction, upon whom the end of the ages has come. Therefore let any one who thinks that he stands take heed lest he fall. No temptation has overtaken you that is not common to man. God is faithful, and he will not let you be tempted beyond your strength, but with the temptation will also provide the way of escape, that you may be able to endure it.

THE LENTEN LIFE

TEMPTATION AND THE VULNERABLE BELIEVER

Text: God is faithful, and he will not let you be tempted beyond your strength, but with the temptation will also provide the way of escape, that you may be able to endure it. *I Corinthians 10:13b*

Let me give you a little context for the text this morning. Paul is writing about the children of Israel and their wanderings in the wilderness, the various temptations to which they fell, and of the surpassing work of God in the middle of their tempted state. This is what he says:

> "Now these things are warnings for us, not to desire evil as they did. Do not be idolators as some of them were; as it is written, "The people sat down to eat and drink and rose up to dance." We must not indulge in immorality as some of them did, and twenty-three thousand fell in a single day. We must not put the Lord to the test, as some of them did and were destroyed by serpents; nor grumble, as some of them did and were destroyed by the Destroyer. Now these things happened to them as a warning, but they were written down for our instruction, upon whom the end of the ages has come. Therefore let anyone who thinks that he stands take heed lest he fall. No temptation has overtaken you that is not common to man. God is faithful, and he will not let you be tempted beyond your strength, but with the temptation will also provide the way of escape, that you may be able to endure it."

I don't know about you, but Lent always makes me feel vulnerable. It makes me feel exposed, in some sense open to temptations and devices and insidious seductions which most of the year I can somehow keep at bay, or at least imagine I have some control over them. They don't seem as important or significant as they do now, but come Ash Wednesday and my habitual invitations to you to keep a godly and a holy Lent, my good advice to you as to what you should and shouldn't do, my constant harping about the journey and the pilgrimage and all of this, and I suddenly feel terribly vulnerable. I am open very much to the fact that when God sets you high up — and he has set me up here in the pulpit ten feet above contradiction — you are vulnerable, and the very virtues that I would preach, the very example that I would try to set, the very goodness that I would try to invoke in you might turn to dust and to ashes in my very mouth, and I might be a millstone around your neck as surely as you are millstones around mine.

Lent makes me vulnerable, and I shudder and try to protect myself with various Lenten disciplines, various bits of minor little abstinences: no wine, no cigars, no red meat, no imported movies, and so on and so forth. My view is that if I deny myself a lot, which I do, for I take up five things that I am not going to do during Lent, make a list, and post it on my desk, then if I fail in two or three of them that's not so bad because there are two perhaps left that I can hold on to; but if I undertake only a single bit of abstinence, just one thing, knowing how vulnerable I am I know that if I fail in that one thing I will be destroyed. So, Lent makes me vulnerable, and if it makes you feel vulnerable, let us be vulnerable together.

Now, the reason that the first lesson that we heard this morning is always appointed for the first Sunday in Lent is that it indicates that we are not alone in our vulnerability. Our Lord is vulnerable, the image of the vulnerable Jesus is clear and unforgettable, and that is a portrait of Jesus's vulnerability in the wilderness where he is alone in a wild and desolate place and exposed not only to the claims of nature and to the natural pains of hunger but also to the most subtle workings of the devil. It is important to remember that Jesus's most vulnerable moment came just after his most pious moment of spiritual power. If you know your gospels you know that Jesus is taken into the wilderness by the spirit just immediately after he has been baptized. Remember, the heavens open, and if there are orchestras in heaven they are playing violins, and the dove descends down upon Jesus and the water, and God says: "This is my beloved Son, in whom I am well pleased." It doesn't get any better than that: you, God, the dove, the water, the violins — that is spiritual power!

From that moment on you should be invincible, and in fact pagan notions of Christian baptism assume that as soon as the baptismal waters touch you or you fall into the baptismal waters, you have an invisible shield that protects you from temptation and from sin, a kind of spiritual deodorant: nobody can see it but nothing can get through; you're all right, in theory.

The gospel writer places Jesus's moment of utter vulnerability immediately after this moment of utter spiritual triumph, and it is to tell us to beware of those moments of sublime strength, of sublime beauty, of sublime power, for those are the very moments in which we become our most vulnerable. It is the fashion on this first Sunday in Lent to go through those temptations and to see how that wily, foxy devil manages with subtle logic and honeyed words to try to seduce Jesus into — in every case — doing the right thing for the wrong reason, an artful combination of deception and vanity. Because we like heroes and Jesus is our hero, when we hear this story, of which we know the end, we rejoice in Jesus's virtue; we know that Jesus wins, and we like that. Jesus meets the devil on the devil's own ground, and Jesus wins, and the emphasis in this story seems often to us the invincibility of the one who is born and baptized in the spirit. I think, however, that we miss the point if we miss the fact that this is the story about a vulnerable and not an invincible believer. If Jesus were an invincible believer there would be no contest at all: he would rise from the waters of baptism and go on from strength to strength, conquering now and still to conquer. We have to be reminded that this is a story about vulnerability, not about invincibility. Jesus could not win if he were not tried, and the victory would not be real if the struggles were not equally real. So, if the first lesson from the gospel is about Jesus's vulnerability, the second lesson is about our vulnerability.

St. Paul is writing here neither about moral heroes nor to moral heroes; rather, he is writing about vulnerable, fallible human beings who stumble along the way of the first wilderness for forty years, and who do the right thing in the wilderness only when they have exhausted every other possibility. He is also writing to his Corinthian brethren and sistern who are vulnerable in the same way, and he does this in order to remind his listeners that the hope of the vulnerable believer is not in his or her superior ability to conquer or to overcome, or even to endure. That is not the moral of the story. The moral of the story has to do in every case with the faithfulness of God. Vulnerable believers and a faithful God: that is the story.

In the gospel reading we are tempted to admire what we imagine to be the moral heroics of Jesus — we could see him perhaps engraved by someone like Durer, or painted by a heroic, romantic portrait painter, holding his hand up against the subtle, insinuating Satan — but in the epistle St. Paul, ever a practical pragmatic man who knows his audience, warns us against moral heroics on our part. That is what St. Paul means when he says: "Therefore let anyone who thinks that he stands take heed lest he fall." (I Corinthians 10:12)

We as believers are vulnerable in the oddest of places. I have said this to you before, and I will say it again to you at the beginning of this Lent, that we are more vulnerable to our virtues than we are to our vices. An old friend of mine once said that a quantity of virtue is more dangerous than a quantity of vice. Why? Because a quantity of virtue is not subject to the constraints of conscience. When you're so good that you are good enough, there is nothing good enough for you. Think of that. We are more vulnerable to our virtues than we are to our vices. In other words, Satan is smarter than you and I are: don't ever forget that, Satan is very very smart, and flourishes in communities of smart people — don't forget that, either. Satan, who is very smart, enters into our hearts and minds not at our weak points, not at our vulnerable points, but at our strongest, most well-defended points. How can this be? Well, if you know what your weakesses are — and we all do, and if you're not sure, somebody right next to you will tell you what your weakest points are — you are smart enough to guard those weak places. You will put up the necessary defenses to protect them; and if you have some sense of your strengths, well, they are your strengths, so you don't need to guard against them and you can take the material used at the moment and guard that vulnerable point of your weaknesses. So, while you pile up all the furniture in front of the weakest point of entry into your line of defense, Satan marches boldly in through the front door.

That is why, by and large, virtuous people — I hope we haven't many here — tend to be so unpleasant, not much fun to be around. Now, I don't like to be partisan here, but there's been such a wonderfully vivid example of virtuous people before us in recent days, I just can't resist, they're like the House Managers! I see those House Managers of the recent impeachment process who in their righteous virtue gave virtue a bad name, not because they were wrong, and I think history will judge that they were more right than they were wrong, but because there came out from around them an odor of virtuous sanctity, so certain were they of their legal and moral positions, so righteous, that they did not see that Satan, who was smarter than they were, was using their very virtuous outrage against them, making their legitimate concerns seem petty and self-serving, and self-indulgent. It was like a lighter wrestler with a heavy wrestler letting the heavy weight of the heavyweight wrestler work against him. That, in an inadequate analogy, is what appeared to be happening there. They were guarding all the peripheral entrances to the house of virtue and of course left the front door wide open. Literature is filled with virtuous people whose sense of their own virtue got in the way of themselves and of God: if there was trouble, Satan did it; if there was prosperity and virtue, I did it. There is a kind of myopia, a moral myopia, to which St. Paul is speaking when he talks about the real points of our vulnerability.

Now you think I make this up, but no; look at those things of which you are most proud, in which you take the most confidence, in which you are most secure — whether it is in your ability to tease out the truth of a difficult text, or your ability to do sums in your head, or your ability to spot a fraud at twenty feet, or your capacity to make clarity out of complexity, or your sense of fidelity, your sense of integrity, your sense of truth, your sense of modesty in all of these elements. Look at those things which you take up in a private audit, just you and your mirror, when you say, "Well, I'm good at these things, I feel pretty strong about this, I'm glad I'm not like that, I think I can handle this, I think I can handle that pretty well:" we can all run through that audit; then remember that Satan, who is smarter than you are, knows better how to use those strengths for his own purposes than you know how to use them for yours, and if there ever was an invitation to modesty, that is it. Let him who boasts be careful, lest he — or she — fall to the ground.

If we take today's lesson seriously, and take it as a pattern not only for Lent but for life, we will see that in the final analysis temptation is not simply about us or about our temptations, failures, or successes in overcoming those impulses that keep us from God; temptation and the vulnerable believer — that means all of us — is first and last a story about God, and about how greatly God cares — not for principle, not for ideology, not for ideas, not for ideals but for us, for individuals. Paul reminds us as he reminds the Corinthians that temptation is not an exceptional thing but a normal thing; we are tempted every day in every way. This is what he says: "No temptation has overtaken you that is not common to man." (I Corinthians 10:13) You are not the first to be singled out by temptation, you are not the first to be tempted by worldly power or human fears and artful seductions. Who are you to think that God has stayed up all night thinking of a most ingenious vulnerable way to make you burdensome, make you feel difficult, make you feel guilty and overwhelmed? No, no temptation has overtaken you that is not common to everybody. You are not in a 'special victim' class, you are neither the first nor the last to be tested in the wilderness.

If you look at those who have been tested in the wilderness before you, you will notice one constant theme throughout the wide variety of temptations: they may have failed from time to time, but God never failed them. They may have abandoned God and each other, they may have indulged in strange bizarre rites, they may have lost their sense of worth and purpose and self-confidence, but God never lost his confidence in them. That is the faithfulness of God. We lose faith but God never does: "God is faithful, and he will not allow you to be tempted beyond your strength..." (I Corinthians 10: 13) In other words, God does not free us from our burdens but gives us the strength that we need to carry every burden that comes our way. What is the proof of that? You are still here, and you have been given strength by God, who cares enough to help you carry your burden. This does not mean, as some may suggest, that God sends us trouble, little pricks of pain just to see how the human experiment gets on with it: God does not send us troubles, God sends us the strength to deal with the troubles that inevitably attend our way. Temptation is not about the virtues of the believer. Temptation is about the vulnerable believer and the faithfulness of God who, even in our worst moments, will not let us go.

It has often been asked why it is that the poor and the oppressed, and the marginalized in the world, those who have nothing to claim in this world, maintain, by and large, a lively faith. How can they believe in a God who has either abandoned them or sent them a squadron of troubles? The answer is simple: in their troubles, in their deprivation, even amidst the injustices that surround them on every hand, they have discovered that they are not alone and indeed that they are near to God, who helps them both to endure and to overcome. What they have in fact discovered is that even when the world abandons them, and the systems fail, and all the analysis fails to deliver the goods, God does not abandon them, for God is faithful. When you have nothing, and when you're going nowhere, you have time and opportunity to realize that God and 'I' are going through this together.

How out of sorts this is with our modern conception of the world and with what we train you here to think and to do because we want to be invincible, we want to be free from desire, we want to be protected from danger or consequence, we want to be free from temptation or anxiety, and our prayer is: "God, make me so virtuous that I cannot contemplate, much less commit, sin." As St. Augustine once so wisely pointed out, "Virtue, in the absence of the opportunity for sin, is not virtue." Think of that. In other words, we are meant to be vulnerable. Remember that marvelous chapter in the book of Genesis, on the creation story in the Garden of Eden? Adam and Eve are getting along happily and wondrously, then they have that little snack on the apple and they discover that they are naked — 'nekkid,' as they say in the south! Naked, they are starkers, and that doesn't mean, unfortunately as St. Augustine suggests, that they suddenly become aware of all these conflicted sexual ambiguities and desires; no, I don't think the word had yet been invented. What they were aware of was that they were vulnerable. There was nothing to protect them from each other or from God. So, they sewed fig leaves to make themselves invincible. We make our fig leaves out of sheepskin, and we hand them out at great cost to make you invincible out there in the real world, but the gospel invites us to the fact that we are vulnerable. To be vulnerable, then, is to be open not only to Satan, who in fact often turns our invincibilities against us, but even more importantly to be open to God, who in our faithlessness is faithful to us, who never abandons us, and who, even in our deepest moments of despair, will not let us go.

God's promise to us is that wherever we go God will go with us, whatever we are called upon to endure God will help us to endure, wherever our wilderness is, there is God beside us. We may be tempted to give up, we may be tempted to give out, we may be tempted to give in; we are vulnerable to all of that on every day in every way, but when we are vulnerable we are also open to God, who will not finally leave us to our own devices. When we fail in the best and highest things that we attempt, as inevitably we must whether out of fear, frustration, or fatigue, the God who loves us, who knows no fear, who knows no frustration, who knows no fatigue, is there with us to help us to endure and to overcome. How do we know? "God is faithful, and he will not let you be tempted beyond your strength, but with the temptation will also provide the way of escape, that you may be able to endure it."

That is good news for vulnerable believers, good news at all times, but especially good news in the wilderness at the beginning of Lent.

Let us pray:

O Love that will not let me go,
I rest my weary soul in Thee;
I give Thee back the life I owe,
That in Thine ocean depths its flow
May richer, fuller be. Amen.

February 21, 1999

THE LENTEN LIFE

MODERATION AND THE DISCIPLINE OF OUTWARD THINGS

The Second Sunday in Lent

The Lesson

Philippians 4:4-14 (KJV)

Rejoice in the Lord alway; and again I say, Rejoice. Let your moderation be known unto all men. The Lord is at hand. Be careful for nothing, but in every thing by prayer and supplication with thanksgiving let your requests be made known unto God. And the peace of God, which passeth all understanding, shall keep your hearts and minds through Christ Jesus.

Finally, brethren, whatsoever things are true, whatsoever things are honest, whatsoever things are just, whatsoever things are pure, whatsoever things are lovely, whatsoever things are of good report; if there be any virtue, and if there be any praise, think on these things.

Those things, which ye have both learned and received, and heard, and seen in me, do: and the God of peace shall be with you.

But I rejoiced in the Lord greatly, that now at the last your care of me hath flourished again: wherein ye were also careful, but ye lacked opportunity.

Not that I speak in respect of want: for I have learned, in whatsoever state I am, therewith to be content. I know both how to be abased, and I know how to abound: everywhere and in all things I am instructed both to be full and to be hungry, both to abound and to suffer need.

I can do all things through Christ which strengtheneth me.

Notwithstanding ye have well done, that ye did communicate with my affliction.

THE LENTEN LIFE

MODERATION AND THE DISCIPLINE OF OUTWARD THINGS

Text: Let your moderation be known unto all men. *Philippians 4:5*

I begin with a confession, and that confession is that one of the things I like most about Lent is the permission it gives me to aspire greatly. Lent doesn't guarantee that I'm going to achieve my aspirations, it doesn't provide me a fool-proof, sure-fire way of getting from one day to the next, let alone from one life to the next, but it gives me license to aspire to those things which otherwise might seem naive and unrealistic, pretentious, pompous, and spiritually arrogant. It gives me permission to try for what the collect frequently refers to as the "amendment of life." Here I think I have a chance to try to catalogue my needs, my wants, and my desires, and to put them in some way into conformity with what I believe to be the divine intention and the divine image in me. Lent gives me permission to do that, and that is why I like this season, and I think it may be why so many of you are drawn to this season as well, when opportunity presents itself to look at the inner life and to conform the outward and inward life in some sense to the divine plan.

Sometimes when one thinks of making up lists of things one wants to do, and places one wants to go, and people one would really like to be and to become, one is embarrassed, but this is the season in which we can move beyond embarrassment, and so today I have decided to take up a topic in which I have a keen interest. I wish to learn to cultivate the quality of moderation, the quality of spiritual moderation, the virtue of gaining stability and perspective in a shaky and unstable world, a world in which you and I are driven by every imaginable ideology, passion, pot-stirring idea, every conceivable claim to an extreme point of view. I want somehow to be able to overcome the temptations of those extremes and to practice some kind of moderating, stabilizing influence on my soul; and the way that I think I can do this is by the discipline of outward things. Now that's where I hope to end up, and if you get there before I do just wait for me, I will get there soon enough.

Let me illustrate a dilemma of this, and something of the problem. On Presidents' Day, which I still refer to as George Washington's birthday, *The Boston Globe* ran a large piece on the editorial page listing a series of virtues that George Washington as a young man copied out of a commonplace book in general circulation among the well-bred, well-read young men of his day. In his series he listed very carefully in his own hand the virtues and qualities to which he aspired, resolving to live by them. There were such ideals as punctuality, clean fingernails, truth-telling, modesty in manner, modesty in dress, deference to elders, the prompt response to correspondence, fidelity in financial matters, and the like. Maybe you saw this list, it went on and on, and I remember seeing similar lists drawn up by Benjamin Franklin in *Poor Richard's Almanack*; Queen Victoria in her journal as a young girl also made such a list; and Booker T. Washington composed such lists for himself as a young boy, as I read in *Up from Slavery*. I even made up such lists myself when I was a young boy, and they are still recorded in my journals which I have not yet burned, as I intend to do. As I look over the lists of the things that I aspired to, in my childish spidery hand, I am sort of embarrassed, for they make me feel queasy, thinking what an odd child I must have been, as my friends constantly remind me. Perhaps some of you kept such lists as well, perhaps some of you have little scraps of paper on which the virtues to which you aspire are either written down or clipped from something else.

As I looked at Washington's list I saw something naively embarrassing about it, something literally out of another age, when a man thought that he could make something of himself by making lists of things that he should and should not do, a kind of rearranging of the outward, external things, as if that had something to do with the arrangement of internal and invisible things. Well, in the same newspaper was a discussion of what the curators of Mount Vernon are trying to do, explaining that they were trying to brush up — or should we say "brush down?" — poor George's image. He seems too much a paragon of virtue, so we are told, and they want to make him more human, more vulnerable, more accessible, more user-friendly, and so they show in Mount Vernon the bed unmade as if George had just stepped up to go to the loo, or something or other; and they show various bits of his study in disarray to try to give us a more human image. They want us to see him as a figure more prone to the passions and calamities of his age and less a tedious, boring soul with ill-fitting false teeth and an intimidating sense of propriety who was first in war, first in peace, and first likely to bore us all to death, which is the current verdict. It was said that of all the classical virtues, moderation was the one that most appealed to our founding father — and that is enough, alas, to give moderation a bad name. Thomas Jefferson's stock has risen — have you noticed? —since we have discovered his hanky-panky with Sally Hennings. He is no longer the hermetic architect down there at Monticello but up to no good in the wood-shed: we sort of admire his human qualities. People admired Warren Harding, they called him the "second Lincoln," if you can imagine that — Warren Gamaliel Harding a second Lincoln — because they admired the fact that they knew he was a rogue.

Moderation, like modesty, as Winston Churchill might have said, is "for those who need it," yet like so many of you I aspire after those virtues, however unfashionable or unobtainable, that will give some balance, some perspective, some order to my life. I do not like being at the end of somebody else's string, or at the end of the string of my own passions, my own appetites, and my own anxieties. Lent is the season in which we are allowed to attempt to redefine ourselves, to re-create ourselves, to allow ourselves to be re-created in the image of our aspirations. You see, I believe, I am convinced, I am persuaded, that we each have within us a sense of who and what it is we really would like to be, an image of our inner and our better self, our ideal, even our divine self — that part of us that is made in the image of God. I think each of us possesses a clue as to what that is. We know who that person is, we have had a glimpse of that person in our moral mirror — through a glass darkly, yes, but we have a hint — we see something of that to which we aspire in our admiration of others, but often we conclude that it is just not possible for us to allow that inner person, that inner image, of the divine goodness to come forward; we simply cannot afford to be as honest as our inner self is, to be as simple as our inner self is, to be as innocent as our inner self is, to be as honorable and responsible as our inner self is, and our life consists of a conflict between what we believe what we ultimately and immediately are, and what we must immediately and unavoidably do. That, it strikes me, is the human dilemma. Lent allows us the moment to suspend that dilemma, it allows us by the discipline of outward things to pay some attention to our inward being, and one of the ways of doing this is by the virtue and the practice of moderation.

When St. Paul says to his friends the Philippians, "Let your moderation be known to all," he is not simply inviting them into some abstract moral discourse; he is saying: "Let everybody see how well-balanced you Christians are." J.H. Phillips translates this verse as, "Have a reputation for gentleness." The Revised Standard Version of the Bible puts it, "Let all know your forebearance;" and the New English Bible translates it, "Let your magnaminity be known to all: the Lord is at hand." Let your forebearance, your moderation, your gentleness, your magnaminity bc known to everybody: the Lord is at hand. Another way of putting it: "Because the Lord is at hand, maintain your balance, and because the Lord is at hand, you can do so." Do not be excited or agitated by everything little whim or fantasy that this world can cook up for you. When the world is drawn by its anxieties and its passions, its fightings within and its fears without, that is just the moment for you, the faithful in Christ, to exercise that moderation, that magnaminity, that gentleness, that forebearance which means that when others "stumble to and fro like a drunken man," as the psalm puts it, you, we, are able to stand stable and secure. We do not fall for everything because we stand for something. Let your moderation be known to all.

Now, I know that this is easy to say, easy to write, even easy to read, but it is hard to sell and even harder to buy. We live in an immoderate age in an immoderate world. Moderation has a bad name. Think of the Republican "moderates," so-called in the impeachment process in the House of Representatives. 'Moderate,' in the overheated jargon of American idealogical politics, means wishy-washy, neither hot nor cold; "lukewarm," as the book of Revelation says with such contempt. Moderates are people who see at least two sides to everything and can never act on either. We have heard those characterizations of moderate people. 'Moderation,' in what is still our raw frontier culture in America, and despite all the veneer we paint over it, it is still a raw frontier culture, suggests an unwillingness to take sides. It's the whining schoolteacher in the western movie, the wishy-washy minister in the western movie, the weak-kneed sheriff who doesn't dare take a stand in the western movie: we're all waiting for Clint Eastwood to come in and clean the whole mess up, and he is moderate about nothing. Thus in our culture we are seduced by an American willingness that says that we must take sides, we must do so immediately, and we must let the immoderates contest and prevail. Remember Barry Goldwater's famous war cry when he was accused of extremism? "Extremism in the defense of liberty is no vice, moderation in the pursuit of justice no virtue." Fortunately, from my point of view, he lost the election but, alas, he won the rhetorical point, as our present politics amply displays, but it's not just in politics, it's in everything that we do. It must be the loudest, it must be the fastest, it must be the biggest, it must be the richest, it must be the noisiest of whatever it is, and anything less than that is simply not good enough for us. That is why here at Harvard people are so stressed-out. They're so busy, everybody is running hither and yon — finals, faxes, Coop books, appointment books, parties — people now have to put their engagements on computers, so complex and demanding are they. "Blessed are they who go round in circles, for they shall be called Big Wheels." That is our fundamental temptation and our ultimate destruction in a community like this.

Yet I cannot help but believe that most of us, while perhaps we think of moderation as one of the more luxurious virtues, wish in our heart of hearts that we could afford it, for moderation suggests a balance in lives more often described by fragments and extremes. Would it not be good to calm down those demons that drive, those anxieties that make us caricatures of ourselves, those forces which we think we control but which in fact control us? Remember, in *Godfather III*, where the young Corleone wants to practice a life of honor, decency, and moderation unlike his ancestors, but struggles with the awesome power he possesses and which in fact possesses him? Here is a man, seemingly a master of his universe after the fashion of Tom Wolfe, who is in fact a victim of both his circumstances and his appetites.

Alumni often ask me, when I go out travelling for Harvard, "What is the chief difference nowadays between the undergraduates whom you experience now, and those whom you first encountered thirty years ago?" I tell them that there are two very clear differences, and that the first is that they are a lot smarter than you are and were, a lot brighter than the first class I encountered, the class that took its degree in 1971. The second big difference, I tell them, is that they have much less time than you did. These undergraduates — you undergraduates — are so incredibly wound up and frantic that you don't have time for lunch, and you certainly don't have time for dinner. We ought to close the dining-halls and simply have the food delivered by Internet or some other way: no one has a moment to pause because we are all driven by our appetites, our demons, our passions, and we long for the illusion, the ideal, of moderation — "but," we say, "I'll have that when there's nothing else to do."

There's no point in having moderation when there's nothing else to do; the point of moderation is that which gives you stability and order in the midst of everything to do. That is what we aspire to.

Think of King Solomon, in the first lesson, known for his wisdom, his prudence and his power, beloved of God, and his first request when God asked him what he wanted, just at the moment of his crowning, was a plea for wisdom: "Help me to know how to do the right thing." Well so much for smart people doing the right thing. Here, when we encounter Solomon, he is defined by his appetites and his passions — all those wives, all those concubines, all those princesses, all those false gods — and it cost him his kingdom save for one little portion left to his son. Perhaps there was something within him that aspired to the inward discipline, but it was outmaneuvered by the chaos of his immoderation, the tyranny of outward things.

In my freshman English class at Bates College many years ago, I was subject to the totalitarian rule of a dreadful martinet, our professor of composition, Robert George Berkelman. "Bobby Berkelman," we called him, not out of affection but out of sheer terror. We thought, at eighteen and nineteen, that we were adults and should be treated as such. He of course knew better, and treated us as children. He insisted upon periodic spot-checks of our notebooks to see how we recorded his lectures, and our own notes on the reading. At his command the notebooks would have to be presented for his inspection, and as he looked at our doodles, scribbles, and inchoate jottings, Bobby Berkelman would say, "Messy notebook, messy mind." The taking of notes was for him a sacramental thing, that is, the "outward and visible sign of an inward and spiritual grace;" and if your notes were a mess, he reasoned, so likely was your mind; and if your mind was a mess, so likely was your world. I hated Bobby Berkelman for his condescension and persnicketyness, but he taught me something of the discipline of outward things, which was no small lesson for a freshman in college to learn, or anybody else, for that matter.

It would be lovely to be able to renovate our spiritual and intellectual interiors, to re-order our souls, if you will, to supply within us those qualities we most admire and of which we have an inadequate supply: patience, wisdom, charity, common sense, and moderation, but even science has not yet figured out a way to do that. Moderation, however, allows us to exercise the discipline of outward things, to impose some sense of order out of chaos, to give purpose, perspective, proportion, to those parts of our lives over which we do have some control. In Lent we become aware of just what we can and cannot control in the outward things of our little worlds, and that is why Lent places such emphasis upon the management of little but visible outward things.

We cannot, for example, control the way in which our appetites rage at us, but we can control how we respond to those appetites. We cannot control those things about which we are anxious, which get into our brain somehow and niggle away at us, but we can control how we respond to those anxieties. We cannot control the chaos and the tumult that surrounds us every day in school, at work, or in the world, but we can control how we respond to those assaults upon our bodies, our souls, and our spirits. That power is in the hands and the mind and the wills and the hearts of every one of us, it is not elusive and exclusive power. We may not be able to change our circumstances but we certainly can determine how we will respond to them. We have more control than we think for, to paraphrase Dietrich Bonhoeffer, facing life and ultimately death in a Nazi prison: "I cannot control life or death, but I can control how I respond to life and death."

Moderation is not the only virtue and, as Ecclesiastes tells us, there is a time and a season for everything under heaven: for passion, for anger, for joy, and for ecstacy. Moderation, however, is the essential art of putting things into perspective. It orders the inward life by exercising control over the outward life.

In Lent we are given permission to consider the discipline of those outward things over which we do have some control, and a way to begin is to ask yourself in the privacy of your own closet what part of your life is out of control. What part of your life runs you instead of you running it? What would you like to do about it? What can you do about it? What will you do about it? Are you drinking too much? Are you playing too much? Are you working too much? Are you worrying too much? Are you partying too much? Do you spend too much time on the Internet and not enough time with your friends? Do you spend too much time with your friends, and not enough time in study or meditation? Do you talk too much? Do you gossip too much? Do you listen too much? Where are your lives out of control, and what can you do about them?

I have an old friend in Plymouth who told me that whenever she feels her life spinning out of control, too much of too much, she cleans her pantry, she re-lines her shelves, she re-orders everything. I asked her how it works, and she said that she has the cleanest house in town. The doing of something that she could do with visible, tangible results that were an improvement, she said, helped to restore a sense of order and proportion to her inner life. The discipline of outward things helped maintain some kind of balance within. When that sort of thing happens to me, in winter I reorganize my desk, and in summer I weed the garden.

When St. Paul tells the Philippians to be anxious about nothing and to let their moderation, their gentleness, their magnaminity be known to all, he wanted them to let their outer life, that which is visible to the world, reflect the inner confidence that they had in the nearness of the Lord. Rather than be frantic or ecstatic about the end of the world or the nearness of the Lord, the Christian is to display that sense of balance and perspective which would give him stability — staying-power, if you will, in the middle of chaos and confusion. There is a prayer of which Dean Sperry was fond, which begins, "Fix Thou our steps, O Lord, that we stagger not at the uneven motions of the world..." It speaks to the discipline of outward things which reflect an interior stability, and the key to that discipline is moderation.

So slow down, my busy, big-wheeled friends, take a deep breath, relax and take long views: that is what St. Paul is really saying. The Lord is at hand, and because we believe we therefore can live and act with confidence, taking our time, not rushing to and fro like flibbertygibbets, not subject to every poll, every whim, every fantasy, every appetite. What will be the result? "The peace of God which passeth all understand shall keep your hearts and minds through Jesus Christ our Lord." That peace which this world can neither give you nor take away from you, which exceeds rational analysis; that peace, that fruit of discipline which is the ultimate freedom. Can you do it? Well, ask St. Paul. His answer is this: "I can do all things through Christ, who strengthens me."

Let us pray:

> *Fix Thou our steps, O Lord, that we stagger not at the uneven motions of the world, but go steadily on our way, neither censuring our journey by the weather we meet, nor turning aside for anything that may befall us. Amen.*
>
> John Austin, XVIIth century English Catholic

February 28, 1999

THE LENTEN LIFE

FRUSTRATION AND HUMAN INADEQUACY

The Third Sunday in Lent

The Lesson

Hebrews 10:32-39 (KJV)

But call to remembrance the former days, in which, after ye were illuminated, ye endured a great fight of afflictions. Partly, whilst ye were made a gazingstock both by reproaches and afflictions; and partly, whilst ye became companions of them that were so used. For ye had compassion of me in my bonds, and took joyfully the spoiling of your goods, knowing in yourselves that ye have in heaven a better and an enduring substance.

Cast not away therefore your confidence, which hath great recompence of reward. For ye have need of patience, that, after ye have done the will of God, ye might receive the promise. For yet a little while, and he that shall come will come, and will not tarry. Now the just shall live by faith: but if any man draw back, my soul shall have no pleasure in him. But we are not of them who draw back unto perdition; but of them that believe to the saving of the soul.

THE LENTEN LIFE

FRUSTRATION AND HUMAN INADEQUACY

Text: For ye have need of patience, that, after ye have done the will of God, ye might receive the promise. *Hebrews 10:36 (KJV)*

Patient endurance is what you need if, after doing God's will, you are to receive what he has promised. *Hebrews 10:36 (J.B. Phillips)*

Just to make sure, I am going to read my text in two translations this morning, both of which say that patient endurance is what we need.

I have always argued that Lent is a time for honest preaching and honest listening, and I like to think that I preach honestly all the time and that you listen honestly all the time, but I know better, and so do you. Lent, however, is a peculiarly acute season which allows us both to say and to hear things that we would ordinarily not say or hear with the same degree of acuity; and one of the things that we are allowed to say, particularly on this third Sunday in Lent, is that on and by our own we can experience only frustration. We cannot manage by or on our own, and whenever we try to do so we encounter the absolutely unambiguous conflict of frustration that is at the heart of our human inadequacy. It is as Paul writes in his letter to the Romans: "I can will what is right, but I cannot do it." I can will to do the right thing, I know what the right thing is, we are not morally stupid, but we cannot do it on our own, and that is the source of our enormous frustration. I hope you noticed that in this morning's collect, that begins, "Almighty God, who seest that we have no power of ourselves to help ourselves..." an astonishing statement in this culture, this climate, and this community of self-help, self-affirmation, self-ennoblement, and self-esteem.

All of you here will proudly boast that you are here on your own, that you got here on your own, you stayed here on your own, and you'll leave here on your own. We all at Harvard boast of the fact that we owe no one anything, we're uniquely self-enabling people. Oh, some people have helped along the way, although we think they didn't have to for we would have got here anyway, but we fundamentally *are* on our own, and then we discover that in our solitary splendor on our own and by our own we know absolutely nothing but frustration. "Almighty God, who seest that we have no power of ourselves to help ourselves..." as Cranmer said; and St. Paul said: "I can will what is right, but I cannot do it." These are not some theological or biblical theories; these are the facts of life — of my life and of your life — staring us in the face. They are always there, but somehow at Lent we allow ourselves the risky privilege of staring back at the facts and acknowledging them, frustration and all, as our own.

Two Sundays ago, on the First Sunday in Lent, I preached on vulnerability; last Sunday I preached on moderation and our desire for discipline; and today we have *Frustration and Human Inadequacy*. I don't know whether such titles reflect more on the congregation or on the preacher, but I do think that we recognize ourselves, or at least our neighbors, in each of those concerns. Nowhere do we more recognize ourselves than in the frustration we experience daily between what we want to do and know is right, and what we find ourselves doing and know to be less than right or good. I *know* that I should balance my checkbook, but I don't do it; I *know* that I should not make snap judgements of people on the basis of first appearances, but I do; I know that I *should* commit myself to less and that I should give full attention to what I do, but I don't.

The difference between intention and achievement nags and frustrates: it will not go away. Call it compulsive, call it nagging, call it conscience, call it what you will: whatever it is, I am reminded daily that I live in a world of frustration and human inadequacy. How often do I find myself saying of others, whose shoddiness or bad form gets in my way: "Why can't they do the right thing?" How often do I find myself saying to and of myself: "Why can't I do the right thing?"

On Friday I had the great pleasure and delight of speaking in the Science Center at the opening assembly of Junior Parents Weekend; some of you were there, I see you here this morning and I'm delighted to see you again. I enjoyed the assembly, it's my kind of scene: I had a large and lively audience paying attention to what I said, generous in their response, and easily, by and large, persuaded of the wisdom of the speaker! Most of all, what I enjoyed about that occasion were the questions that the parents were free to send in my direction. One of the parents asked me, "Do our Harvard children know how to deal with failure?" The diplomatic answer, the one doubtless approved by both the Dean and the Development Office, is, "Of course not. Harvard students don't have to deal with failure because being Harvard students they never encounter it." Remember the old light bulb joke? "How many Harvard students does it take to change a light bulb? None, because Harvard students glow in the dark." Now Harvard students may do many things in the dark, but they do not glow.

The real answer is that Harvard students, like the rest of us, find failure very difficult to deal with, a source of enormous frustration, for we live in a culture of winning. You parents have brought your children up in a culture of winning. They are meant to win the soccer game. Now, you want them to play well and they should be decent losers, but basically you want them to win. Why else have you spent all that money and wasted all that gas? In the Olympics, only the gold counts; silver and bronze are for losers, nobody stands up and very loudly applauds the silver and bronze, it's the gold that counts, and nothing else. Silver and bronze may be close but this, after all, is not horseshoes.

So, when we find that our best efforts and our best intentions do not always produce the desired result in the required time-frame, we become frustrated. That is a relatively easy kind of failure, however, for there is always somebody or something to blame. You know how the questions about grades go around here: the comment is either, "I got an 'A,'" or "She gave me a 'B.'" A more difficult kind of frustration, even here in Cambridge and certainly among the faithful everywhere — and this kind of frustration is the one that is at the heart of our personal dilemma and far more compelling than plain old-fashioned failure — is the frustration that comes from within us, between what we know and will to do and what we actually end up doing. It is the conflict which St. Paul describes as the struggle, inadequately translated but adequate for our purposes, between our subjugation to the flesh on the one hand and the spirit on the other. Now, I don't want you, because Paul does not want you, to think of this as purely a division between the physical and the spiritual, for it is not: it is between what is fundamentally human but which is incapable of fulfilling divine purposes and the divine purposes which we as humans are capable of understanding but not of achieving on our own. That's the conflict to which St. Paul is referring in Romans 7, and to think of it as just some abstract theological issue is to fail to recognize what a fundamental description of frustration it is for the human condition. All of us know what St. Paul is speaking about.

Moral maturity, I suggest, comes not when we always know the right and act upon it — a kind of Dudley Do-Right version of public or private virtue — but rather when we honestly recognize that we are conflicted within ourselves between what we know to be right and our inability on our own to do that right. The question is not so much how to live with failure as it is how to live with frustration, and it is to this intensely human dilemma that St. Paul speaks in the seventh chapter of his letter to the Romans.

If you have the same image as I have, or even a fraction of it, Paul — Saul of Tarsis, St. Paul, the apostle of the Gentiles — does not come across as very user-friendly, or as the sort of person you sidle up to at a coffee hour or a cocktail or tea party, or as somebody you would write to for friendly advice on how to resolve some of life's more difficult or moral problems. He doesn't come across as a touchy-feely, empathetic, sympathetic kind of guy, he's not a sweater kind of a person, he's a suit and tie kind of a person; but here in Romans 7, he is so much in touch with his feelings — to use a current phrase — and with ours, and he so acutely feels his pain, and ours, that it is scary. Can this be the rigorous, hair-shirted Paul before whom grown men and women weep? This is the Paul who writes that he has the will to do good, but not the power. This is the Paul who says that he doesn't accomplish the good he sets out to do, and the evil he really doesn't want to do he finds himself doing. This is the Paul who says that his conscious mind wholeheartedly endorses the Law, yet he observes an entirely different principle at work in his nature. This Paul sounds as if he has much more in common with Bill Clinton than with Kenneth Starr, don't you think?

Speaking of our president, the one in Washington, that is, I recall hearing during the impeachment proceedings some very angry critic, of whom there were many, commenting with some annoyance on CNN on the frequently reproduced photographs — each Monday morning— of the president, Bible in hand, coming out from services at The Foundry Methodist Church in Washington. I was so interested in what this woman said that I wrote it down. She said, "I think it is outrageous that a sinner like that should be seen coming out of church." Now she didn't get it, but Bill Clinton got it and Paul got it, and perhaps you and I get it as well. This frustration between our natures, between what we will to do at our highest moments and what we actually do or cannot restrain ourselves from doing at our lowest moments, or don't do at all, is the source of our human identity, our human dilemma, our human frustration, and it is for such people as ourselves that such places as the church of Jesus Christ exist. Paul, in the King James Version of the Bible and in the Revised Standard Version, calls himself, in this situation: "Wretched man that I am!" In the Phillips translation he describes his condition as "an agonizing situation;" and in the New English Bible he says, "Miserable creature that I am." Wretched. Agonized. Miserable. This is not the result of external persecution or peril or nakedness or famine or sword; this misery, this anxiety, this agony, this wretchedness is a result of our internal struggle which usually results in our frustration, our inability to act upon the difficult right in the face of the easy wrong. It is that which makes us agonized and wretched.

Over the years I have, as many of you know, frequently complained about the short-sighted liturgical reformers in the Episcopal Church who, twenty years ago in reforming their matchless Prayer Book, took from the General Confession the phrase 'miserable offenders.' They said that they did it — I talked with some who were involved with the revision — for pastoral reasons and for reasons of self-esteem because they didn't want people beating up on themselves regularly in church and on their knees since people didn't like being required to refer to themselves as miserable. The fact, however, is they are miserable, they were miserable, and they will continue to be miserable, and so are we. 'Miserable' in this sense doesn't mean that we lack character or will or intelligence or integrity, 'miserable' means that we are miserable because we are caught in this frustration of our inability to act on our higher and our upper natures. We cannot do it on our own and by ourselves, and that is why "there is no health in us." When we say that in the General Confession we are not beating ourselves up, we are looking ourselves in the eye; and if we can't do that, there is absolutely no health in us at all. What should we expect? We are miserable, in Cranmer's splendid indictment, because we recognize the frustration and inadequacy of our human condition to act upon the right. As Paul Zahl, our Lenten author and Good Friday missioner, has recently pointed out in a newspaper article about the revised form of the Prayer Book, "Who can take altogether seriously the literary notions of a prayer book produced in the age of disco?" The young, and the rest of us, have to learn how to cope not simply with failure — which is in some respects easy — but with frustration — which is harder because it is enduring — for young people and the rest of us will see more of frustration than of anything else in life.

St. Paul, however, being St. Paul, is not content to remain in his state of miserable wretchedness, he does not regard it as a steady, ultimate, and absolute state, not at all. He sees a way not out but through his all-too-human dilemma. The fact of frustration for St. Paul leads inevitably, but not always easily, to the promise of victory in Jesus Christ, best put in the Phillips translation of Romans 7, where Paul says: “It is an agonizing situation, and who on earth can set me free from the clutches of my own nature? I thank God there is a way out through Jesus Christ our Lord.” (Romans 7:25) The eighth chapter of Romans goes on to describe the nature of that way out through Jesus Christ, and we should reflect just a little bit about what he means about the “way out through Jesus Christ our Lord.”

As long as the self is bound to and defined only by the selfish interests; in other words, as long as we alone are the subjects of our own discourse, as long as it is about only ‘me’ — about *my* hopes, *my* fears, *my* loves, *my* hates, *my* anxieties, *my* frustrations, *my* promises — as long as it is focused only on us, our will and our desires are defined by that self-interested trap and there is no way out. If *you* are the only subject of your discourse, you are trapped forever with a tedious lifelong companion, namely *you*.

Have you listened to the songs that define our popular culture these days, the songs that get prizes at the Grammy Awards, for example, just given out this last week? I will not pretend that I am a *connoisseur* of the hip-hop culture, for I am not, and if I said I was you would have every reason not to believe me; but this last week as these awards were given out and it was impossible to avoid them either on the television or in the paper, I took a little advantage of learning about the songs that people think are important, of the subjects that describe our wall-to-wall sound-contaminated universe in which the young are particularly mesmerized. The young are sold these things by the not-so-young who make an enormous profit out of them, and I discovered in the songs that I listened to and heard about, and in the lyrics that I could decipher, that they were all about ‘me.’ They are all first person personal pronoun-centered songs. They never move beyond the frustrations of the first person singular, and it appears that neither sex nor drugs nor an unremitting beat and intolerable volume can stave off the incredible confession of absolute frustration. If I believed half of what I heard on the basis of these songs I would conclude that our young people are miserable, that they live in a world of absolute frustration and terror, that there is no way out for them, and that the longer they sing and the louder they sing and the harder they party and the merrier they appear to be, the more trapped and miserable they are; and we celebrate these songs as vital and relevant and full of energy when in fact they are the songs of a culture of death and despair. Mrs. Gore is more right than I ever thought she was, and you might agree too, if you could bear to listen to some of these songs.

Now, Paul says that the only way out of a culture of death and despair and frustration is not by 'me,' 'myself,' and 'I,' but through Jesus Christ. This is the promise given to the faithful, that through Christ who confronts and transcends the culture of death, no matter how artfully or artificially packaged, we too may be called to newness of life here and now. The culture of death and diversion, which is what the modern entertainment industry really comes down to and celebrates and sells, and what we buy, does not help us in our struggles. It doesn't even articulate those struggles very well, it helps only to illustrate and define the nature of our frustration. The Temperance Movement in America once had a slogan about drink that went like this: "Alcohol doesn't drown your sorrows, it only irrigates them." There is something to be said about the nature of our popular culture which, in trying to divert us from the tyranny of ourselves, simply irrigates that frustration. The only way out of the culture of misery, as St. Paul would put it, is through the mercy of Jesus Christ.

Not so fast, though. Up to this point this could be your usual evangelical commercial for giving up everything that's fun and getting on with everything that's difficult and miserable. Jesus paid it all, all you have to do is cash in your check at the cross and it will all be sorted out for you. It is far too easy to say that Jesus solves it all, far too simple to claim the victory and the promises now, that all we have to do is simply to put all our troubles in his hands and they will go away. They won't. That is too simple an answer for you, too simple an answer for me, and it is too simple an answer for St. Paul, and he does not give it. There is a distance, a long interval, between the *fact* of frustration and the *promise* of victory, and how we make our way between that fact and that promise is in essence how we live our lives. That distance is undertaken through the practice of patience, of "patient endurance," which is how the writer of Hebrews puts it. If you want to get from here to there, my dear friends, young, middle-aged, old and beyond, you are going to have to practice the patience of endurance. It does not come in the twinkling of an eye or at the snap of a finger or by exercising some pious formula, and if somebody tells you that it does you have reason to suspect his credentials as an honest, functioning human being in this life and in this world.

It's hard to sell patience in a world where impatience appears to be the thing that gets things done. Some will say that patience is what you practice when you can't do anything, or that patience is a poor substitute for action. I looked up 'patience' in one of my quotation books, and after all the prosey-dosey stuff of Emerson and Wordsworth and all of the other dead white males, was a wonderful aphorism about patience by Baroness Thatcher, whom I have always admired. Mrs. Thatcher says about patience, "I can be patient about anything as long as I get my way in the end." She may not have got her way in the end — she got hers in the end, alas — but nevertheless that is an attitude that most of us have, and if there is an antidote to frustration and the pervasive sense of human inadequacy, it is in the patience that it takes to pursue the promises of God, the patience that it takes to allow us to gain victory over ourselves through Christ. Frustration acknowledges the tyranny of the short-term, the tyranny of the present moment, the things that have to be done yesterday; patience is the key to the long-term; frustration is the witness of the day; patience is the testimony of the ages.

Early on in the deanship of Henry Rosovsky, that wise and true sage and somewhat cynical grand rabbi of Harvard in the 1970s, I remember when some undergraduates in the predecessor of the present Undergraduate Council came and demanded some immediate change in some absolutely wicked policy of Harvard, some perverse and stupid way in which the University had been going. The dean said to them, "You are here for four years, we are here for life, and Harvard is here forever." This certainly poured sufficient cold water on the immediate urgency of the moment, and it raised a much larger question: if you are hearing about change and reform either institutionally or individually, what is required is not so much your moral outrage as it is your capacity for patient endurance and persistence. Institutions do not change willingly or readily, ever, and they certainly do not change without a long dose of enduring patience; and neither do individuals. This is what Hebrews means in the Phillips translation, when our text says, "Patient endurance is what you need if, after doing God's will, you are to receive what he has promised."

St. Paul knew the problem of the short attention span, he knows our late twentieth century American culture not because he was a prophet, but because our culture is not so different from his own. Our frustration arises in part from the fact that if we finally and fully decide to do good, we want an instant result. If we are to endure any pain or suffering we want a quick assurance that all will be well, and on our terms and in our time.

It is said that we have no taste for foreign policy in this country because it takes time and patience to cope with cultures not as addicted to the quick fix as we are, and so we are frustrated in Northern Ireland, the Balkans, the middle East, and we are frustrated in Africa, not so much because we lack empathy with the peoples in those troubled lands, but because a simple, agreeable, and instantaneous solution is not readily in sight.

My father was a farmer. His principle crop was cranberries, but he also kept a large vegetable garden in which I was taught the fine and demanding art of the farmer's patience. Father taught me that if you plant and weed carefully and do all that you can, in the end you must have the patience and the trust that nature will take its course and a harvest will come in the fullness of time. Those are hard lines to tell to a six-year old boy eager to see the immediate results of his labor and of his harvest, and one of my father's most favorite lines, which I hated then but appreciate now, was this: "My boy, the carrots will not grow if you keep pulling them up to see how they are getting on."

Christ Jesus promises us a new life in this life which is not dominated by the demands and frustrations of our old life. We are promised a victory over our worst nature, the triumph of our better selves, but that victory is not easily accomplished, not cheaply won. It takes time to live and to work toward those promises that what we will to do and the good that we do do are the same. It takes time to achieve that synthesis in spite of all the frustrations to the contrary, and there are times for most of the faithful when in doing what we believe to be God's will that instead of being rewarded we suffer, we are persecuted, they talk about us, they write letters to the editor about us, they write letters to us about us, they persecute and say all manner of evil against us falsely. When our good efforts do not produce the instant good result, indeed when our good intentions turn to dust and ashes, when on behalf of a good cause or a good person we suffer and are persecuted, when we have done all that we can and it is not good enough — it is in that frustration, in those moments of misery, that more than ever we need what Hebrews calls 'patient endurance,' or, in other words, 'staying-power.'

Some years ago, in one of my 'Sermons for Seniors,' I said that the one thing I wished them almost more than anything else, more than wealth or fame or reputation or achievement, more even than happiness, was endurance, staying-power in the face of the adversities that they were sure to encounter. I received a letter from one of those seniors two or three years after her Commencement, and in it she said that hers had not been an easy way since graduation, although her glitzy job on Wall Street would suggest otherwise to the casual observer. She said that of the qualities most necessary to the survival of her soul in a soulless place and time, patient endurance was the quality she most needed, and she was glad that she had been wished it on the morning of her Commencement.

I hope you will give me credit and agree with me that over the years I usually try to avoid simple and simple-minded formulations for complex matters. As I want you to remember the essence of what I have said today, however, I am going to leave you with a formula: 'The fact of frustration and the promise of victory generate the need for patience.'

God's intention for us is that we should succeed in the victory over our frustrations for his sake, and for ours, which is Paul's great claim in all of Romans; and the way God has given us to do it is by patient endurance until the victory comes, which is the promise of Hebrews. Patience is what we practice when what we do doesn't work; and what makes patience plausible is the certainty that it is God's desire for us that we be saved from our frustration and our human inadequacy. Knowing that that is God's will, and knowing in whom we can trust, we need know nothing and no one else.

Thus we can say as Hebrews says, at the end of Chapter 10: "We are not of those who shrink back and are destroyed, but of those who have faith and keep their souls."

For that we should praise and thank God. Amen.

March 7. 1999

THE LENTEN LIFE

ABUNDANCE

The Fourth Sunday in Lent

The Lesson

Luke 6:32-38 (NEB)

"If you love only those who love you, what credit is that to you? Even sinners love those who love them. Again, if you do good only to those who do good to you, what credit is that to you? Even sinners do as much. And if you lend only where you expect to be repaid, what credit is that to you? Even sinners lend to each other if they are to be repaid in full. But you must love your enemies and do good; and lend without expecting any return; and you will have a rich reward: you will be sons of the Most High, because he himself is kind to the ungrateful and wicked. Be compassionate as your Father is compassionate.

"Pass no judgement, and you will not be judged; do not condemn, and you will not be condemned; acquit, and you will be acquitted; give, and gifts will be given you. Good measure, pressed down, shaken together, and running over, will be poured into your lap; for by whatever measure you deal out to others will be dealt to you in return."

THE LENTEN LIFE

ABUNDANCE

Text: "Good measure, pressed down, shaken together, and running over, will be poured into your lap; for whatever measure you deal out to others will be dealt to you in return."

St. Luke 6:38 (NEB)

This passage comes from Jesus's second set of beatitudes, the Sermon not on the 'Mount' but on the 'Plain.' Over these Sundays in Lent we have been speaking of vulnerability, moderation, and frustration — appropriately self-improving and self-confronting topics, and I am grateful that so many of you have taken the trouble to tell me that you have seen yourselves addressed in these issues, that you have recognized your concerns, your longings, and your vulnerabilities, if you will, in these sermons. Who here doesn't feel vulnerable, or desire moderation of our voracious appetities, or feel frustration? If you preach to neurotics there is always enough neurosis to go around, both for preacher and for preached at: one cannot lose with topics like these in a place like this, with people like you and a preacher like me.

Today, however, on this Fourth Sunday in Lent, Refreshment Sunday, we take an announced and admitted break from our neuroses and instead of problems to be solved we have a promise to embrace. Turn your problems in at the door, accept your promises at the altar. We are promised abundance by a generous and giving God, "fullness of joy," as the New Testament puts it. It is God's intention that we not suffer, that we not be frustrated, that we not be vulnerable, that we not be consumed by our apptetites; it is God's stated desire for us that we should flourish, that we should have life, that we should "have it abundantly," as Jesus says, although you wouldn't know from the way Christians talk, the way Christians act, and particularly from the way Christians look, that it was God's intention that we should have abundance of joy, so frequently do we define ourselves by our problems and our neuroses. It is as important for you to discover as it is for me to say that that is not God's design or plan. We are not to be defined by the alchoholic in Pew Ten, or the abuser in Pew Fourteen, or the failed economist in Pew Forty-seven, or by whatever set of difficulties; and if I've hit the money on the head I'm sorry, but you are not meant to be defined by that, you are meant to be defined by the promises, and you are here and are intended to claim them. That is what God wants for us, and we must be reminded of it.

In today's text, our Lord's manifesto, if you will, on the Plain, or the 'Level Place,' in St. Luke's gospel, he tells us, "Give, and it shall be given to you; good measure, pressed down, shaken together, and running over, will be poured into your lap; for whatever measure you deal out to others will be dealt to you in return." Give, and the promises will be yours.

Now I know that that sounds almost too good to be true. You have been offered pie in the sky so many times by so many people and have been disappointed, that most of you, most of us, are shrewd and discerning in the promises that we accept, even if they are promises that come from God; and we know from sad experience that when it sounds too good to be true, it usually is. Shrewd, sensible people, whether we are born in New England or not, we are all cultural Yankees, we bite the coin to make sure that it is real, we do not expect something for nothing. Perhaps you have been following, as I have, the congressional hearings investigating Publishers Clearing House and all of the other entities that through the mail try with extraordinary promises to separate us from our money. "P.J. Gomes, of 21 Kirkland Street, you have won $10,000,000.00!!" Now I have received my fair share of letters from Ed McMahon telling me that I have won $10,000,000.00, and if it were true you would be listening to Dr. Meyer this morning, and not to me. You and I know better. We are not easily taken in.

We are people who take problems much more seriously than promises. Have you ever looked at the titles of graduate theses submitted for the Ph.D. in this university? I have, I look at them on Commencement morning. There is a book published that is placed on our chairs, and during the long conferrals I read the Ph.D. titles just to amuse myself, and I would say that fully one third of them begin, "The Problem of..." or "Looking at the Problem of This..." or "Attesting to the Problem of That..." We churn these people out regularly, defining these problems. You can fill any number of Harvard lecture halls during the week with a lecture on the problem of this or the problem of that, the problem of pain, or the problem of gluttony, or the problem of whatever, but you would find it very difficult to find many mid-week takers for a lecture on, say, "The Promises of Heaven..." or "Standing on the Promises..." or anything of that sort. That sounds too easy, too televangelistical, too much offering of something that we are not altogether sure is real or even that we really want. Part of this is that we don't want to set ourselves up for disappointment, but for too many of us reality is defined by the problems rather than by the promises that we articulate. We accept the notion that religion is for the sick and not the healthy, that faith is for the weak and not the strong; we accept that we are being 'mature,' 'healthy-minded,' 'sophisticated,' 'grown up,' when we accept as a given law of physics that the glass is always half-empty and never half-full. That protects us, that is our shrewd, cynical discerning: we may cloak it in ironic humor or foul language or a certain kind of indifference and aloofness, but it is our protective armor against promises too good to be true that might seduce us and leave us like a one-night stand.

Well, if that sounds like something of your perceptions of rationality and reality, something of your perceptions of yourself or others, if it sounds like something you have been going through this Lent, then listen up, for mid-Lent, Refreshment Sunday, is time-out from that kind of thinking, time-out from that sense of being defined by problems, neuroses, anxieties, frustrations and concerns. Refreshment Sunday is meant to break the claims of a stingy therapy upon us and free us, indeed liberate us to accept the promises of an abundant life here and now in Jesus Christ. It is offered to you fully and freely, and this is the place, the hour, and the moment, and you and I are the ones to accept the promise. It cannot be said too often, and alas, it is not too often said that we worship a generous and a giving God. You wouldn't know that by our articulation of the nature of God — we used to have a course in the Divinity School called 'God the Problem' — but that wasn't the problem, the problem was that we declined to accept the notion of God at face value as gracious, generous, giving, and loving us. We almost said, "If God is gracious enough to love me, that's not a very sensible and discerning God," a version of Groucho Marx's line about any club that would accept him was not a club worth joining. Well, my advice to you is not to be inhibited by the problems but invigorated by the promises. Take them as given. We are not meant to take life as it is as gospel; we are meant by the gospel to transform and be transformed, as God means it to be for us.

The more I read, the more I study, the more I become convinced that Jesus meant precisely what he said when he said that he came that we might have life, and that we might have it more abundantly. He said that, if you remember, in the context of thieves and robbers and bad shepherds and false prophets in the gospel, and all of the allusions and blandishments of this life. He said, "I have come that you might have real life, that you might enjoy it and flourish in it without limit..." Christians are meant to luxuriate, to be enthusiastic, to be filled with the kind of abundant energy that will make the world wonder what your secret is, what you have that makes you, in the middle of all of this, so happy, so blessed, so pleased, so energized. Remember that old line, "If Christianity were a crime would there be enough evidence to convict any of you?" If Christianity were a contagious disease, would anybody catch anything from you? You know the cautious reply that might come: "Ours is not an antiseptic faith, ours is an abundant faith;" and it is in that context of promise of abundance that we must look carefully at our second lesson today, and our text.

Some of you are doubtless familiar with the verse in St. Matthew's beatitudes where the matter is put, "Ask, and it shall be given you." I hope you heard in today's lesson from St. Luke, that the verse that initiates the discussion on abundance has a subtle but significant difference: "Give, and it shall be given you." Did you notice that? There is a big difference between 'ask' and 'give,' and that is the burden of our text this morning.

> "Give, and it shall be given to you; good measure, pressed down, shaken together, and running over, will be poured into your lap; for whatever measure you deal out to others will be dealt to you in return."
>
> (St. Luke 6:38)

That means, simply put, that generosity begets generosity. If you are open-handed, open-hearted, open-pursed, open-lived, filled with generosity, giving even what you haven't, you will get back with interest. I know that that's an incredible statement to make but it's true, and if you don't give, if you go through life with clenched fists, pursed lips, closed and beady eyes, and a sense of holding on to what's yours — I got it and it's mine and I'm not going to give it to anybody under any circumstances — that is exactly what you will get back. Nothing. You will get clenched fists from clenched fists, for you respond and will be responded to in the same way. You know how it works in interpersonal reactions: if you feel hostile, negative, put-upon and angry, and communicate that, strangely enough, the person who comes upon you will be hostile, angry, and put-upon, and you'll say, "I knew it wasn't good to be good today because this person is so hostile, so nasty, so unpleasant..." and so it goes, and if that kind of anger and anxiety and repression is contagious, Jesus is saying that generosity, open-handedness, open-heartedness, open-lives, are also contagious, and if you're going to catch something in this life it is better to catch that than anything else.

The key to abundance, the key to fullness of joy, the key to that exuberance of which the gospel speaks with such clarity and conviction, is generosity: not God's generosity to us but our generosity toward others. Instead of asking God to bless us so that we might receive, we bless others, and both they and we receive. You and I have the opportunity to initiate blessings by blessing others, you and I have the opportunity to initiate abundance, pressed down, running over, by giving and sharing with others. Now that's a radical new spin on all our relationships, a new way of looking at ourselves, at others, at our world, and at our God, for it sort of breaks the claim of territory and turf and priority and suggests very clearly that if we are to receive generously we must give generously, and we must do the giving before we can do the receiving.

Remember how the lesson reads? I invite you to look it up and follow along, if you wish. See what Jesus is saying in announcing this brave new world, this new world order? Jesus says that the normal way of doing things, the received or conventional wisdom, simply is not good enough either for the kingdom of heaven or for the kingdom of believers on earth, which is to reflect the kingdom of heaven. Then he begins to illustrate, very practically. He says that if you love only those who love you back, what is so interesting about that, what is so novel or brave about that? If you just love people who are supposed to love you, and you love them back in a kind of partnership deal, that's not very inventive, that's not very demanding, even sinners do that, he says. If you like only those who like you, if you like only those who look like you, if you like only those who are like you, what good is all of that? It takes no rocket scientist to figure out that like likes like; that is a no-brainer. What have you gained or done that is interesting, risky, new, demanding, or exhilerating? Nothing at all. Ethnic ethics will not do. You get no credit for liking people who like you.

That's a risky enough start, but what about this one, where Jesus stops preaching and begins to meddle, in the next few verses? "If you lend to those from whom you hope to receive, what credit is that to you? Even sinners lend to sinners, to receive as much gain." Now don't look perplexed, erase those frowns, you know perfectly well what he says, and you know perfectly well what it means. It's not that you don't understand that upsets you; you understand perfectly well, and that is what upsets you. Is Jesus saying here that there is no moral credit in lending with an assurance that the loan will be repaid? Yes, that is exactly what he is saying! You heard it right the first time: Jesus is not running a bank here, not even a Savings and Loan. Jesus is suggesting that you give not because you expect to receive it back, but because the person who asks you needs it.

The Jesus we are all fearful of meeting, the social revolutionary, the man who redefines credit, the man who would be unwelcome in most of our churches, probably including this one, that very Jesus says that if we want to get any moral credit in this world we must do good and we must lend, expecting nothing in return. What happens if you do this? Those of you in Economics 10 know the answer: economic chaos and moral upheaval is what happens, according to the custodians of the *statue quo* both in the Economics Department and in all our social and political institutions. Jesus, however, says, "Do good and your reward will be great, and you will be children of the Most High." If you want the key to an abundant, generous life, the key is neither in asking nor in saving: the key is in giving, in sharing.

Just as a small little footnote: what are you hoarding up that should be shared? What have you got locked up somewhere, waiting for that rainy day where it will never rain enough before you are prepared to share it? On what are you holding back? I once knew a person whose dining-room linen was never good enough to be used in ordinary times, she was saving it up for that special guest who was never special enough, for that special day that was never special enough, and when she died she left a sideboard full of magnificent linen that had never been used. We all know stories of people like that. What love are you storing up, waiting for someone to deserve it, to be good enough to receive it from you? What treasures are you keeping so clutched in your spiritual savings-deposit box that it is weighing you down, when there are people who could live off of the love and the life that you could share, if you only would initiate that process? You can think, over lunch, about what you're hoarding.

Now, in the first lesson, from the first book of the Kings, we heard that marvelous story about the prophet Elijah and the barrel of meal and the cruse of oil. There was a great famine in the land brought on in fact by Elijah, who invited God to punish the land, and God was busily doing so and so the people were suffering. Here was Elijah himself suffering, and he asked the widow for a cake and something to drink, and the widow replied that she had just enough to feed herself and her son so that they might have the strength to die. Consider that, the "strength to die." The prophet, however, being the prophet, insisted that she share and reassured her with the promise that in giving the last of what she had, her supply of oil and flour would never run out. "The cruse of oil shall not fail, neither shall the barrel of meal;" and we know how the story ended: because she trusted the prophet it was so, and they had food and drink for many days. Her abundance was triggered by her giving, her abundance was triggered by her sharing.

That, of course, is the story of the feeding of the five thousand, in St. Luke's gospel, a few chapters after today's lesson, as if to prove the point of today's text on a big and mega-scale. People were as impressed by big numbers in Bible times as they are today. Feed a widow and her child? That's nice, a little act of charity; but five thousand people? That gets on the Six O'Clock News! There was not enough food on the plain, but because the little boy gave his loaves and his fishes not only were the five thousand fed but, as if to make the point of our text, St. Luke says, "And all ate and were satisfied. And they took up twelve baskets of broken pieces." Not only was there satisfaction, there was surplus. Not only was the meal adequate, it was abundant. What is the point here? Is it like the miracle of Cana? Always invite Jesus and you'll never run out of food and drink? Is that the miracle? The miracle was trusting in the promise that if we give, we receive more than we require. Our God wants us to prosper rather than to suffer, our God wants us to give so that others may have, our God promises that if we learn to share, we will have much to spare. The key to generosity is generosity and the remembrance of God's generosity to us.

Did you notice, in Psalm 77, where the first part of the psalm is the usual complaint, the psalmist is always complaining: "God, you promised this and you didn't do that, I'm feeling so low and I don't know what I'm going to do, and I've lost my faith, and it's cold and hot out here, woe is me." Those are usually the first third of the verses of a psalm, and then it turns and it says, "But I remember not only your promises but the fulfillment of your promises;" and the whole mood shifts and the psalmist is back on balance when he remembers that God has never forgotten to remember.

That is easy to say, but not as easy to do. We come back to the fact that it is easier for you and for me to be defined by our problems than to be stimulated by the promises of God. Let me tell you what I have learned to do. Some of you have noticed that on occasion, when people say to me, "How are you?" I reply, "I flourish!" It always catches them offguard. They don't know what to say, they don't know how to respond to that. "You do?" or "That's nice;" or "I'd better get away from this guy, he's about to testify or do something very very strange." Now, I never say it when I don't mean it, but when I mean it I say it. It is so easy, I have learned, to define your day, your life, even your faith, by the things that don't work, by your problems, by your frustrations, by your difficulties, by what has not happened, like the psalmist, or by what God has not yet done for you or somebody else has done to you. Somebody has set your day off in the wrong key and you're going to sing in that foul key all day long. Well, I don't want that to happen to me. I am no Pollyanna, I hope that is well known to all of you, but I have decided that God has done more for me every day than I can do for myself; God has done more good for me than others have done harm to me. I have discovered that God wants me to prosper, God wants me to flourish, God doesn't want me grovelling on the floor saying, "Woe is me;" God wants me standing on my hind legs and saying, "Praise the Lord!"

God wants to know that I am flourishing, and he wants you to know that I am flourishing, and he wants me to know that you are flourishing; and so when I think that I woke up this morning — as the old black prayer put it, "I thank God that I woke up this morning in my right mind and not in my winding sheet" — and that I'm able to stand on my feet, I speak with my lips the praises of God. When you ask me how I am, I answer that I flourish, because God has been so good to me. I rejoice, I flourish in the abundance of his mercies. Morning by morning, I can name them chapter and verse, and the remarkable thing is that you can too, if only you will. Everyone here flourishes and has been blessed by God beyond the power of our imagination. Every one of us here, no matter how weary, how fatigued, how beaten down, how burdened, how oppressed, how taken-over — everyone here has reason to bless the Lord; and you can do that not abstractly but concretely.

What is the consequence of this knowledge? I must give much because I have been given so much, and the more I learn to share — not just my disposable income but my life, my heart, my soul — with others, the more I realize how much God has chosen to share with me. God wants us to know the abundance of life, and the only way we will know that abundance is not by what we save, but by what we give. You are rich not by what you have but by what you have shared. That's the story of the little boy and his fishes, that is the story of the widow and her dying son, and that is the story of Christ Jesus himself; and it is your story and it is my story.

What we give when we let go and let God we are promised we will get in "good measure, pressed down, shaken together, and running over." That which is so abundant in our own lives will be poured into our laps — and remember, when you pour something into your lap the experience is such that your lap cannot contain it — "for whatever measure you deal out to others will be dealt to you in return." I flourish, and so do you, and you are meant to do so, and to give the praise to God.

Let us pray:

> *O God, who hast prepared for them that love Thee such good things as pass our understanding: pour into our hearts such love toward Thee that we, loving Thee above all things, may obtain Thy promises which exceed all that we can imagine or desire. Through Jesus Christ our Lord. Amen.*

March 14, 1999

THE LENTEN LIFE

BETWEEN OUR SINS AND THEIR REWARD

The Sunday of the Passion

or

Palm Sunday

The Lesson

Ephesians 2:11-17 (NEB)

Remember then your former condition: you, Gentiles as you are outwardly, you, the 'uncircumcised,' so called by those who are called the 'circumcised,' but only with reference to an outward rite, you were at that time separate from Christ, strangers to the community of Israel, outside God's covenants and the promise that goes with them. Your world was a world without hope and without God. But now in union with Christ Jesus you who once were far off have been brought near through the shedding of Christ's blood. For he is himself our peace. Gentiles and Jews, he has made the two one, and in his own body of flesh and blood has broken down the enmity which stood like a dividing wall between them; for he annulled the law with its rules and regulations, so as to create out of the two a single new humanity in himself, thereby making peace. This was his purpose, to reconcile the two in a single body to God through the cross, on which he killed the enmity.

THE ABUNDANT LIFE

BETWEEN OUR SINS AND THEIR REWARD

Text: Your world was a world without hope and without God. But now in union with Christ Jesus you who once were far off have been brought near through the shedding of Christ's blood.

Ephesians 2:13 (NEB)

Our brothers and sisters in the Christian church throughout the world keep Passion Sunday by reading, as we have just done, the Passion according to St. Matthew. In choosing a text upon which to preach on Passion Sunday, popularly known as Palm Sunday, it is also the custom of some great antiquity to take one of the epistles and use it as a pointer, or lens, if you will, through which we can take an appropriate glance at the story of the Passion which in itself as a whole is almost too large, too grand, too powerful, and too risky for us to undertake. So today I do as I have for many years, which is to take one of the epistles as a way of looking at the Passion. Hence I take as my text the thirteenth verse of the second chapter of the epistle to the Ephesians: "Your world was a world without hope and without God. But now in union with Christ Jesus you who once were far off have been brought near through the shedding of Christ's blood."

A world without hope and without God, a means of bringing those of us, who once were far away, nearer to Christ through the shedding of his blood: if we are not careful, this Passion story can be all be too tidy, all too neat, and all too artfully contrived. The finest artists in the world have committed the Passion to canvas, the finest glaziers in the world have committed it to stained glass, the finest poets and dramatists have committed it to literature; and we know in this church because we are particularly blessed here, that the finest musicians have committed this story to music. If we're not careful this story can become the perfect aesthetic experience: suffering relieved and annotated by beauty, a wonderfully distancing enterprise. I often think of the authentically correctly performed performances of the Passions that abound all over Boston in this season of the year, given annually by the most exacting of our choral societies and choirs to standing-room only *connoisseurs* of the very best of the very best, and sung safely in Latin or in German lest anyone really understand what is really going on in the cadences....

It can become too tidy, my friends, too neat, too carefully managed, and it can also be too familiar; and if you are not careful you might join in with that cynical saying of the young, "Been there; done that." Many of you have been here before on Passion Sunday, I know, because I have been here with you; and you have done this before: you have come and received your palms, you have shouted your 'Hosannas,' and your 'Crucifys,' and then you and I have all gone home to a good lunch. Passion Sunday, however, is not meant to be quite as tidy as all of that. Passion Sunday is not meant to be an aesthetically-experienced enterprise in repose with perfect choreography; Passion Sunday is not meant to be something like a televised war in which we sit in front of our screens and have the action accurately narrated by some disembodied voice while disembodied carnage takes place elsewhere: Passion Sunday is not meant to be an antiseptic experience.

Each year some of you write me well-meaning letters after Easter, telling me how you found the service on Palm or Passion Sunday a little grim, a little intense, and that it is a good thing the children are downstairs in the Church School lest they hear the shouts of 'Crucify!' and see their parents and their friends assuming rather frightening roles. We do nothing to try to typecast anybody here, by-the-way, and you should know that last year's Jesus was this year's Judas. Somehow there is a sense that we should be distanced from the Passion Sunday story, we don't want it too up-close, we don't want it too real and too immediate, and therefore we want to cloak the parts that hurt — the parts that are a little too true, the parts that are a little too close to the bone — in something else; and if we can't cloak them we will avoid them. That is why most of you, alas, will find some excuse not to sit at the foot of the cross on Good Friday. There will be a third of you here for most of the time, and that is good, but the rest of you understand the point I'm trying to make as you consider skipping over the 'grim,' hard parts of Good Friday, thinking to yourselves: "It's just too much, it's just too close, I was there on Palm Sunday, doesn't that count? I'll be there on Easter Sunday, surely that counts?" It doesn't, though, it doesn't count; and that is why today we rehearse the great mystery of our redemption.

On one Sunday of the year, and that Sunday is today, we are meant to contemplate with full recognition the whole story of the nature of our sins and their reward, and the redemption won for us between our sins and their reward by God's redeeming act in Jesus Christ. Contrary to the image of the Passion, we are not mere spectators or extras or voyeurs in the drama, we are not mere onlookers, watching others play their parts or play our parts for us, we are the story. 'Toys 'R' Us' is a wonderful slogan and it works. 'Passion is Us' is equally true and applicable today. The story is about us. We are its cause, we are its subject, we are its objective. Perhaps what I am trying to convey is better said in the letter to the Ephesians from which my text is taken: listen to Ephesians 2:1, in the plain-speaking translation and unambiguous English of J.B. Phillips:

> "To you who were spiritually dead all the time that you drifted along on the stream of the world's ideas of living, and obeyed its unseen ruler (who is still operating in those who do not respond to the truth of God), to *you* Christ has given life. We all lived like that in the past, and followed the impulses and imaginations of our evil nature, being in fact under the wrath of God by nature like everyone else. But even though we were dead in our sins, God, who is rich in mercy, because of the great love he had for us, gave us life together with Christ."

The immediate purpose of the letter is to remind the non-Jewish believers, the Gentiles, that before God's love brought them together with Jews in Christ, they — and we should always add 'we,' for we non-Jews are Gentiles — were "spiritually dead and drifting along on the stream of this world's ideas of living." Our world, then, as you remember our text puts it, "was a world without hope and without God."

So, this world without hope and without God is the very world in which and to which the Passion speaks, the very world into which God chooses to enter and in which he chooses to participate. It is a world which appears to be self-sufficient, even contented, to drift along on its own self-defined way — a world that you and I know only too well. Let me ask you a question. What do you think are the two largest industries that surround us today? You would be wrong if you said manufacturing, you would be wrong if you said commerce, you would be wrong if you said the military/industrial complex; and even those seniors here who are sucking up to Wall Street know that it pales in comparison with the two leading forces in our culture today: entertainment and sports — which is in itself entertainment. We like to think of these two as 'leisure industries' — is that an oxymoron? — but we know better: they are the colossal diversions, the colossal fantasies that we have labelled 'industries,' that we have constructed to delude ourselves into thinking that we are happy, and that will take us out of ourselves and the routines of everyday life. These contemporary and immensely profitable 'Bread and Circuses' serve to protect us from the fact that we live in a spiritually dead world, and that we ourselves are spiritually dead.

In such a world passions take place all of the time, for life is cheap and human emotion raw. Have you followed the Massachusetts debate on the reinstatement of the death penalty? It has been in all the papers, and on the six o'clock news, and I find it a frightening spectacle when the Chief Magistrate of the Commonwealth, the Governor, sees state murder — for that is what the death penalty is — as necessary to the good order of the common wealth and the welfare of the people. Sympathetic as we all may be to those who have been both victims and survivors of violent crime, our fragile public order cannot be overwhelmed by their leaders' cries of vengeance. I stand heartily with Cardinal Law, who has taken what I think is a heroic and appropriate stand, as he reminds us all, not only Roman Catholics, that state murder does not enhance life, and that it must not be permitted.

Spiritual death allows us to cheapen all life, for lives where diversion takes precedence over devotion are lives in which we can so easily be indifferent to the suffering, sorrow, or sadness of anyone other than ourselves. It was and is to save ourselves from ourselves and from the consequences of our own folly, our own freedom, our own foolish pride, that God entered the world in the form of one of us — in Jesus, whom we call Christ — literally to save us from ourselves. Left to our own devices and desires — that wonderful phrase in the Book of Common Prayer — we would destroy both our neighbors and ourselves, practicing every day on a personal level that old Cold War strategy of Mutual Assured Destruction, whose code name appropriately was 'MAD.' Our sin is the notion that we as morally impaired individuals can save ourselves, and the reward of our sin, if God has a sense of humor worthy of the occasion, is to let us try to do so.

God, however, does not choose to waste his resources: over and over again God takes the initiative and comes to us, and says that he wishes us to have life and love and not death and hate. God says that he will do whatever he has to do in order to save us from ourselves and for him, and thus it is this God who gives himself in Jesus for the life of the world. This is the incredible tale that we revisit and renew every time we look at the cross, and every time we look at ourselves. As the old hymn says:

For, lo! Between our sins and their reward
We set the Passion of Thy Son, our Lord.

This is the point that Ephesians makes with such urgency in a time and to a people much nearer to Jesus and his Passion than we are. Lest we forget the temptation to which Christians have historically so easily fallen, to lay the Passion and the Crucifixion solely upon the shoulders of the Jews, and on that basis to have provided for the terrible sins of anti-Semitism, let us remember that in Ephesians the unity of Jew and Gentile by God's action in Christ is celebrated and proclaimed: the cross has made the enmity between Jew and Gentile utterly irrelevant, the war is over, and in Phillips's phrase, "And it is through Him, that is Jesus, that both of us — Jew and Gentile — can now approach the Father in the one Spirit." If that message of reconciliation was urgent and true then, in their world, and necessary for people to understand if they were to be recalled from spiritual death to a life of mutual service and peace, then it is even more urgent and true now, in our fractured world, for those of us who continue to drift along the stream of this world's ideas of living.

As if writing directly to us in these last days of the second Christian millennium, Ephesians says, "Your world was a world without hope and without God. But now in union with Christ Jesus you who once were far off have been brought near through the shedding of Christ's blood."

Let us pray:

Look, Father, look on his anointed face,
And only look on us as found in him;
Look not on our misusings of Thy grace,
Our prayer so languid, and our faith so dim:
For lo! Between our sins and their reward
We set the Passion of Thy Son, our Lord. Amen.

Canon William Bright, 1874

March 28, 1999

THE NEW DAY

The Sunday of the Resurrection

or

Easter Day

The Lesson

Psalm 30 (KJV)

I will extol thee, O Lord; for thou hast lifted me up, and hast not made my foes to rejoice over me. O Lord, my God, I cried unto thee, and thou hast healed me.

O Lord, thou hast brought up my soul from the grave: thou hast kept me alive, that I should not go down to the pit.

Sing unto the Lord, O ye saints of his, and give thanks at the remembrance of his holiness. For this anger endureth but a moment; in his favour is life: weeping may endure for a night, but joy cometh in the morning.

And in my prosperity I said, I shall never be moved.

Lord, by thy favour thou hast made my mountain to stand strong: thou didst hide thy face, and I was troubled. I cried to thee, O Lord; and unto the Lord I made supplication.

What profit is there in my blood, when I go down to the pit? Shall the dust praise thee? Shall it declare thy truth?

Hear, O Lord, and have mercy upon me: Lord, be thou my helper. Thou hast turned for me my mourning into dancing: thou hast put off my sackcloth, and girded me with gladness;

To the end that my glory may sing praise to thee, and not be silent. O Lord my God, I will give thanks unto thee for ever.

THE NEW DAY

Text: Weeping may endure for a night, but joy cometh in the morning.
Psalm 30:5

Last Sunday we brandished our palms and cried out "Crucify!" and "Hosanna!" as we kept the Sunday of the Passion; on Thursday, Holy Thursday, I gathered with others of my small local church in Plymouth in the dark of a Maundy Thursday Communion service; on Good Friday, I am so happy to report, a large number of us sat here at the foot of a cross draped in black, and meditated for three hours on the Seven Last Words of Jesus from the cross; and last night, at eleven o'clock, many of us gathered here for the Easter Vigil, first in the cold and dark outside in Harvard Yard and then inside in the dark and empty church which we filled with our bodies and lighted by the power of the small candles that we held in our hands. We then celebrated the first Eucharist of Easter, and the baptism of two young girls born again before our very eyes of water and the risen Christ.

The cycle now is complete. Here you are, here we are, on Easter morning, many of us here again and some of you perhaps for the very first time, and all of us whether or not we understand or can articulate it, keeping today the habit of hope, embracing the dawn, celebrating the new day, rejecting the night, and claiming for ourselves, if only for a moment, an instance of new birth, new hope, new confidence, new life. You have followed your instincts, which sometimes lead you astray, as mine do, but today have led you aright to the right place at the right time. No matter how bad yesterday was, or how difficult it has been to bear the burdens of the past, or how hard the blows of affliction, this is the new day, this is, in that old cliche, the beginning of the rest of your life. What was, was; what was yesterday is there: today is the new day. The psalm writer knew what he was talking about, as is always the case, for if you take the psalms seriously you will realize that they are the most honest songs in the Bible, or perhaps anywhere. If you want candor, you who are as hard-bitten and smitten as you are, read the psalms. It is what the psalmist says for us this morning that counts: "Weeping may endure for a night, but joy cometh in the morning."

Three times in the last week I listened to the Passion narrative: on Sunday, on Thursday, and again on Friday. When as a young child and then as a young Christian I first heard the accounts of the suffering and death of Jesus they intrigued me, and I was eager to get on with the story to the victorious end that I knew awaited, to get to the moral of the story, the happy ending: I could not wait to get to Easter. As a Protestant of a certain type I was brought up to remember that in our churches the cross was empty, as a sign of victory, and that the Catholics of course got it all wrong with their crucifixes and horrific images of the shattered body of Jesus affixed to the cross. Like the women who loved Jesus, however, and the disciples who followed him, I discovered that I could make sense of the cross and the awful death upon it, and the older I got the more the cross and its burden reflected the reality of a crucified world. We may try to avoid death in this life-affirming, death-denying culture of ours, filled as it is with the icons of youth and the seductions of material immortality, but we know that death and suffering are real, for reality in television is conveyed by the numbers of deaths, particularly of violent deaths, that we see.

So, death and suffering are "really real," as John Silber likes to say, and in a strange sense the passion of Jesus, awful and difficult as it may be, makes sense, as this world understands sense. Think of it. A good guy tries to do good things and he is betrayed by his friends, done in by his enemies, and crucified for it, dying as an example to all who would try to change, or who would try to change the system. We understand that, we understand that that is reality, and that those are the things which fill the airwaves and the newspapers; and to this reality both we and the followers of Jesus very quickly become accustomed, for it is the way of the world. The other day I actually overheard someone say, "Isn't it a pity that Kosovo will spoil Easter this year?" and the point of view was not so much that Easter would be spoiled for the poor Kosovars but that the images of death, destruction, and violence would spoil our images of Easter quiet and tranquillity, and that we would be disturbed by the sounds and sights of an imperfect world.

We, however, are quite used to the sounds and sights of an imperfect world. We are realists, you and I; and if in a contest we have to bet on whether good or evil will prevail, the smart money will be on evil. Take professional wrestling, for example, which terminology alone — 'professional wrestling' — used to be an oxymoron before the election of Jesse 'The Body' and now 'The Brain' Ventura was elected governor of Minnesota. Now, I confess before God and before all of you here today that I have followed professional wrestling for years! It is cheaper than therapy and a great way to work out one's aggressions and fantasies, and over the years I have noticed that the increase in popularity of what used to be a minor and slightly shabby diversion is directly proportionate to the cultivation of villains and anti-heroes in the ring. When I was young you actually cheered for the guy in the white tights who fought fair and who, after a series of near-death, bone-crushing experiences, would win, and win honorably, against a chair-smashing, hair-pulling, foul-mouthed, overweight villain. Today the rules and roles are exactly reversed, and the industry flourishes. Heroes are meant to lose, and the villains — the more vicious and menacing the better — are expected to win, and usually by foul means and in the face of a distracted referee; and we cheer because this approximates more closely the way that life actually is.

I used to think that it took courage to be here in church on Good Friday and not much courage to be here on Easter, but, as a friend recently pointed out, "I don't like Good Friday but it makes sense; I love Easter, but it doesn't." I think that that is exactly what the women who followed Jesus must have felt. They didn't like Good Friday, and all of our preaching of the cross would not have made it any easier for them to understand, but they could eventually accept it, in a similar way as when Margaret Fuller once announced that she had finally accepted the universe. To that Bronson Alcott is said to have responded, "By God, she'd better."

It was with acceptance and a hearty dose of what the world continues to call 'reality' that the women passed the Sabbath in their first hours of mourning. They no doubt spent the night in weeping, and in the early morning they set out upon their final mission of mercy, to do the last thing they could do for Jesus. They didn't come to the tomb to see if he was still there for they knew that he was still there: where else would he be? It was not curiosity, then, but duty — sad, somber, realistic duty — that brought them on their early morning errand.

You know how the story goes: they did not find what they expected, and what they expected was not to be found. What did they find on this first Easter morning? Joy, glory, conviction, conversion? Not at all. St.

Luke's sparse account tells us that the women were perplexed and frightened, and when they did as the angels instructed them, and told the disciples what they had heard and seen they were disbelieved, and the men wrote it all off as an idle tale. That is not a very impressive start to Easter morning, and that is the way it must be if we think of Easter morning as simply the end of the tragedy of Good Friday or, in our terms, the happy ending to a grim Lent. No. What intriques me about St. Luke's account is the fact that the new day, Easter day, begins not with an explosion of conviction, not with the triumph of trumpets and a sure and swift victory over darkness and the night, over doubt and over death, but rather as the dawn itself arrives after the long night, slowly and perhaps even tentatively, but eventually and ultimately. The dawn, if you have ever watched and waited for it, comes in its own time: it cannot be rushed, it will not be easily nor cheaply proclaimed, but finally, when it is day, and fully so, the night holds no contest to it. "Weeping may endure for a night, but joy cometh in the morning." Day will not be put down by night but comes in its own time, and on its own terms.

Many years ago an explanation of the Maundy Thursday, or Tenebrae, service was offered to me. The occasion of that service was as impressive as it was last week, and I remember that we sat in a darkened church illuminated only by candles, one for each of the nine appointed readings. As each reading was concluded another light was extinguished until we sat in Stygian darkness, and this was meant, I was told, to represent the utter desolation and loneliness of Jesus, the darkness of the tomb, and the death of the world. It was Christian and, I might add, Protestant doom and gloom at its best — the only church I know of that feels good about feeling bad.

Years later I learned from a scholar of medieval liturgy a different version of this same experience, and participated in one. The proper medieval way of doing it, I learned, was to maintain an all-night vigil, not a cheap hour or two, and we went through the same process that I had gone through before except with one notable difference, which was that the candles were extinguished over the course of the entire night, and when the last one had been put out we were not in darkness but in the light of the new day, for we had waited through the watches of the night and had lived to see the new dawn, the new day, the true light. We had the sun, and there was no need of any other light. What a difference a few hours makes! "Weeping may endure for a night, but joy cometh in the morning."

From what you have experienced and not from what I say I think you know and understand this. Remember how long the night is when you are sick, or waiting and watching with someone who is? I can remember my mercifully few stays in the hospital, and how long the nights seemed that I spent in Stillman Infirmary, and how I longed for the first rays of the early morning grey-ish pink light, for as the light grew stronger I felt stronger and better: having lived through the night I felt I could triumph in the day. You know what this is like. This is why St. Paul calls Christian believers "children of the day, and not of the night," why creation begins at dawn, why the sun is the greater light and the moon the lesser, why Christianity is called a religion of the dawn, why Easter is a morning religion of light, why we celebrate the women as witnesses of the morning, and why we long for and celebrate each new day. We know in a thousand ways that "weeping may endure for a night, but joy cometh in the morning." It takes courage in the night to hope for the day.

Living as we do in the darkness, and waiting and hoping for the day, we know this to be true to our own experience, but what does it mean to be a child of the day, an heir of the dawn? What claims does the new day have upon us?

It is very important, my dearly beloved ones, for you to know that Easter is not an exercise in argument or in evidence but is meant to be an experience in which you can and must participate now. If Easter is simply one more unique event in the unique life of Jesus, then it is no more our experience than Jesus's walking on water, turning water into wine, or multiplying the loaves and the fishes, which are nice tricks if you can do them, and we can't. No. The church teaches that what God has done in Jesus by raising him from the dead he can and does do for us; and if Jesus is the "first fruits of them that sleep," then we are meant to follow him in his new life. That means new life for us not at some future time but here and now.

By raising Jesus from the dead God redeems history by claiming the future. Easter is not a re-run of the past where this time the good guys win, for the momentum and direction of Easter is forward: the gospels all tell us that "He goes before you, even as he said." We don't find Jesus in history, and that is why the 'Historical Jesus' craze is so wrong-headed. The place where Jesus is, the risen Christ, is Lord of the future. What God says to us in the risen Christ is that no matter how old we are, or how young, how tired or how energized, how cynical or how believing; no matter who and where we are, or what our condition, our best years are ahead of us, our best time is the time we have not yet spent or experienced; and in a world obsessed by the present, ignorant of the past, and fearful of the future, that is perhaps the most radical thing that one can say or believe.

We are a culture of doers: what can we do? What can be done? What practical claim can this conviction have on our lives here and now?

The epistle has the answer for St. Paul understood the question, and what he said to those early, anxious believers in Colossia, those ancient children of the dawn who needed to know, is the same answer that he gives to us: "If then you have been raised with Christ, seek the things that are above, where Christ is, seated at the right hand of God. Set your minds on things that are above, not on things that are on earth. For you have died, and your life is hid with Christ in God. When Christ who is our life appears, then you also will appear with him in glory." (Colossians 3:1-5)

The life God ratified by raising Jesus from the dead is the life to which God invites you now: you can walk in the light as a child of the day; you can begin today, and you don't have to die to do so.

Thanks be to God who gives us this victory, through Jesus Christ our Lord. Amen.

April 4, 1999

PART FOUR

Sermons for After Easter and Before Commencement

LIFE BEFORE DEATH

The Fourth Sunday of Easter

The Lesson

Ezekiel 37:1-7 (RSV)

The hand of the Lord was upon me, and he brought me out by the Spirit of the Lord, and set me down in the midst of the valley; and it was full of bones. And he led me round among them; and behold, there were very many upon the valley; and lo, they were very dry. And he said to me, "Son of man, can these bones live?" And I answered, "O Lord God, thou knowest." Again he said to me, "Prophesy to these bones, and say to them, 'O dry bones, hear the word of the Lord.'" Thus says the Lord God to these bones: "Behold, I will cause breath to enter you, and you shall live. And I will lay sinews upon you, and will cause flesh to come upon you, and cover you with skin, and put breath in you, and you shall live; and you shall know that I am the Lord."

So I prophesied as I was commanded; and as I prophesied, there was a noise, and behold, a rattling; and the bones came together, bone to its bone. And as I looked, there were sinews on them, and flesh had come upon them, and skin had covered them; but there was no breath in them. Then he said to me, "Prophesy to the breath, prophesy, son of man, and say to the breath, 'Thus says the Lord God: Come from the four winds, O breath, and breathe upon these slain, that they may live.'" So I prophesied as he commanded me, and the breath came into them, and they lived, and stood upon their feet, an exceedingly great host.

Then he said to me, "Son of man, these bones are the whole house of Israel. Behold, they say, 'Our bones are dried up, and our hope is lost; we are clean cut off.' Therefore prophesy, and say to them, 'Thus says the Lord God: Behold, I will open your graves, and raise you from your graves, O my people; and I will bring you home into the land of Israel. And you shall know that I am the Lord, when I open your graves, and raise you from your graves, O my people. And I will put my Spirit within you, and you shall live, and I will place you in your own land; then you shall know that I, the Lord, have spoken, and I have done it, says the Lord.'"

LIFE BEFORE DEATH

Text: "Son of man, can these bones live?" *Ezekiel 37:3*

Do you believe in life after death? That is the question which God puts to the prophet, and to ask such a question in the abstract is provoking enough, but to do so in the vivid context of the Valley of the Dry Bones is pretty provocative indeed. Death is real, and these bones are really dead: can any life come out of them? Is there hope here in the face of this unremitting reality of death? What could be more improbable than the possibility of life in the midst of the reality of total death?

We know a little more of the reality of this scene than we might care to after the events of this week, of the past seventy-two hours, when we look at the senseless carnage in Littleton, Colorado, with evil and death on every hand, and we ask whether new life can emerge out of all of this. Can we live again? Can life ever be the same again?

Lest we be tempted to easy answers, to cheap church talk, as I call it, or to the simplistic analysis which passes as punditry, let us remember that the prophet does not give a clear answer to the Lord's question, "Son of man, can these bones live?" He answers, "O Lord God, thou knowest." We might call that a nuanced answer, the kind to which we are accustomed in court proceedings, but the prophet is not being evasive. What a brilliant answer! "O Lord God, *thou* knowest."! He doesn't know the answer to the question but he does know that God knows; and we know that very shortly God will show him the answer when the impossible happens and the spirit blows across that dry-as-death place, the bones begin to knit together and kick up, and life returns. The prophet and we ourselves are amazed, as well we should be.

Here we might rest awhile. Ezekiel has learned that with God all things are possible, and that out of the worst things the best things can happen. Appealing as this moment may be, however, and challenging as the question may be, we must move on to what is for the Christian believer — on this fourth Sunday of Easter — an even more challenging question, which is not so much whether one believes in life after death but rather the Easter question, which is whether one believes in life *before* death. That, I believe, is the perennial question of Easter. Have you a life worth living *before* death? We know what God can do with the dead; the question is, what can God do with you and with me, the living?

An epitaph on a tombstone in Vermont puts it famously:

HE LIVED WITH HIS WIFE FOR SIXTY-THREE YEARS
AND DIED IN THE HOPE OF A BETTER LIFE

That doesn't tell us much about the life to come, but it does suggest a great deal about the life that those two might have lived together.

Easter, I suggest, is about the life that you are living here and now. It is not simply a lesson in history or an exercise in futurology, for Easter is not about Jesus, it is about you. Easter is not about the past, it is about the present. Easter is not about death, it is about life.

If Ezekiel is asked about the possibilities of life *after* death; in the story of the raising of Lazarus from the gospel of John we are invited to confront the possibilities of life *before* death.

You will recall the story, you have all heard it from the time of Sunday School, and if you don't recall it, I will tell it to you again. Lazarus had been ill, sick unto death, and his sisters Mary and Martha had sent for their close friend, Jesus of Nazareth. Clearly they had expected Jesus not simply to comfort them but to do something for their ailing brother, for they knew of his reputation for healing the sick, and if he could heal perfect strangers, then who better to heal than his sick, dying friend? Jesus, however, is late. He doesn't get there on time, and the sisters are very much annoyed, ticked off. Twice they rebuke him, "Had you come when we asked you to come, our brother would not have died;" and we can only imagine Lazarus's last words: "Where is Jesus?" The gospel writer is at pains to make it clear that Lazarus is dead, really dead, as dead as those dry bones in Ezekiel's valley, for he points out that Lazarus had been sealed up in the tomb for four days, and when Jesus proposed to roll the stone away the sisters warned that there would be an odor. As depicted in a little plaque on a cathedral in Europe, "He stinketh," in the unvarnished prose of the King James version. This point is wonderully demonstrated by a famous misericord in a medieval French cathedral, which shows an imp standing before Lazarus's tomb and holding his nose.

So, as we know, Jesus calls Lazarus to come forth from the tomb, and he does. The on-lookers are commanded to unbind him and let him go from the grave clothes in which he had been wrapped for his burial, unwinding them from his body and removing the cloth from over his face; and we can imagine a scene of great rejoicing.

Here the story ends, however; there is nothing further written about it and we think that we have a tidy miracle and a little resurrection on our hands, but what we would most like to know, I think, the text does not tell us. What, for instance, was Lazarus's reaction to all of this? Was he grateful to be called back from the dead to the land of the living? Did he say, "Oh, I'm glad to be back!" or did he say, "Oh no, not this all over again, life with my sisters?" The real question that intrigues is this: what would Lazarus do with the new life now before him? What would he do with his second chance, his second opportunity? He was not given immortality, for unlike Jesus, Lazarus would die again, and so the great question is not about life *after* death, but now it is about life *before* death.

Was he more sensitive, more loving to others, more sensible of the fewness of his days? This is the Easter question, for in Christ we have each and all been given a second chance, a new opportunity: now what will we do with our new life, our new opportunity, our second chance, before death?

We may not know exactly the quantity of life left to Lazarus after his resurrection since the scripture is silent on this point, but we do know the quality of life that Jesus intended for him, and intends for all of us who are called to live life before we leave it. Elsewhere in the gospel of John, Jesus says, "I am come that they may have life, and that they may have it more abundantly." By this he does not mean quantity time, he means quality time, the fullness of life lived with the benefit of the second chance.

We may not know what to make of Lazarus or the dry bones, but we all know what to do with Ebenezer Scrooge. Dicken's classic character in *A Christmas Carol*, I submit, has been placed in the wrong season. His is not a Christmas story, his is an Easter story, for he is called back from death and the grave, he is given a new chance to live life before death, and he does it, according to Dickens, with gusto and brio. He was not the same man any more, and he didn't have to die to experience new life.

We are given second chances every day, and Easter reminds us of that. Each morning is resurrection morning for us, and we can resolve to make more precious the time that is before us. Who of us does not cherish the opportunity to try again, to have a second chance, to have a second bite of the cookie, if you will? Who of us would not willingly rise from dry bones to what Jesus calls 'newness of life?' Remember, it was Mae West who put it best: "It is not the men in my life, but the life in my men, that counts."

Our images earlier this week from Colorado were of violence and death, lives cruelly, wantonly destroyed by boys already dead, but the ironic fact is that even as we speak new life is claiming victory over old death. The frailty of life reveals its precious quality, and when we realize how precious life is we want to live it as fully as possible, taking nothing for granted and cherishing everything as the gift of God for the people of God. The murderers join the ghouls' gallery: they have had their grisly revenge on life and they are dead, but death will have no triumph over life as long as we embrace the abundant life before death.

So, dear friends, no matter how much time you may or may not have, your best years are before you, the best is yet to come, and to know that is to know no fear but only courage and joy. That is the power of resurrection which overcomes Calvary and Littleton and all of the little Calvarys and Littletons which beset us on every hand. It is for this, and for us, that Jesus gave his own life a ransom for many, and it is because of this that we are called to newness of life here and now. "Son of man, can these bones live?" You bet they can. So, then, get on with it, for Christ's sake and your own.

Let us pray:

> *God grant me life until my work is done, and work until my life is over, for the sake of Him who has called us into the new life, even Jesus Christ, our risen Lord. Amen.*

April 21, 1999

THE SPLENDOR OF GOD

The First Sunday after Pentecost

The Lesson

Revelation 4:1-4 (NEB)

"After this I looked, and there before my eyes was a door opened in heaven; and the voice that I had first heard speaking to me like a trumpet said, 'Come up here, and I will show you what must happen hereafter.' At once I was caught up by the Spirit. There in heaven stood a throne, and on the throne sat one whose appearance was like the gleam of jasper and cornelian; and round the throne was a rainbow, bright as an emerald. In a circle about this throne were twenty-four other thrones, and on them sat twenty-four elders, robed in white and wearing crowns of gold. From the throne went out flashes of lightning and peals of thunder. Burning before the throne were seven flaming torches, the seven spirits of God, and in front of it stretched what seemed a sea of glass, like a sheet of ice.

In the centre, round the throne itself, were four living creatures, covered with eyes, in front and behind. The first creature was like a lion, the second like an ox, the third had a human face, the fourth was like an eagle in flight. The four living creatures, each of them with six wings, had eyes all over, inside and out; and by day and by night without a pause they sang:

> 'Holy, holy, holy is God the sovereign Lord of all, who was, and is, and is to come!'

As often as the living creatures give glory and honour and thanks to the One who sits on the throne, who lives for ever and ever, the twenty-four elders fall down before the One who sits on the throne and worship him who lives for ever and ever; and as they lay their crowns before the throne they cry:

> 'Thou art worthy, O Lord our God, to receive glory and honour and power, because Thou didst create all things; by Thy will they were created, and have their being!'"

THE SPLENDOR OF GOD

Text: "Thou art worthy, O Lord our God, to receive glory and honour and power, because Thou didst create all things; by Thy will they were created, and have their being!" *Revelation 4:11(NEB)*

That enigmatic and vividly vague splendiferous fourth chapter in the book of the Revelation of St. John the Divine is a chapter which someone has said describes the author in a trip to the moon, over-the-top, exceeding with description and adjectives the fact of being in the presence of God surrounded by all of those thrones, by those angels casting down their golden crowns. It is a cacophony of metaphors, similes, images, and visions, almost too much for sensible dour Protestants like ourselves to take in, and even too much for Pentecostalists to take in: it is an overwhelming set of images, and yet they are the images which are presented to us on Trinity Sunday. We heard the chapter from the beginning; my text is from the end, and it sums up why those twenty-four elders do what they do. All of the splendor, all of the majesty, all of the glory, all of the golden crowns, all of the cherubim and seraphim forever singing — all of this is done because of what God has done for us, creating all things; and in God all things have their being. That is a splendid God, that is a God who resides in splendor, that is a God who requires all that we have of thanks and adoration and praise. That is the context for Trinity Sunday.

When our Holy Mother the Church gave us the doctrine of the Trinity she did not do so in order to confuse us although that, alas, may be the consequence for many of us. If you hear a great grinding, groaning sound over the course of the next hour or so it will be the collective minds of the ministers of Christendom trying to explain to their people the nature of the Trinity, and there will be an even deeper, greater growling sound on the part of their people who, like you, are resisting every opportunity to learn. The Church did not give us this doctrine to confuse us; it gave us this doctrine in order that we might have a better, more comprehensive means of worshipping God. The Trinity is meant to be a functional exercise to help us, not to intimidate us, to clarify rather than to confuse, and to give us a handle, if you will, on the immense, immeasurable capacities of God. As believers it is important for us to remember this at all times, but never is it more important for us to remember than on Trinity Sunday, the only Sunday in the entire liturgical year devoted to the celebration and the adoration of a doctrine. It must be taken very seriously, and very joyously, and I hope we can do both this morning. We do not worship the doctrine — that is a human conception — the doctrine is designed to help us better to worship the living God. The Trinity is meant to help us to enlarge our thought of God, to expand it beyond the tiny little purview of one's own pet God, one's own domesticated Deity. The Trinity is meant to break out of that small box and help us to enlarge our thought of God. That is what the hymn writer Frederick Lucian Hosmer meant when he wrote:

One thought I have, my ample creed,
So deep it is, and broad,
And equal to my every need —
It is the thought of God.

The thought of God. It is that which opens hearts and minds and imaginations, and it is the thought of God that we are meant to fully consider on Trinity Sunday, the Sunday on which God, in all of the fullness of the godhead, is addressed.

Now, I realize that this is heavy lifting: thought itself is sometimes put on hold in church, and all of you who have thought about it at all have some thoughts or two on why the Trinity may or may not be your cup of tea. Why should we have to deal with this on a lovely spring Sunday? Why not talk about Decoration Day, or the weather, or some of the lovely reasons we all have to be grateful? This, instead, is rather heavy sledding.

Well, let me make certain first that we know what the church is not saying about the Trinity, which might help us to clear away some of the theological cobwebs. It does not teach us to have confidence in three gods or to offer worship to three gods, for we are talking about a unity in which three are combined. As my predecessor Charles Price used to say from this very pulpit, "The Trinity sits on a throne and not on a bench." We do not worship three gods, nor are we free to choose which of those three gods we prefer. I know that some of you like God, some of you like Jesus, and many of you have cozied up to the Holy Spirit; well, Trinity Sunday is meant to correct those understandable but basically unsound and wrong views. We are trying to do that today.

The essential character of God is unity, not division, a single entity rather than a constellation. The classic language of the doctrine is that God is one nature in three persons, just as we sang in the first hymn this morning, *"God in three persons, blessed Trinity!"* Perhaps a minor point of grammar will help here, although I realize that grammatical allusions are lost in this sad and bedraggled age: when we speak of the Trinity we always speak in the singular, never in the plural. We do not say "The Trinity are here this morning;" we say, "The Trinity is with us."

Our confusion, however, is easily understood because for us in the age of the 'id' and the 'ego' and the 'supergo;' for us in the age of 'I' and 'me,' the notion of a 'person' suggests a complete and autonomous self-contained individual. Therefore 'three persons' would suggest several 'me's,' and hence we think of each character of the Three Stooges, the Three Tenors, or the Three Blind Mice, as a single, separate, totally self-contained entity. That is a fine concept for the Three Stooges, the Three Tenors, and the Three Blind Mice, but it is neither accurate nor sufficient for what the church teaches us about God. The purpose of the doctrine of the Trinity is to help us to imagine, not necessarily to understand but to imagine, the comprehensiveness of God, who in one person contains three distinct but related functions or faculties by which that one person is made more accessible to us.

I hope you notice that I have used the word 'imagine' rather than 'understand.' We in this University are devoted to things that we can understand, and if we can understand something it therefore must be true, and if we cannot understand it, it therefore must not be true, or not worth studying or considering. Understanding is a very limiting concept. I do not, for example, understand what they do in Mallinkrodt Laboratory, the Chemistry Department: I never have, I never will, but that does not mean that what they do is not true or real just because I do not understand it, or that I couldn't imagine what they do even though I cannot understand it. So too is it with the Trinity. It is not meant as an explanation, it is meant as an experience to be imagined, and that is why everything that we have is meant to be open to the imagining, the imaging, of God in three persons.

St. Augustine tells us that we can understand the nature of God in the

Trinity if we consider our own single personality, our own single being, within which is to be found memory, intellect, and will. All three, Augustine says, are critical parts of who we are. Our memory is a vital part of us: in fact the older we get the more important our memory becomes because we are connected to worlds we no longer experience; our intellect is that which helps us to make judgements, which deals with what we know and understand; and our will is that which instructs us and causes us to take action and responsibility for our actions. These are three distinguishable characteristics which all combine to make the one being which is our personality. We exercise each of these — our memories, our intellects, and our wills — we do not confuse them, and we are in serious trouble if we do; and each of them is our self but no one of them alone is our self. Helpful, is St. Augustine, up to a point.

Medieval theology liked analogies, metaphors, and similes to explain the notion of the three-in-one. The medievalists understood that literature and its devices, far more than science and its evidences, is the way in which the imagination works, and the way by which the inconceivable can be imagined; and in one of their favorite syllogisms the Trinity is the fist, the finger, and the palm of the hand, all of which are essential and each of which must work together to perform an action, but each of which is quite different, unique, and has a different function. Interesting, as far as it goes. The example which appeals to me most, however, is the example which I have chosen to demonstrate for you this morning by bringing this light from the holy table into this pulpit. I know that some of you liturgically quirky people are thinking, "Oh yes, this is an ancient symbol on Trinity Sunday, the preacher always takes the light from the holy table into the pulpit, it goes back to some medieval practice." Well, that's utter nonsense, I just thought of it during the sermon hymn, and thought that this would be a good way to illustrate the point I wish to make this morning. This illustration — much beloved by Calvin — is that the Trinity and the relationship of its three persons to the one is as the wax, the wick, and the flame of a candle which together compose one source of light whose purpose is to destroy the darkness. When you see a candle lit, and when you go into a room illumined by a candle, you don't ask about the relationships of the bits and pieces that make it happen, you see the unity, you appreciate the benefit, and you glory in the light which has banished the darkness. Each of the three elements is unique and distinct: it is only in their relationship and their totality that we take the benefit of what they do. Music consists of the notes, the sound, and the instrument through which it all comes into being; art consists of the idea, the worker, and the work. You get the picture.

Now, you might think that all of this was designed to confuse you and to celebrate the complexity of God, and by even this brief explanation this morning I may have won one or two souls to the University's old and prior Unitarian tradition, always a risk here at Harvard: you might find one God simply too much to comprehend. Rather than an invitation to complexity, however, the Trinity is meant to be an invitation to unity, to sovereignty, and to splendor. We are meant to see the thing that is larger than the sum of its parts. We are meant in art to see and to take in the beauty of the painting; in music, the glory of the sound; in architecture, the power of the space. If we were to say one thing on Trinity Sunday about God, it is that God is greater than the sum of God's parts.

I remember my first encounter, many years ago, with Lincoln Cathedral in England. Lincoln is not on the hot 'Freedom Trail,' if you will, of English cathedrals: you have to leave London in order to see Lincoln, you have to go northward toward the North Sea to Lincolnshire, that rather flat and damp lowland area around the North Sea called 'The Wash.' You go to Lincoln only if you have reason to go to Lincoln, and I had reason to go to Lincoln because our mother city of Boston is located in Lincoln, and the Pilgrim Fathers, to whom I'm devoted, came from that part of England, and I had read about Lincoln Cathedral as a great and splendid and not frequently visited place. So I made my way across the flat tulip-land, 'New Holland,' it is often called, to the village of Spaulding and on to the plain. Then almost in a vision that I imagine might be true of Mont St. Michel in France, off in the distance over the flat horizon one could see the mounded city of Lincoln, and in the center of that mounded city the three misty Gothic towers far off in the distance — a wonderful subject for amateur landscape painters. As one drew nearer to the city the city seemed to be dominated by those three towers, which must have descended down into the bowels of the cathedral itself. As one drew nearer and nearer and finally got into the city, breeching the wall around the cathedral close, there was no place near to it where one could see the whole thing, it was so crowded about by medieval and modern buildings, cheek by jowl. There was all this Gothic fantasy, impossible though it was to look up fully to see the tower, impossible though it was to take in the whole west front, but there it was and I went in, and it was quite splendid inside, damp and musty the way a cathedral ought to be. One could see quite clearly the different periods of the cathedral's construction, the remarkably different functions of its spaces, and marvel at the ingenuity of its builders and the beauty of the liturgy that takes place there. The concept of the cathedral, the idea of the cathedral, however, is greater than the sum of all of its splendid parts, and in fact the only way to take it all in is not to get up close to it but to see it as I first did, from afar, its wholeness transcending its particulars, the clarity lost in the enormity of the vision.

Perhaps it was the great art historian Erwin Panofsky who said that "First we have the idea of the cathedral in our heads or in the heads of those who constructed it; then we have the reality of the cathedral, the thing in itself; and then we have the image of the cathedral, that thing which is larger than conception or construction." The cathedral is not one of those parts alone but all three of them and then some, and by this we understand instinctively, without any doctrine of art to explain it to us, what is happening in those relationships. The whole is greater than the sum of its parts; the sum of its parts is significant and the parts themselves are magnificent. The Trinity in its idea, its reality, and its image of God, is meant to leave us with a sense of the immensity and the splendor of God, the need to get up close and to stand back, and to take in the awe of it all. What is the most natural thing to do in the presence of incomprehensible splendor, majesty, beauty, and power? It is to fall down and worship it. Never explain it; only experience it.

When you go to a rock concert or an athletic enterprise, or to some other orchestrated mob scene, your natural reaction is to scream and to cheer and to be a part of the whole thing: it exists because you exist, you exist because it exists, and there's a kind of chaos, an energy, an almost primitive set of forces unleashed on the field, in the stadium, or in the concert hall. You know what that is. Your natural reaction there is not to fall on your knees and say, "My God, my Lord, my God, what an extraordinary thing!" That, rather, is the response you have when you go into the Gardner Museum and behold in quiet one of the many magnificent treasures hidden around the corner; that is what happens when you go into a cathedral and are suddenly overwhelmed not only by the immensity of it but by the idea; that is the thing that happens to you without trumpets and drums rolling, without screaming and amplified crowds, without blood, guts, and violence. When you come into the presence of the incomprehensible your first reaction is not to cheer but to fall on your knees and say, "Holy, Holy, Holy is the Lord God of Hosts, Heaven and earth are full of Thy glory."

That is what happened to Isaiah, going about his routine in the temple, about whom we heard this morning in the first lesson. My students in preaching know that there's a good deal more to Isaiah 6 than that marvelous theophany and manifestation of God, but in the first place one must realize that it is not about 'me,' nor even about Isaiah: it is about God. What is the response of this professional holy man — Isaiah is paid to be in the temple, he's not just devout, he's a hired hand for God — what is his experience? He falls to his knees, and he recognizes that he himself is unworthy to be in that place. I think that nobody ever feels unworthy to be in Fenway Park, unworthy to be at Worldwide Wrestling, unworthy to watch the Patriots play, after their fashion — in fact I think many of us go to these events because we feel superior. That's the differnce between spectacle and splendor; that's the difference between entertainment and worship. The most natural thing to do in the presence of the incomprehensible is to fall down and worship it. Experience it; don't explain it.

Here's a footnote to those of you who travel: never enter a cathedral for the first time with a guide, never join a group to see a cathedral, wander in on your own, don't buy the guide book at the beginning, and resist any temptation to be taken round by anybody with a badge. Refuse it. Stumble on your way, discover, like Scott or Byrd, wherever it is you're going to go: take it all in, stop, pause, think, wonder, and after it has had its way with you then buy the book, take the tour, hire the guide, take the pictures. See where you have been and then let the explanation follow the experience, not be the experience. That's a free footnote to those of you who are travelling this summer: you will be driven to your knees. Then, upon reflection, you might like to have explained what you have experienced.

On Trinity Sunday we are meant to be reminded that, for once, the sermon is not about us, and has less to do with what we are supposed to do than with what has been done for us. I say this because at just about this time practical, sensible sermon-tasters like you are saying, "Well, that's all very well, splendid images, wonderful pictures, very good analogies, I might say, but what am I now to do?" You are accustomed to being given marching orders, because of course the kingdom of heaven depends upon you and what you're going to do in the next forty minutes. Well, for once, my brothers and sisters, this is not about you; it is about God in three persons, blessed Trinity. When we look at this text we realize that the sermon is not about us and that it has less to do with what we are meant to do than with what has already been done for us. This is a retrospective rather than a prescriptive text, and here is where our text is intended to instruct us. Do you notice, for example, that the text is making the case for the worthiness of God, that God is worthy of our praise, worthy of glory and honor, because of what God has already done? We worship God; that is, we pay God that of which God is worthy, because all things, including ourselves, owe their being to God. We worship God not because of what we hope God will do but because of what God has already done, of which you and I and all that is, are living, standing proof.

It was for the comprehension of the splendor of God, splendid in his works and in his being, that the old adage was invented which says "Don't just do something: stand there." Comprehend, if you dare, the splendid mystery by which the unity of God is made clear by the particular functions of God: God the Father, who creates us; God the Son, who redeems us; and God the Spirit, who sustains us. Do you notice that it is God in each of these three cases who is doing it? God has not appointed deputies, assistant gods who redeem, associate gods who sustain; God has not done that. It is God himself who has done all of these things. In Trinity we have not merely a collection of useful functions, useful though they doubtless are; rather, in Trinity we have a set of relationships into which we must enter, for each of us has been created and our being here this morning is testimony to our very existence; each of us has been redeemed, our lives called back from the depths and the edge of the pit by Jesus Christ; and each of us can give hourly testimony as to how we have been sustained daily by the work of the Holy Spirit. The Trinity is no abstract theory, the Trinity is alive and at work in you and in me every hour of every day. In the unity of those relationships we are made whole, which is where the word 'holy' comes from. All of these parts are put together.

When you think of it, however — and I hope that you are still thinking — we come to our knowledge of the Trinity via our own experience, and that experience of Trinity often works in reverse of the order with which we are familiar. Our lives, for example, are a daily testimony to the sustaining power of the Holy Spirit, and that is where we first encounter God at work — in our daily sustenance against all odds. We know of and admire Jesus Christ, the son of God, for by his example we are inspired and by his sacrifice we are redeemed. We encounter Jesus by the same spirit that was in him, and we come to God the Father, the Creator, out of an acknowledgement of our own creation at the hands of one who loves. Trinity is how all three of these work in relationship to each other, and in ourselves.

St. Paul puts it famously and differently when in his blessing, which we use as the grace every Sunday, he speaks of "The grace of our Lord Jesus Christ, the love of God, and the fellowship of the Holy Spirit," as the way in which we experience God's three actions on our behalf. Grace, and who of us knows nothing of grace? Love, and who of us has not been sustained by love? Fellowship, or community, and who of us can exist without one another or without fellowship with God? They are done for us, but they reflect once again the splendor of God.

William Ralph Inge — which rhymes with 'sting' and not with 'cringe,' as he was fond of saying — the so-called "Gloomy Dean" of St. Paul's Cathedral in London in the first quarter of this century, once said that it was the "easiest thing in the world to say the word 'God,' and mean absolutely nothing by it."

That is so, and it happens every day. On Trinity Sunday Christians are meant to say the word 'God' and to mean everything in this world and in the world to come by it, for the Trinity is the way by which we express the limitless options of God, the splendor, indeed, of One who was and is and is to be, and in whose image we are created.

> "Thou art worthy, O Lord our God, to receive glory and honour and power, because Thou didst create all things; by Thy will they were created, and have their being!"

For this the whole church must say, "Thank God: Father, Son, and Holy Ghost." Amen and Amen.

May 30, 1999

BEFORE IT'S TOO LATE

The Second Sunday after Pentecost

Sermon for Seniors

Last Sunday of Term and of the Academic Year

The Lesson

Romans 8:31-39 (KJV)

What shall we then say to these things? If God be for us, who can be against us?

He that spared not his own Son, but delivered him up for us all, how shall he not with him also freely give us all things? Who shall lay any thing to the charge of God's elect? It is God that justifieth. Who is he that condemneth? It is Christ that died, yea rather, that is risen again, who is even at the right hand of God, who also maketh intercession for us.

Who shall separate us from the love of Christ? Shall tribulation, or distress, or persecution, or famine, or nakedness, or peril, or sword? As it is written, For thy sake we are killed all the day long; we are accounted as sheep for the slaughter. Nay, in all these things we are more than conquerors through him that loved us.

For I am persuaded, that neither death, nor life, nor angels, nor principalities, nor powers, nor things present, nor things to come, nor height, nor depth, nor any other creature, shall he able to separate us from the love of God, which is in Christ Jesus our Lord.

SERMON FOR SENIORS BEFORE IT'S TOO LATE

Text: If God be for us, who can be against us? *Romans 8:31 (KJV)*

This is the last Sunday of the Term and of this academic year, and for some of you on either side of the screen this morning it is the last Sunday of your career as a Harvard or Radcliffe undergraduate. As your pastor I have some things to say to you about the Christian faith, about your Harvard experience, and about your life to come, and I wish to say them to you before it is too late, before this teachable and listening moment passes and you are incapable of further instruction or of further advice.

It has been my experience over twenty-nine years here, that in these last days of the last week of the last year of one's college experience, rather than being indifferent to advice or counsel or thought, seniors tend to listen with an intensity, an eagerness, a hunger that they have not known since the opening days of freshman week. Many of you listen so intently at the end of your careers here in College because you hope that there is something more than you have already received or heard. You hope that there is something more to life than what we have taught you here at Harvard and Radcliffe Colleges; you hope that there is more significance, more meaning to your being than can be signified by the granting of the diploma on Thursday morning. You, more than anybody else, know that it is possible to fool a lot of the people a lot of the time, and you have done your share of fooling, but you have also had your share of being fooled.

This last Sunday, these last moments, are among the most precious moments that you have, and you listen with the hope that maybe somewhere somehow out of the torrents of words that will descend upon you in the coming days, something will be said that will be useful, that will be true, and that will get you beyond Thursday morning. After this morning, I can tell you, there is nobody else who will ever be obliged to tell you anything for your own good. You are literally on your own, dependent upon *The New York Times* and Ted Koppel for your moral advice.

It is therefore a sense of both urgency and opportunity that provokes this last sermon to you on this last Sunday of your last year and week at Harvard, about things that I wish to say to you, things that I want you to hear and to remember before it's too late. Before it's too late there are two things for me to say to those of you who worship here, two things that you must know before you leave. The first has to do with failure, and the second with fidelity: it is failure and fidelity about which I will speak this morning.

I've been in this business long enough to be able to read minds, and I am reading your minds at this very moment as I speak, and they are asking, "Why failure? Why does one mention the 'f' word on an occasion such as this? Aren't we supposed to be upbeat at this time of year?" Aren't we, in other words, supposed to tell you who listen that you can do anything because we have prepared you for everything? Did not your parents bargain with the devil himself in order to get you in and through Harvard because somebody said that that would guarantee success in life? Somebody must have said to you that the important thing about Harvard is not what you learn here — and some of you have taken that advice rather literally — but who you meet here. Connections, networking; that is what it is all about: "I met old Todd, he went down to work for Dewey, Cheatham, and Howe, his nephew was in my House and we played on the soccer team and we're working up a little deal....." You know how it all falls into place. Have you considered that the reason certain women advertise for Harvard sperm in *The Crimson* is not because they want brains for their baby — although they might want brains too — but because they want connections, they want access to the Alumni Directory? That's what they want. After all, Harvard people don't have to be smart, we just have to be smart enough to hire smart people from MIT.

Well, my guess is that most of you after four, and in some cases five, and in one or two cases six years, know more of failure now than you did when you got here. Nobody who got to Harvard knew much of failure in high school, but here you have encountered your fair share of it, and that is an important, constructive lesson because — and I'm willing to be quoted here by all and sundry — you will experience more of failure than of success in your life after Cambridge: that is a guarantee. If you are unacquainted with failure and how to deal with it you are unprepared for life, and you may want to join the rest of us who are unprepared for life and get tenure and stay here forever, but there's no room for you, you must go on. So it is necessary for you to be able to come to terms with failure because it will be failure more than success that will define your life, your life experience, and your life's work. The wisdom, therefore, to be gleaned from this experience is not how to market success but how to cope successfully with failure.

What will you do, for example, when you don't get the interview, you don't get the job, you don't get the promotion, and others far less worthy than you scamper up the greasy pole in front of you? What will you do when that happens? What will you do when Mr. Right turns out to be Mr. Wrong, or Miss Right turns out to be Miss Wrong? What will you do if your children turn into monsters and you regret the moment of their conception? What will you do when Mr. Greenspan's bubble eventually and inevitably bursts? You will live to see it, and what will you do when that happens? The test of a man or a woman of faith comes not on the mountaintop of victory but in the valley of defeat, where most of us spend most of our time. You've heard the phrase that "life consists of little victories." It does: when somebody gives you the correct change, that's a little victory; when somebody smiles at you, that's a little victory; when you get a human voice on the telephone, that's a little victory, and the reason that we accumulate these little victories is because we are surrounded by huge defeats, failure on every hand, and we have to be able to cope with it.

Tom Wolfe calls people like you candidates for degrees on Thursday, 'Masters of the Universe.' It is a contemptuous phrase uttered by a non-Harvard man, of course, and while there may be a certain tinge of envy to it, there is a pound of truth in it. 'Masters of the Universe' means that you have been trained here to expect the best, to believe in yourselves as part of the best, and to accept nothing less than success. As Margaret Thatcher once famously said, "Failure is not an option." It is not to Baroness Thatcher, however, but to the gloomy prophet Isaiah that I wish to direct your attention as we consider the nature of failure, and what it is that you are up against. I hope you listened to that first lesson from Isaiah this morning.

Remember how the lesson began? "Now, therefore, hear this" — it sounds like a naval announcement — "you lovers of pleasure who sit securely, who say in your heart, 'I am, and there is no one beside me.'" I will never know sorrow or sadness, is what it says; and then the prophet says, "Yet suddenly, in a single day [calamity] will come upon you." In case you don't get it, he then goes on to say, "Secure in your wicked ways, you thought, 'No one can see me'" — I can get away with murder, I can do anything. "It was your wisdom and knowledge that led you astray," says Isaiah, "you said to yourself, 'I am, and there is none other.'" That's a rather strong indictment, and those of you who did listen might have thought it a rather heavy note on which to play on this last Sunday for seniors. After all, the people who should hear this sort of thing are elsewhere, sunning themselves on the Charles, or recovering from last night's debauch, or coping with their parents: why preach to the choir? Why tell the people of these dreary things, who were good enough to come this morning?

The prophet here, in Isaiah 47, is not speaking of an individual, not condemning a particular arrogant or self-centered solicistic individual, he is speaking quite specifically of a culture, of society, of an environment so full of itself, so secure in its powers and in its pleasure, so convinced of its inevitable rightness, that just at the moment when it feels itself most secure the bubble will burst. He is speaking of Babylon, Babylon the Great. Babylon, that incredibly urban, urbane, sophisticated culture the likes of which the world had not seen before. Here is the place that can hire anybody it needs to do anything it requires, here is a place so self-contained, the only superpower standing which can define the standard of living and death for everybody. Here is Babylon: this is the city to which Isaiah 47 speaks, a place of such fabulous power and prosperity that it could be equalled only to the power, the prestige, the prosperity of our own age and our own culture and our own time. This is Babylon, and we Babylonians are sitting in the middle of calamity.

Now, you won't read that in *The Wall Street Journal*, you won't read that in *The Boston Globe*, you won't even see pictures of it in *The Boston Herald*. Babylon, according to Isaiah, put its faith in wizards, in sorcerers, in magicians, and in wise men engaged to save them by foretelling the future — that's the reference to the sorcerers, the diviners of future prophesies. This is of whom Isaiah speaks when he says, "Stand fast" — an ironic statement — "in your enchantments and your many sorceries, with which you have labored from your youth...you are wearied with your many counsels; let them stand forth and save you, those who divide the heavens, who gaze at the stars, who at the new moons predict what shall befall you." You want to put your confidence in these soothsayers, in these magicians, in these people who read the tea leaves and predict the weather; you want to put your confidence in them? Well, go ahead, you who depend upon such as those will be disappointed. "So much for your magicians, with whom you have trafficked all your life; they have wandered off, each his own way, and there is not one to save you." You will not be rescued by these prophets, by these diviners, these magicians, these wise men.

Unlike Isaiah, and Babylon, I have no desire to invoke disaster upon you just to prove my point or his point, or to get you to see sense, but when disaster comes, as it inevitably will, I pray that you will be strong enough to stand and endure and overcome. If, however, your faith is dependent upon a world made safe by the policies of Alan Greenspan — to take a magician, for example — then we live in a very precarious world indeed, where we had better be prepared to learn as much from adversity as from prosperity. During one of the great economic crises of the early twentieth century some economic reporter went to the wisest, wealthiest, and most powerful financier, J.P. Morgan, and he said, "Mr. Morgan, you have known more than anybody else about the economic cycles of the world. What advice and observation have you to give us about these precarious circumstances?" Mr. Morgan said in reply, "Either the market will rise, or the market will fall." So much for the soothsayers, the magicians, the wise prophets of prosperity. The gospel of success does you no favors, especially when success is determined by somebody else's standard, and that very success itself may prove elusive or, when achieved, unsatisfying.

A few weeks ago, during dinner at Sparks House for my students in Religion 42, one of the waiters came to me during the progress of dinner, and whispered in my ear the following news. He said that while they were waiting to lay on the courses the staff in the kitchen was watching the Emmys on television, and that after nineteen years of nomination Susan Lucci had at last won an Emmy for playing Erica Kane in 'All My Children.' I rejoiced, for I have watched 'All My Children' for nineteen years, and if anyone ever deserved an Emmy for acting, it was Susan Lucci, but she had become a byword for failure; she was to acting what Harold Stassen was to presidential elections. That night, however, after all of the years and false hopes and real disappointment, she actually won. She could have given up along the way — some said that she should have given up along the way, others said that she never should have begun along the way — but we came to know her over these many years not because she was a winner, which she was not, but because we watched how she coped with the consistent and public display of her losing. I would suggest, not to put too fine a point on it, that she was more formed and improved by those years of failure than she was at that supreme moment of success, which is so momentary and elusive.

For most of you, my dear young friends, there will be no Emmys, but what will make your success in life will be how you cope with your failures when they surely come. Now, what makes that coping possible, I suggest, is the subject of my second and final point, and it is the substance of the second lesson, from St. Paul's epistle to the Romans: fidelity. Fidelity — faithfulness, is what it is all about. Faithfulness will get you through. It is fidelity that got you to this moment, it is fidelity that will get you to the next moment.

Now, again I see very clearly what is going on in your minds, you are thinking, "Sure, we're supposed to have faith; that's what he's supposed to say and that's what we're supposed to hear, faith is a great thing, and that is what it's all about, believing, as the Red Queen says in *Alice in Wonderland*, in "six impossible things before breakfast." You've heard that all of your life; faith this, faith that: faith.

Faith indeed is the subject, but in Romans 8, as you noticed carefully as it was also read to us this morning, St. Paul here is not talking about your faith in God, for that is not the subject: St. Paul is talking about God's faith in you, and that is very different. "If God be for us, who can be against us?" That is very different from saying, "If I'm for God, who can be against me?" No, this is not about your affirmation of God, it is about God's affirmation of you. It is God who has faith in you that makes the difference. It is God in Romans 8 who is the faithful one. It is God who in spite of our failure does not ever lose faith in us. "If God be for us..." If God believes in us, if God is on our side, who or what can be against us? What failure can endure if God still believes in us? If God Almighty has confidence in you and will not abandon you in the pinch, what does it matter what others may think, or what others may feel, or what others may do? That pinch is pretty considerable, as we read on in Romans 8, for it includes tribulation, distress, persecution, famine, nakedness, peril, sword. "Nay," says the King James translation, "in all these things we are more than conquerors through him who loved us."

Then, I think, comes the greatest summary of the Christian faith anywhere under any terms, when St. Paul virtually shouts from the rooftops, "For I am persuaded that neither death, nor life, nor angels, nor principalities, nor things present, nor things to come, nor height, nor depth, nor any powers, nor anything else in all creation will be able to separate us from the love of God in Christ Jesus our Lord." God has so much faith in us that nothing will be permitted ultimately to come between God and ourselves. Because of God's investment in us, made by his hand, created in his image, designed for himself, he never loses faith in us and therefore there is nothing past, present, or future, that can separate us from his love. Even in the bowels, in the depths of failure, of the worst that the world can do to you, nothing can separate you from the love of God. That means that he loves us when we are down, he loves us as well when we are up, he loves us when we are lovable or lovely, or not. That means that there is no place beyond the reach of the love of God, and it has nothing to do with who we are or what we do but everything to do with who God is and what God does, You wil be tempted to forget this, like those Babylonians, but I hope you do not: for the sake of your souls, I hope you do not.

I think it was Billy Graham who some years ago after his return from Russian reported on the remarkable and wonderful survival and revival of the Christian faith, the Orthodox church, after seventy years of systematic and rigorous Soviet repression. He talked with an old woman of the Orthodox faith who had seen and endured the persecutions, and he asked her how it could be that under such terrible circumstances the faith could survive. She said, in translation, "The people were tempted to abandon the faith, but God was never tempted to abandon the people." Fidelity, you see, faithfulness — God's fidelity — is the companion of human adversity. I want you to remember that.

Because God has such confidence in us and shows such love toward us we are meant in return to have that confidence and love for God, and to share that love and confidence with our brothers and sisters wherever and whenever we may encounter them. Faith does not begin in what we do or believe about God, faith is not a credal formulation; faith is not denominational loyalty, faith is not religious passion. Faith begins in what God has already done for us and believes about us. That is why that great early twentieth century hymn of William M. Runyan, that the Baptists sing so often, is so true:

Great is Thy faithfulness! Great is Thy faithfulness!
Morning by morning new mercies I see;
All I have needed Thy hand hath provided —
Great is Thy faithfulness, Lord, unto me.

We are faithful to God because God has always been faithful to us. This, then, is truly good news, and that is why they call it the gospel.

This is the gospel message, and I beg you, I beseech you, in St. Paul's language, to accept God's affirmation of faith in you as sufficient reason for faith in yourself, and ultimately for faith in God. In your prosperity — and I wish that for each of you — such faith will help you to be grateful to God and modest, and humble; and in your adversity, which I cannot prevent from happening, such faith will help you to endure with courage, with dignity, and with imagination. You must hear this, you must believe it, you must live it, and I am telling it to you today before it is too late.

You have heard the word of the Lord, you have heard the words of scripture and the words of the hymns describe an inconstant world, an ambitious devil, and a faithful God. Before it is too late reconcile yourself to the God who has never left you, and who never will. That is something that you must know before it is too late.

Let us pray:

> *We thank Thee, O God, for these days of struggle and of preparation. Now send us forth ready for Thy service and free from every fear, for the sake of him who gave us his life that we might fully enjoy ours, even Jesus Christ our Lord. Amen.*

June 6, 1999

PART FIVE

Addresses for Daily Services of Morning Prayers

SMALL PIETIES

Morning Prayers
Opening of Term

Text: For who hath despised the day of small things?
Zechariah 4:10 (KJV)

Zechariah is not among the great prophets, in fact he is distinctly among the minor prophets, but he is a minor prophet with a great message: through the hand of the curiously-named Zerubbabel small and ordinary things will be used to accomplish the great work of the Lord, and those who despise the "day of small things" shall live to see this great work accomplished. The angel explains to Zechariah the word of the Lord to Zerubbabel: "Not by might, nor by power, but by my Spirit, says the Lord of hosts..." will the will of the Lord be accomplished.

Life consists in the maintenance of little pieties, the little duties, chores, and tasks by which body and soul are literally held together. To think of these things is to think of nothing earth-shattering: no sonic booms here. Yesterday, for example, as did many of you, I went to vote in my Town House, doing my civic duty along with hundreds of my fellow citizens. I didn't expect my single vote to make much of a difference, and I said as much to one of the elderly wardens at the polls. She smiled and said, "I know what you mean, but suppose we didn't do the little we could, what would happen then?"

She was right, of course. Life, we are told, is what passes by while we wait for great things to happen. It seems to me that anybody can aspire to greatness, there is a whole cottage industry in greatness, and it is what we are best at thinking about here. Since most of us will have few great moments, however, and will have many more moments when we are less than great or brilliant, the burden of life consists in how well we make use of those ordinary, undramatic, non-climactic moments in which we spend most of our time.

As the world becomes less and less civil, less humane, and less accomodating on a human scale, the small pieties take on an even larger importance. A civil greeting from a shop attendant, a human voice at the other end of the telephone instead of a menu, even an insincere "Good Morning," or the ubiquitous "Have a nice day," take the sharp edges from a brittle civility.

Marriages, we are told, calculate their breakdowns not from great moments of anger or betrayal, or from epic acts of infidelity or violence, but from the erosion of the little courtesies, the little pieties and niceties, and that erosion indicates that we no longer care to take time to care.

This chapel service is a little piety, a small thing in the cosmic scheme of things. More symbol than substance, by these ritually repeated words and gestures we anchor ourselves and our souls against the great indifference. It is a small thing that we do, and heroics in this place are neither expected nor encouraged, yet by our fidelity in this small thing of the spirit we remind ourselves of the prophet's words: "Not by might, nor by power, but by my Spirit, says the Lord of hosts..." will the will of the Lord be accomplished. Those who despise the day of small things, who place no hope in the little pieties or the modest gesture, who fail to do what is possible because they hope to do the impossible, will soon weary of these morning devotions. To those who persevere, to those who recognize that great adventures, including college, consist in the faithful discharge of small duties — to you, to us, will come the sure conviction that the only way to build sure foundations for living life is to do so brick by brick, stone by stone, and prayer by prayer.

Every day is the day of small things. That is why we begin each day with this service of prayer, so that rather than despise the day of small things we rejoice, and are glad in it.

Let us pray:

> *O God of beginnings, we have come again to a new day and a new year. Help us wisely to use Thy precious gift of time, and grant that this day we may catch a glimpse of the divine in that which is most fleeting and most ordinary. Amen.*

September 16, 1998

REMEMBRANCE AND THANKSGIVING

Morning Prayers

Text: Let them thank the Lord for his steadfast love, for his wonderful works to the sons of men! *Psalm 107:8*

Admiral Samuel Eliot Morison, '08, opened his 1936 address at the begining of Harvard's Three Hundredth year with this elegaic description of the month of November:

> "Autumn has crushed her vintage from the wine press of the year. November has come, the days of family reunions and New England anniversaries. In November the Mayflower sighted Cape Cod, and the Compact was signed; it is the month of Thanksgiving, the important football games, and John Harvard's birthday. *The Old Farmer's Almanac* advises us to observe November by taking in cabbage, casting up accounts, and filling the cellar with good cidar, 'that wholesome liquor.'"

A thoughtful people are a remembering people, and November is the month of remembrance, beginning with the remembrance of All Saints and All Souls on the first two days and proceeding with the remembrance of the war dead and of our benefactors. Then there are the Pilgrim Fathers and the Pilgrim Mothers to be recalled, and the Indians as well.

For my generation, November is also the month in which we remember where we were on that day thirty-five years ago this Sunday when Mr. Kennedy was shot, and the innocence of our world shattered and lost forever. I remember the leaden sky, the cold snap in the air, and the sense of a culture in shock and in mourning; and I remember that as Thanksgiving Day approached that year we wondered what on earth we had to be thankful for.

The twentieth of November is a day for other remembrances as well: on this day in 870 St. Edmund was murdered by the Danes in Bury St. Edmund's, England; the Nuremberg War Crimes Trial began in 1945;

and on this day in 1947 Princess Elizabeth of England was married to Lieutenant Phillip Mountbatten in Westminster Abbey. In November 1974, twenty-four years ago, I was inducted as Minister of this Church.

November was and is the month of remembrance, and thus of contemplation. I was in London last Wednesday, November 11, and witnessed for the first time in that place the two minutes' silence at eleven o'clock in the morning, commemorating the eleventh hour of the eleventh day of the eleventh month of the year 1918, when the guns stopped and the armistice agreement ending the 'war to end all wars' was signed. Big Ben rang out, trains and cars and buses and trucks stopped wherever they were, store clerks stopped transactions, lawyers stopped pleading, and people stood still. It was an astonishing moment, an act of remembrance.

Memory is a powerful emotion, giving us participation in worlds we cannot see and allowing us in the present to reclaim something of the past. Memory thus adds a dimension to our existence, and reminds us that we are not alone and that our present moments, however pleasant or sad, are not our only moments. The young are wisely advised to cultivate both the present and a sense of the past, so that they will have something to live on when they are old. "Lay down good thoughts now," they are told, "so that when you can no longer think in the present you will be able to live off the store of your remembrance."

Remembrance, therefore, is of the essence of thanksgiving, for the first act of thanksgiving is always an act of recollection. To be thankful is to remember and be reminded of that by which we have been sustained, renewed, and kept whole. We give thanks, in essence, because we are still here to give thanks, not so much for what we have, but for that we are. Memory is the gift God gives us in order that we might know that for which we are thankful; and thus the one who remembers remembers to be grateful.

The Lord has provided far beyond our needs or our capacity. When we remember that we have remembered everything, and our only natural response is to give thanks not only with our lips but with our lives. I invite you to remember that around the festive board next week.

Let us pray:

> *Help us to remember that in all things we are to be grateful. Through Jesus Christ our Lord. Amen.*

November 20, 1998

TIME AND CHANCE

Morning Prayers

Text: Again I saw that under the sun the race is not to the swift, nor the battle to the strong, nor bread to the wise, nor riches to the intelligent, nor favor to the men of skill; but time and chance happen to them all. *Ecclesiastes 9:11*

Today is the feast day of two disciples of St. Benedict, Maurus and Placid, a rather minor feast day in the Anglican calendar. Of somewhat more importance to us is the fact that today is the last day of the winter reading period, and examinations for the Fall Term begin tomorrow morning, whether or not you are ready. It is no secret to many of you that I have always enjoyed the reading period: when I was a Divinity School student here over thirty years ago, in that winter of 1966 I found my first reading period to be a remarkable encounter. I was terrified of what I did not know, and of how soon that which I did not know would be discovered, and so I looked forward to the expanse of days in January in which classes would not get in the way of my education. I rose early, organized myself and my tasks, and expected to accomplish fourteen weeks' worth of work in two.

That was before the days of computers, the Internet, and all of the technological accessories which present day students take for granted; and, believe it or not, it was even before the days of Xerox. Paper, pencils, and the required reading were the tools of the trade, and the days were spent in purposeful toil assisted by a certain amount of constructive panic and the bonding that occurs with similarly situated colleagues. It was what I imagined life had been in that small life-boat on the black North Atlantic on the night the Titanic went down, or perhaps as the fellowship among the doomed men in Scott's heroic but tragic adventure at the South Pole.

Some of my colleagues adopted odd eccentricities such as not changing their shirts for the duration, or of always sitting in the exact same chair in the library. I gave up shaving. Demanding times stimulate strange and exotic rituals.

When the days of reckoning came, of facing blank blue books in the unrenovated, cavernous space of Memorial Hall, I discovered that by and large I knew more than I knew that I knew, and was able to occupy the time and fill up the book. It was reassuring to know that even at Harvard I could still fool some of the people some of the time.

Neither an exceptionally clever student nor a particularly gifted one, I was grateful for the biblical wisdom contained in today's lesson — that the race is not necessarily won by the fastest person nor the battle by the strongest fighter, that the wise do not necessarily get their bread, and riches do not necessarily go to the intelligent. These anti-meritocratic verses strike at the heart of an entitled community such as ours, and the assumption, not easily demonstrated, that we should get what we deserve.

Usually I have been grateful that I did not get what I deserved; indeed, usually I have got more. Some are quick to cry, "Foul!" and "Unfair!" but to anyone who has ever had the benefit of the doubt given them in an exam, in a relationship, and in life itself, this reward that is contrary to merit and expectation is an act of grace and of mercy which only we who have received it can fully appreciate.

The examination period, consisting as it does of both preparation and of pressure, is indeed a season of time and chance, yet it can also be one of grace. It allows us the discovery of what we do know and of what we do not know, and, even more, it allows us the opportunity of taking advantage of both discoveries. The lesson upholds wisdom as superior to might, which I take to mean that both examiner and examined should regard mere information — "just the facts," as it were — as merely the means to their wise interpretation and application. The one who knows more may not necessarily prevail, for in examination as in life it is not how much you know that counts, but how well you are able to manage that which you know. This, then, is your chance and time to discover this wisdom, and that in itself is an act of grace.

So, don't panic. Trust in God and let the pressure bring out the best in you, for the result of irritation and pressure is diamonds and pearls. May God grant you both time and chance to harvest a few of each out of the work of the coming days.

"Again I saw that under the sun the race is not to the swift, nor the battle to the strong, nor bread to the wise, nor riches to the intelligent, nor favor to the men of skill; but time and chance happen to them all."

Let us pray:

> *In our toil let us remember that we labor not simply for now nor for ourselves, but for that day and time in which all that we know and do can be lent to Thy service and the common good of Thy people. This we pray through Jesus Christ our Lord. Amen.*

January 15, 1999

THE REALITY OF FALSE GODS

Morning Prayers
Opening of Spring Term

Text: Thou shalt have no other gods before me. *Exodus 20:3*

For many of you who have discovered the habit of these services at the beginning of each morning, Morning Prayers is both a precious and a quiet time, fifteen minutes snatched from the jaws of the day. If you had to describe to somebody who had never been here just what it is that makes this service 'go,' and makes you go to it, I suspect that you would not find it easy to do.

Those who do discover what goes on here beneath the bell have often commented that the service of daily Morning Prayers is one of Harvard's best-kept secrets. Thus it will perhaps come as as much of a surprise to you as it did to me that there are people here at Harvard who are apparently afraid of what we do, and consider both us and this expression of public and private piety threatening, and even subversive. I read this in the newspapers, and so it must be true. A former president of the Undergraduate Council is quoted in The Wall Street Journal of January 20, 1999, as follows:

> "There is a large community of Harvard students who are extremely suspicious of and feel threatened by organized religion. Certainly, there is a prejudice against Christianity here more than against any other religion."

Well, religion is certainly 'organized,' as opposed to 'disorganized,' in The Memorial Church, a point perhaps of dangerous pride for those of us who manage it; and the principle traditions of this church and chapel are Christian. So, if our well-placed student leader's observation is correct, there is any number of undergraduates who tremble every time the bell disturbs their slumbers at 8:40 a.m. each day — and at 10:50 a.m.

on Sundays — at the thought of what we do here. Part of me — the lower part, I must admit — is delighted by the thought that our devotions may cause some of the brightest and best some trepidation, for it is reassuring that our efforts, which we tend to underestimate, may in fact have a greater impact than we might possibly imagine.

One of the things that most annoyed the pagans and the Gentiles about the ancient Jews was their unwillingness to acknowledge the legitimacy of any gods but their own. For the Jews it was simple — the God who had delivered them was the only God to whom they owed any loyalty: "I am Jehovah thy God, who brought thee out of the land of Egypt, out of the house of bondage. Thou shalt have no other gods before me."

Jews and Christians worship a God who has done great things for them, and put nobody and nothing in place of that relationship. The Romans objected first to the Jews and then to the Christians because neither would place Caesar or Rome at the heart of their loyalty; the Greeks thought Christians silly because they preferred the worship of God to the worship of ideas; and Hitler opposed any religion that made God superior to the German spirit or state.

We do ourselves and our faith no service when we fail to acknowledge the reality of false gods whose worship is not worthy of us. False gods abound on every hand, even here at 'godless' Harvard where one can easily worship the 'scientific method,' democratic pluralism, socialism, republicanism, feminism, rationalism, truth, beauty, or whatever other fashionable ideology we are meant to encounter in as lively and diverse a place as this. Perhaps the most annoying thing about Christians, in a place of so many tempting partial visions, is our unwillingness to mistake the partial — no matter how interesting — for the whole. We are prepared to concede that it all neither ends nor begins with whatever may be discovered in Mallinkrodt or conjured up in tutorials. Perhaps we are too smug in our quiet knowledge that now, as St. Paul has so beautifully put it, we know only in part; and perhaps we seem naive when we declare that it is our ambition to know the whole, the holy, and that that can be only when we are fully and finally known. Until that day we cannot take the University and all that happens in it as seriously as it takes itself or as others take it, and that, perhaps, is what makes people nervous and even threatened. It has always been so and it is maybe a mercy that we now know that it is so, even in this seemingly tolerant place.

On February 8, 1961, Professor Gordon Allport gave a talk in this chapel entitled, 'The Seductive Idolatry in Academic Life,' in which he argued that "in academic life the temptation to worship the Part instead of the Whole is subtle, and rationally appealing." The part, wondrously available to us here by the means of the mind, is not false but, in his words, "only seductively incomplete." How, then, he goes on to ask, does one at Harvard obey the First Commandment? Here is what he says, "A simple answer — which I would offer figuratively as well as literally — is to start the day at 8:45 with the whole, and not merely at 9 o'clock with the part."

Perhaps upon reflection you will agree with me that this is a secret too good to keep just to ourselves.

Let us pray:

> *O God, who hast ordained that whatever is to be desired should be sought by labour, and who by Thy blessing bringest honest labour to good effect, invigorate our studies and direct our inquiries, we beseech Thee, and let us not linger in ignorance, but enlighten and support us, for the sake of Jesus Christ our Lord. Amen.*
>
> Samuel Johnson, 1709- 1784

February 3, 1999

LIFE AFTER DEATH

Morning Prayers

Text: "Unbind him, and let him go." *John 11:44*

The story of Lazarus is about as dramatic as it gets in the New Testament, and it is no small story to hear just a little more than a week before Easter. As a child I was fond of this story in John's gospel, not so much because I was interested in either Lazarus or the resurrection, but because it contained the shortest verse in the Bible: "Jesus wept." (John 11:35) That was a useful verse to know in the Bible competitions which were regularly held in our Sunday School.

As I recall the lesson, two things of interest but beside the point, stand out. The first is that Jesus is late. We know this because twice the sisters rebuke him with the words, "Lord, if you had been here, my brother would not have died." Jesus had no good excuse, despite the best efforts of the evangelist, and his tardiness reminds me of the gospel song:

You can't hurry God, No! you just have to wait:
You have to trust him and give him time, Child,
No matter how long it takes.
He's a God you just can't hurry,
He'll be there, so don't you worry;
He may not come when you want him,
But he's right on time.

It might not have seemed so to Lazarus, however, whose last words might have been, "Where's Jesus?"

The second thing we note along the way is that Lazarus is really really really really dead; and to make clear that this is the case, for he had been in the tomb three days, the King James Version has Martha say to Jesus, "He stinketh." There is a wonderful medieval carving depicting this moment through an image of an imp holding his nose.

The point that captures my interest, however, begins with Jesus's command to Lazarus's friends: "Unbind him, and let him go." The image in my childhood's mind's eye was of someone holding one end of Lazarus's binding cloth and Lazarus spinning around and around like a top until he stood naked as the day he was born. Here we could make the sound point that Jesus defeats the holds and claims of death and literally sets Lazarus free, but after this first death Lazarus will surely die again. The point is, what does he do with his new life, with this second chance that he is given? Does he wake up and say, "Oh no, not this all over again, life with my sisters?" Does he say, "I am born again, and perhaps I can get it right this time?" Does he simply pick up where he left off? Who knows?

Both the text and Lazarus are silent, but this story gives us an opportunity to reflect upon the new chances for life and living that we are given every day. It gives us a chance to ask the question not so much of whether there is life after death but, of more immediate importance, of what we do with life before death.

Lazarus, at Jesus's command, experiences freedom *from* death, and now, by that same command, he is to experience freedom *for* life. Freedom from and freedom for: which is it to be? We cannot speak for Lazarus but we can speak and act for ourselves, remembering that for the faithful in Christ, Easter is an every day experience, an act of freedom *for*. So may it be for us all.

Let us pray:

> *Cause us, good Lord, to live each day as if it were our last, and to rejoice in it as if it were our first: for the sake of Jesus, our living Lord. Amen.*

March 26, 1999

LAUGHTER

Morning Prayers
Visitation Weekend

Lesson: When the Lord turned again the captivity of Zion, we were like them that dream. Then was our mouth filled with laughter, and our tongue with singing: then said they among the heathen, "The Lord hath done great things for them. The Lord hath done great things for us; whereof we are glad. Turn again our captivity, O Lord, as the streams in the south. They that sow in tears shall reap in joy. He that goeth forth and weepeth, bearing precious seed, shall doubtless come again with rejoicing, bringing his sheaves with him." *Psalm 126*

Text: Then was our mouth filled with laughter... *Psalm 126:2*

This morning I take as my subject a rather serious topic, laughter, specifically laughter in church, and in so doing I recall a story of an old Church of Scotland man in the western isles where laughter was not much approved of in the kirk. He had a keen, if not robust, sense of humor. Apparently he made a wry remark one day, and one of his elders warned him after the service not to do it again because, as he said, "It was so funny that I nearly laughed." That, of course, would not do.

In the church of my youth, while tears were permitted and in fact encouraged as a sign of sincere conviction, laughter was frowned upon; and when I first preached at College Evensong now many years ago in the chapel of Emmanuel College in Cambridge University, I was warned by the chaplain that while the Fellows did not believe in God, they did believe that laughter was inappropriate in the house of the God in whom they did not believe.

In my own experience, first of the human and then of the divine, I have come to quite the opposite conclusion. To laugh, I think, is to see the folly and the vulnerability that surrounds us on every hand. Laughter is not the opposite of tears: laughter is another, and equally valid, way of responding to that over which we have no control, which has gone out of control, and which in fact transcends control. I believe that it is a fair rule of human evaluation to say that we should trust no one who lacks a sense of humor.

Queen Victoria was famous for saying, "We are not amused." While she did indeed say it, and the occasion upon which she said it is recorded in the journals of her last Keeper of the Household, that same source tells us that she loved a good joke, could laugh uproariously, and, like many members of the Royal Family, preferred humor to irony.

I have found that humor, as a device, both levels distinctions between speaker and audience and opens relationships in discourse that eventually allow for the weightier matters of the law; and while a book on the humor of Jesus would likely be a very short one, I nevertheless believe that laughter is a way through which we can both hear and receive the good news. You will not take my word for this, I know, and so I will summon to my aid two significant thinkers of our age, neither one of whom could ever be accused of frivolousness or insufficient sobriety.

Last summer when I was in Edinburgh, I read in a Scottish newspaper that my friend and colleague at Boston University, the sociologist Peter Berger, called a sense of humor "one of the signals of transcendence that breaks through into the human situation and reminds us of something beyond." A sociologist, particularly of religion, and particularly a German sociologist, is not given to pulpit slapstick and clerical stand-up routines, and so we must take Peter Berger seriously when he suggests that laughter invades our human solemnity and offers a glimpse of that which transcends our own limits. Laughter, in other words, is the work of angels, and it brings us nearer to God.

Another way of thinking of laughter is to think of it as a form of prayer. It is the sober Reinhold Niebuhr who has written on humor, that "Humor is in fact a prelude to faith, and laughter is the beginning of prayer." What could he possibly mean? Perhaps simply this: that when we laugh we are at our most vulnerable with all our defenses down, and it is only when we are vulnerable, open, that prayer can come from within and God can enter from without. Humor and faith, he argues, have an intimate relationship because they both deal in what he calls the "incongruities of existence."

Laughter, in today's psalm, is the natural response to the deliverance of the people, an act of thanksgiving, the expression of gladness and praise: "Those that sow in tears," says the psalmist, "shall reap in joy." The ultimate weapon, if you will, in the face of evil or sorrow, sadness or death, is not stoic virtue and the stiff upper lip but laughter, for where laughter is, God cannot be far away. That is why at wakes, both Irish or other, the dead are celebrated and sent on their way not with weeping and mourning but with funny stories and irreverent tales — the stuff that takes us from one world to the next; and if that's good enough for the dead, then it is good enough for the living.

Let us pray:

> *Let us smile at the thought of God, and laugh for joy for all of his kindness toward us. Amen.*

Saturday, April 10, 1999

STANDING FIRM

Morning Prayers

Text: So then, brethren, stand firm and hold to the traditions which you were taught by us, either by word of mouth or by letter.

II Thessalonians 2:15

Most of us Christians are creatures of an invincible optimism, despite all evidence to the contrary. We live in a world made famous by Dickens' imperishable character in *David Copperfield*, Wilkins Macawber, who, you will recall, was that lovable but improvident fellow always on the precipice of disaster, who believed invariably that "something will turn up."

Well, even Wilkins Macawber would be challenged by the events of recent days, both personal and public. What does the person of faith say or do in the following three circumstances?

1) I have learned of the impending death by brain cancer of an old and beloved student of mine, and former well-esteemed seminarian on our staff. Roger, a promising young theologian with achievements behind him and a bright future before him, is cut down in his prime by this senseless, invasive, and destructive cancer. He is one of the good ones, in him the gospel of Christ has always shone so brightly, and he would have done so much good for so many that he deserved more and better of God and of life than to leave it so soon. His faith has helped him to cope, as it is helping him to endure to the end. What about our faith? Where will his death leave us?

2) Christian people everywhere are paralyzed by the events in Kosovo, and our confusion in policy reflects

our confusion in prayer. How do we cope with the moral ambiguity of violence in the name of humanity? Had we been more violent in Europe in 1939, might we have saved more of humanity? Are we caught forever between the polarities of Munich and Vietnam? At whom should our outrage be directed? Must we constantly improvise our moral position as we watch the nightly news? On Tuesday of this week I participated at the New York Public Library in a panel entitled 'The Meaning of the Millennium,' where the author Francine duPlessis Gray said in essence that we cannot escape this moral baggage as we imagine the clean new pages of a new century and millennium. Alas, I agree with her.

3) What do we make of the terrible events in Colorado, in which a pre-civilized insanity seems to have taken possession of the young? We have made the devil and evil mere metaphors in this secular age, and yet the most barbarous pagan could not have given more life to the reality of Satan and evil than did these deranged and angry teenagers.

How can one find anything left to believe in, in the face of these facts? That was the persistent question that was put to me on Tuesday, and it is the question that every believer faces in the face of tragedy, grief, and evil.

We must remember, and be reminded over and over again that it was into just such a set of worldly facts as these that the Christian faith was born. Grief, tragedy, evil, were no strangers either to Jesus or to his followers. The New Testament is not a humanistic tract, a Utopia for optimists incapable of dealing with what Hannah Arendt once called "the banality of evil." If Christians wince, blanche, and become paralyzed in the face of this banality, then our faith is of no consequence. The test of faith is the worst of life, and not the best.

St. Paul, that sturdy controversialist, understood this if nothing else, and we should remember him for this if for nothing else. Over and over again he and those earliest believers remind us that the promise is not peace and prosperity and happiness, but rather that if we persist in faithfulness despite the evidence to the contrary, we will not be overwhelmed by the calamaties that surround us. St. Paul reminds us to remember what we have been taught, that we must remember to teach the moral law, love of God and love of neighbor, and hold to it most especially when it seems impossible to do so. "Stand firm," he argues, "and hold to the traditions which you were taught." Our faith, we must remember, was developed in and for times just such as these.

So, what do we do when the unfair and arbitrary hand of death strikes the good and the young? We weep, and we give thanks to the God who permits death and gives life. That is not easy, but it is necessary.

What do we do when faced with morally ambiguous choices in a fallen world? We remember that we are not God, and therefore we must pray and struggle, so that on the basis of insufficient evidence and weak wills we will somehow do more good than harm, enduring in our hope that God's will may become our own.

How do we explain terrible violence, and cope with the "banality of evil?" We do not explain evil, we recognize it and resist it by teaching the practice of goodness over and over and over again, one by one, day by day, person by person, soul by soul.

Our daily devotions here, especially today, may seem of no consequence in the face of terrors great and small. Recall, however, if you will, the inscription, attributed to John Austin, over the door of an English parish church, which was put up at the time of the terrors of the English civil war in the seventeenth century, when it had become routine for Christians to slaughter one another, and to do so in the name of God:

IN THE YEAR 1653
WHEN ALL THINGS SACRED WERE
THROUGHOUT THE NATION
EITHER DEMOLISHED OR PROFANED
SIR ROBERT SHIRLEY BARONET
FOUNDED THIS CHURCH:
WHOSE SINGULAR PRAISE IT IS
TO HAVE DONE THE BEST THINGS
IN THE WORST TIMES
AND
HOPED THEM IN THE MOST CALAMITOUS

So, then, brothers and sisters, stand firm and hold to the traditions which you were taught.

Let us pray:

> *Fix Thou our steps, O Lord, that we stagger not at the uneven motions of the world, but go steadily on our way, neither censuring our journey by the weather we meet, nor turning aside for anything that may befall us. Amen.*
>
> John Austin, XVIIth century English Catholic

April 23, 1999

THOSE WISE RESTRAINTS

Morning Prayers
Last day of Term and of the Academic Year

Text: Oh, how I love Thy law! It is my meditation all the day.
Psalm 119:97

In the mid-summer of 1970, the summer in which I was appointed Assistant Minister in The Memorial Church but well before the time I was to take up my duties in September, I received a telephone call from a Harvard professor at my home in Plymouth. He began by saying, "This is John Maguire of the Harvard Law School; it is not very important, otherwise I would wait for your boss to return, but I think you can do me a kindness." The kindness was to officiate at a memorial service for his late and long-serving secretary who had recently died, and of whose estate he was executor. When in order to prepare a suitable eulogy I asked him about the deceased, he said, in words I have never forgotten: "She was a singularly unpleasant woman who outlived what few friends she had had." We concluded that under such circumstances a eulogy would not be necessary.

I performed the memorial service, my first of many, in the presence of the professor, his wife, and their maid, and thus began a relationship with both Maguires that ended only with their deaths many years later. As I came to know him, I learned that John Maguire claimed for himself only one small Harvard distinction.

At Commencement it is the custom of long-standing for the president to confer degrees upon candidates from the professional schools with an economic phrase describing in essence the work of that school. Architects, for example, are testified competent "effectively to shape the space in which we live;" and doctors are declared "ready to engage in an honorable and merciful calling." Professor Maguire had composed the phrase which the president uses to this day when he confers the several degrees in law, declaring that the candidates are "ready to aid in the shaping and application of those wise restraints that make us free." It is a felicitous phrase and a noble sentiment often out of joint, alas, with bellicose law students and the tattered reputation of their profession. Yet it seems to me that the sentiment deserves to be heard apart from the crowded context of Commencement, as a reflection not just upon lawyers but upon all of us who must take our share, large or small, in the maintenance of civilization: "those wise restraints that make us free."

What is rhetorically appealing about this sentiment is the combination in one sentence of two dissonant concepts: restraint and freedom. The dissonance is all the more acute because most of us assume that freedom is by definition the absence of restraint, and that is the sort of freedom that we are accustomed to celebrating. Thus, for many, it is a strange thing to hear the psalmist say, as we do this morning, "Oh, how I love Thy law! It is my meditation all the day." There appears to be almost a sensual delight in the keeping of the law.

Recently I saw an interview with some super-Orthodox Jews living in an Orthodox community in the Bronx. These were Jews of the most intense observance, living with the black hats and coats of eighteenth century Polish Jewry, rebuking with their every gesture the assumptions of twentieth century American secular modernity. The interviewer was a typically annoying National Public Radio woman, keen to ask the women of the community how they could yield their own individual autonomy to the archaic and absolute rule of religious law. "Don't you feel imprisoned by these regulations?" she fairly shrieked at one Orthodox woman. "The law is my freedom," the woman replied; "when I keep it I know who I am and what God wants of me, and only then I am free." It was an exercise in cultural dissonance.

Perhaps you and I know something of what that woman meant. We know that 'liberation,' understood strictly as 'freedom from' is not all that it is cracked up to be. We know the chaos of a community in which everyone is "free to be me" and there are no inhibitions, no restrictions, and no rules. We know as well the necessity of "those wise restraints" upon our natures, our instincts, and our fears, which help us to achieve a degree of order and self-control without which freedom worthy of the name is neither possible nor desirable. It is no small point to observe that as a sign of his love and promise the most precious thing that God gives to the people whom he chooses is the gift of the law. Their freedom 'from' Egypt is in itself not sufficient: not until they are given the gift of the law have they the opportunity to exercise true freedom. Thus, when the psalmist sings his song of delight and praise in the law, he celebrates those wise restraints that make him truly free to be what God intends him to be.

For the Christian, those wise restraints are among the things that St. Paul invites us to put on when he writes to the Colossians, "Put on then, as God's chosen ones, holy and beloved, compassion, kindness, lowliness, meekness, and patience, forbearing one another and, if one has a complaint against another, forgiving each other..." Against these things, as St. Paul says elsewhere, there is no law.

The relationship between restraint and freedom is the work not just of a Term but of a life, and the cultivation of those wise restraints is the work to which every believer and aspirer is called. That is our daily work here. We are called to love the One who makes us free, and both to cherish and to practice those wise restraints by which our freedom is secured. Nothing more is necessary; nothing less will do.

Let us pray:

> *O God, who art the author of peace and lover of concord, in knowledge of whom standeth our eternal life, whose service is perfect freedom: defend us Thy humble servants in all assaults of our enemies; that we, surely trusting in Thy defence, may not fear the power of any adversaries; through the might of Jesus Christ our Lord. Amen.*

May 28, 1999

SENIOR CHAPEL ADDRESS: OVERWHELMED BY OPPORTUNITY

Commencement Day

Welcome to your last rites. You have come nearly to the end of this extended period of adolescence known as 'Senior Week,' and it is not a moment too soon for some of you who, having got this far, are living proof that it is still possible to fool a lot of the people a lot of the time. Not certain that you will have got away with it, you will open your big red envelope this afternoon very carefully, and not in front of your mother; and then to your great surprise and relief you will discover that there really is a document inside, not merely a library fine or a telephone bill, and that President Rudenstine really has admitted you finally and fully into the company of educated men and women. For a moment you will thank your lucky stars, your guardian angel, and such gods as you dare name. "Amazing Grace!" you might say; "The age of miracles has not passed: praise the Lord!"

Then upon cooler reflection you might believe that you had actually pulled it off by yourself, that nobody had given you anything but that you yourself had earned it all and deserve it all. It is at that moment of alchemy that you will have turned from a grateful undergraduate into an entitled alumnus, a metamorphosis for which there is no known cure. It is then that you will be able to identify with the great American actor John Barrymore who, while not a Harvard graduate, sounded like one when he said of his own acting career: "One of my chief regrets during my years in the theatre is that I couldn't sit in the audience and watch *me*."

Beneath and behind all of this self-congratulatory talk, however, and the promises of success and conquest is, I suspect, the lurking suspicion that in fact you might not be able to make it 'out there' on your own and that, in the words of that great theologian Talullah Bankhead, "There is less here than meets the eye."

To those of you who secretly wonder whether you will be able to cope once you return your rented regalia to the Coop, I have three things to wish for you this morning. First is that you continue to be "overwhelmed by opportunity," which phrase comes from a friend in England who this last autumn won five million pounds in the lottery. When asked how he felt about it he replied that he was "overwhelmed by opportunity." Well, who wouldn't be? Some of you felt that way upon your first arrival and early days at Harvard when, looking at the Course Catalog and its thousands of offerings, you marvelled at how it could be possible to take advantage of all of it with only thirty-two half courses. Then, of course, you had not fully appreciated the implications of asterisks, brackets, sabbaticals, leaves, limited enrollment, lotteries, and even death, not to mention the CORE: you take my point.

To be overwhelmed by opportunity is to be able to appreciate fully what you can contemplate only partially, to be intimate with the immensity of life and not intimidated. If your Harvard consisted only of the facts of what you did rather than the experience of what you could have done, and if your life follows the same unimaginative pattern, then you will have missed out on a great deal and will continue to do so. I wish that you all, therefore, continue to be overwhelmed by opportunity.

The second thing I wish for you is that you join with the "multitude of the wise." Perhaps you have encountered this verse from the Wisdom of Solomon on the Business School side of the Anderson Bridge, where engraved on the eastern pillar are the words, "The Multitude of the Wise is the Welfare of the World." The assumption is that the more of you there are the better for the world, and although I would like to think that that is true, I have my doubts. We have been adding to the multitude of the wise for nearly four hundred years now and the world does not seem much the better for it, although with each new class the chances of making a difference increase rather than decrease. This is your moment, your chance to add to rather than detract from the welfare of the world, for the multitude of the wise is the welfare of the world only when the multitude itself exhibits the virtues that it would share with others.

Finally, I wonder how many of you have ever noticed the stone staircases that lead from the first to the second floor of University Hall? They are a remarkable example of the engineering skills of the building's great architect, Charles Bulfinch, and their particular style is called 'vagrant' because they have no visible means of support. Here are efficient and elegant structures of Chelmsford granite with no visible posts or beams or columns and seemingly in defiance of gravity, yet since 1814 these staircases have carried the business of the College up and down. They are not a miracle but they are a marvel.

My wish for each of you is that you have useful, elegant, and efficient lives without any visible means of support, vagrant lives which will suggest to others as well as to yourselves that you are supported by an inner strength, an inner tension, a source of support that appears to defy the laws of physics but which sustains you and supports others. In other words I wish God for you, that peace which this world can neither give you nor take away from you but will sustain you in this life and get you to the next. My prayer is that you will grow inwardly so that you may thrive spiritually, and serve outwardly.

We have come now to the end of the beginning and the beginning of the end, and soon you will belong no longer to us or to yourselves but to the world. Go out there, then, with courage, grace, and imagination. We give you our love — a word not much used around here, and saved for your very last moments — and we commend you to the love of one another and to the greater love of a loving God. This now, at last, is the best that we can do for you. This is the best that there is and it is yours, so go for it, for God's sake, and for your own. Amen.

June 10. 1999

BENEDICTION

at

The Three Hundred Forty-eighth Commencement

Let us commend now to God and His sure keeping the well-being of this beloved community of memory and hope.

For these young in scholarship who are to depart from us, bearing with them the honors of the day, we give Thee thanks, and pray that their learning will be glorified by their wisdom and their lives amplified by their virtue. For those who have borne the burdens of the day we give Thee thanks for their sacrifice, their service, and their willingness to invest themselves and their treasure in the lives of others. Upon all of us who remain to teach and to serve, and to whom is entrusted this place of ancient and lively endeavor, give that due sense of all Thy mercies, that we may be grateful and faithful stewards.

Upon us all, O God of history and of hope, send now Thy blessing that we may depart in peace, according to Thy word. Amen.

June 10, 1999

**Printed by Harvard Printing and Publications Services,
Harvard University**